On August 17, 1937, at a depth of 125 feet, work on the shaft was abruptly halted. After nearly two centuries since its discovery, with millions of dollars spent, Gilbert Hedden, a wealthy New Jersey native with a fascination for engineering and money to spend, had just seen dramatic proof of what some people still believe is the key to the riddle of Oak Island.

And it had nothing at all to do with the shaft he'd spent all summer digging....

THE BIG DIG:

The $10 Million Search for Oak Island's Legendary Treasure

D'Arcy O'Connor

With line drawings by
Ann Elsdon

Formerly entitled:

THE MONEY PIT: The Story of Oak Island and The World's Greatest Treasure Hunt

BALLANTINE BOOKS ● NEW YORK

*For **my** treasures:*
Miranda and Patrick

Library of Congress Catalog Card Number: 77-21882

ISBN 0-345-35558-X

Manufactured in the United States of America

First Ballantine Books Edition: November 1988

Contents

Illustrations

Preface

Treasure. The very word conjures up images of buccaneer booty buried beneath a desolate island beach; gleaming gold locked in a long-lost vault of some ancient civilization; priceless archaeological artifacts concealed under the canopy of an overgrown tropical jungle, or barnacle-encrusted bullion stacked in the rotting hull of a treasure galleon that has lain at the bottom of the sea for hundreds of years.

All of these images and more are evoked by the possibility of what might be hidden in the depths of a small island off the south coast of Nova Scotia, Canada—site of the world's longest, most expensive, and most perplexing treasure hunt. For almost two hundred years, Oak Island has baffled scientists and madmen, scholars and idiots, millionaires and get-rich-quick dreamers, psychics, engineers, charlatans, and even a former president of the United States. The island has consumed the fortunes, and in some cases the lives, of those who have obsessively set out to unlock its secret. Despite all that, the mystery remains unsolved, and not a single dime of treasure has ever been recovered.

Yet even today the search continues. An estimated $5 million has so far been sunk into the quest; and now the current search group is spending a further $10 million in what may well be the final assault on Oak Island. It is an archaeological dig exceeding anything ever done anywhere for similar purposes, and it may well result in the discovery of one of the world's richest and most historically important treasures.

But this is also a story of people; those individuals who have dedicated years of their lives to discover what was long ago buried beneath this strange island. They are men driven by a lust for gold, by archaeological curiosity, and by their determination to outwit the unknown engineer who was responsible for the Oak Island enigma.

Acknowledgments

The research that went into this book would not have been possible without the generous cooperation of the following people: Dan Blankenship, Gary Clayton, Bill Cox, Arnie Gilson, David Hanson, Dan Henskee, Lavern Johnson, Eugenia Macer-Story, Fred Nolan, Mildred Restall, Bill Sobey and (alphabetically last, but instrumentally first) David Tobias.

For their belief in the project and their editorial guidance I am indebted to Peter Livingston and Bob Wyatt; as well as Beth Rashbaum, who, in a serendipitous way, brought us together.

I also owe thanks to Ty Grevatt, Sonja Larsen, and Terry Mosher for their technical assistance.

But most important, there is Ann Elsdon, who, besides creating the excellent artwork, convinced me that this book should, could, and would be done.

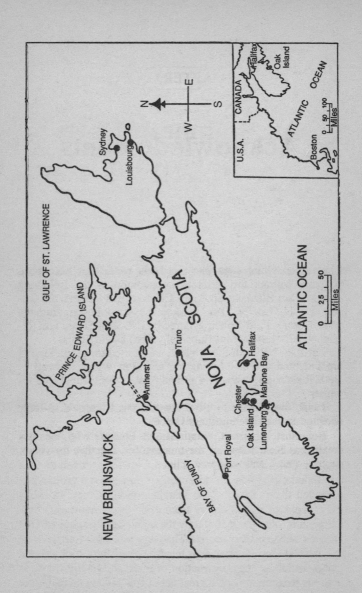

CHAPTER ONE

An Enigma Is Born

ON A SMALL WOODED ISLAND FORTY MILES SOUTHWEST OF Halifax, Nova Scotia, one of the world's deepest and most costly archaeological digs is currently under way. The project, which began in the autumn of 1988, is expected to provide the final chapter to a bizarre story that unfolded quite accidentally almost two hundred years earlier. Moreover, if the expectations of the group digging this hole are proved correct, the $10 million they're pouring into it may be recouped a hundredfold or more. For the members of the syndicate, known as Triton Alliance Limited, believe they are close to recovering the elusive and legendary treasure of Oak Island.

Nevertheless, Triton's optimism is tempered by the fact that it has been pursuing the treasure for over twenty years, and that Oak Island's history is littered with the broken dreams and failed expeditions of dozens of individuals and groups that preceded them. All of those searchers thought they too were only weeks or months away from discovering enormous buried wealth, only to be foiled by the ingenious designer of Oak Island's subterranean secret. That designer, who arrived on this desolate island some four hundred years ago, took special pains, including the construction of hydraulic booby traps, to hide his treasure at such a great depth and in such an elaborate

1

manner that only an obsessed fool or a determined genius would bother to pursue it.

But when the gold bug bites, its teeth sink deep. Little wonder that most who've been bitten by Oak Island have ended up wishing the island's so-called Money Pit had never been found in the first place.

THE DISCOVERY WAS MADE ON A SUMMER AFTERNOON IN 1795 by Daniel McGinnis, a teenage farm boy who'd rowed out from the mainland to explore the uninhabited island. As he was wandering through the island's densely wooded eastern end, he came to an area that appeared to have been worked at some far earlier time. It was a small clearing in which rotted, moss-covered tree stumps were visible. In the center of the clearing stood a large oak tree with a thick limb about fifteen feet up that had been cut off several feet out from the trunk. Below the end of this branch the ground had settled into a shallow, saucer-shaped depression.

Undoubtedly, McGinnis was as aware as anyone in Nova Scotia that pirates and privateers had frequently cruised the waters of Mahone Bay in the seventeenth and early eighteenth centuries, and that the notorious Captain William Kidd was rumored to have hidden part of his treasure somewhere on the Acadian coast. Thus, the young adventurer quickly linked his discovery with the possibility of a buried cache beneath that oak tree. So he returned home and told two friends, John Smith and Anthony Vaughan, what he had found.

The following day the three of them returned to the spot with spades and pickaxes. They set to work digging in the center of the depression and found that their shovels could easily bite into the relatively loose soil. Two feet down they encountered the first of many pieces of evidence that someone had been there before. It was a layer of carefully laid flag-stones—a type of rock that is not natural to Oak Island. (The stones were later found to have originated at Gold River, about two miles up the coast on the mainland.) When they cleared away the earth and removed the flagstones, they found themselves working in what obviously was a refilled circular shaft, about thirteen feet in diameter. A section of the shaft, eventually dubbed the Money Pit, lay beneath the sawed-off limb, which presumably had been used by the original excavators to haul up the earth.

For several weeks the three boys returned to the island and continued to dig. They noticed that the sides of the shaft were of tough clay and that pick marks were visible along its walls. At the ten-foot level they struck a tier of snugly fitted oak logs completely covering the pit and embedded into the clay walls. They pried the logs out and resumed digging, only to hit an identical wooden platform ten feet later. At a depth of thirty feet, another layer of oak logs was encountered. Below it, as was the case with the upper two layers, the ground had settled about two feet. The logs themselves were visibly rotten on their outer surfaces, indicating they had been there a long time.

At this point, the boys realized that the project they'd undertaken was too big to handle by themselves and that they would need to enlist outside help. So far they had found nothing more than evidence that someone long before them had gone to a lot of trouble presumably to hide something more than thirty feet underground. Treasure seemed the only likely answer to what lay below. But how far below? Only years later would McGinnis, Smith, and Vaughan learn how much deeper and more complicated the Money Pit actually was. And even then, they would go to their graves knowing only a small part of the island's extraordinary subterranean secret.

It should be noted that the story of the 1795 discovery and the early attempts to get to the bottom of the Money Pit originated with the journals and verbal accounts of the three boys, all of whom lived till the mid-1800s. Today, the earliest published version of the story is found in the October 16, 1862, edition of the *Liverpool Transcript*, a long-defunct weekly newspaper that served southwestern Nova Scotia. The article was by Jotham B. McCully of Truro, Nova Scotia, who was associated with Oak Island search groups in 1849 and 1861 and interviewed both Smith and Vaughan in their later years. Another account of the discovery appears in the January 2, 1864, edition of the *Colonist*, a Halifax tri-weekly. This article was based on a lengthy letter written to the newspaper by "a member" of the 1861 search group, possibly McCully.

Later descriptions of the find appear in Israel Longworth's "History of the County of Colchester," an unpublished work written in 1866, and in Mather Byles DesBrisay's *History of the County of Lunenburg*, first published in 1870. Both writers borrowed heavily from the article that had appeared in the *Colonist*. However, DesBrisay was a close friend of Mary Smith, John Smith's daughter, and he undoubtedly got some of his facts from her. The next complete account of the discovery is found in the prospectus for an Oak Island search syndicate formed in 1893.

In these and later accounts there are minor discrepancies. But the story of the discovery and early search attempts as I've presented them here contains only facts that are basically common to all versions. One detail, for instance, that appears in a few accounts is that McGinnis found a wooden tackle block fastened to the branch over the Money Pit. This is likely an apocryphal detail added to the story later, and was based on the assumption (probably correct) that the overhanging limb had served as a support for some sort of hoisting device when the pit was originally dug.

Omitting fanciful details, early records agree that the Money Pit was discovered by Daniel McGinnis in the summer of 1795 and that he and his two friends excavated it to a depth of about thirty feet, striking a layer of flagstones at two feet and then three platforms of wood at intervals of ten feet. There they temporarily abandoned the search, not a doubloon richer. But they had launched what would become the world's longest and most expensive treasure hunt.

A Pandora's Box had been irrevocably opened on a seemingly ordinary and inconsequential island—and there were to be many who would sacrifice their fortunes and even their lives in their frustrated attempts to discover just what was in that box.

OAK ISLAND IS JUST ONE OF SOME 350 ISLANDS THAT DOT MA-hone Bay on Nova Scotia's Atlantic coast, and it was so

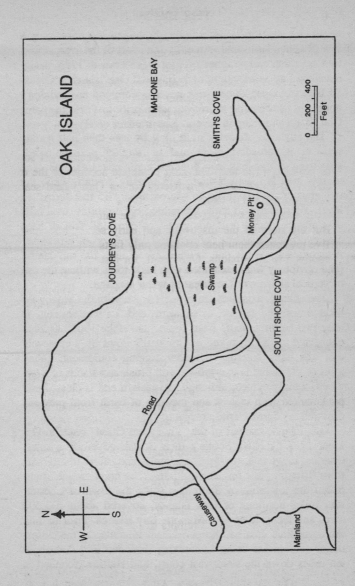

OAK ISLAND

MAHONE BAY

SMITH'S COVE

JOUDREY'S COVE

Swamp

Money Pit

SOUTH SHORE COVE

Road

Causeway

Mainland

N
W — E
S

0   200   400
Feet

named because of its large umbrella-domed red oaks, only a few of which still stand. An early sea chart of the area, drawn by the British cartographer I. F. W. Des Barres in 1776, designates the bay as Mecklenburgh Bay and Oak Island as Glouster Isle. But these names were never in common use and don't appear in later charts. Moreover, even prior to 1776, the name Oak Island shows up in several land-transfer deeds.

The island is almost a mile long by less than half a mile wide at its broadest point and is roughly peanut-shaped, squeezing to less than four hundred yards near its center. The narrow area is mostly swamp and marshy ground, while the two ends of the island rise to approximately 35 feet above sea level. These elevated areas are geological drumlins, oval hills of compact glacial drift composed of over 150 feet of hard clay overlying anhydrite bedrock and carboniferous limestone. A significant point is that in undisturbed areas the soil can be (and obviously was) excavated with hand tools without the use of vertical shoring or the threat of water seepage.

The island's axis runs almost east-west, with the Money Pit located near the eastern, or seaward, end. Its western edge is only two hundred yards from shore, and since 1965 has been connected to the mainland at Crandall's Point by a causeway that was built to transport heavy digging equipment. Today most of the island is overgrown with brush and stands of evergreen, mainly spruce, although the eastern end is cleared and pockmarked with craters and mounds of earth from previous digs and the current Triton project.

Oak Island was part of the "Shoreham Grant" made in October 1759 by Nova Scotia's then British governor-in-chief, Charles Lawrence, to approximately sixty-five immigrants from Britain's New England colonies. The grant, which established the township of Shoreham (now the town of Chester, four miles northeast of Oak Island), covered about 100,000 acres and included several Mahone Bay islands. Prior to this, the immediate area had no permanent inhabitants, the closest major settlements being Lunenburg (founded in 1753) about ten miles down the southwest coast, and Halifax (founded in 1749) some forty miles up the coast. According to a 1763 census, Lunenburg County then consisted of some three hundred families, most of whom lived in and around the towns of Lunenburg and Chester and were primarily engaged in fishing and farming.

The original records show that in 1759 most of Oak Island was granted to New England families by the names of Monro, Lynch, Seacombe, and Young. Accounts of the 1795 discovery of the Money Pit indicate that the island was then uninhabited. Nevertheless, it was probably used by its grantees as a source of lumber and was perhaps even partially cultivated at its western end in the early years after the founding of Chester. And like several other Mahone Bay islands that lay close to shore, it may have been used to pasture cattle in its early years. (Rafting livestock out to a nearby island to fatten them over the summer was a New England practice that eliminated the need for the containment fences that were necessary on the mainland.)

The island was first surveyed in 1762 by Charles Morris, the province's surveyor-general. Its 128 acres were divided into 32 rectangular lots of about four acres apiece, with lots 1 to 20 running down the north side and lots 21 to 32 along the south side of the island.

The earliest existing deed pertaining to Oak Island shows the sale of Lot 19 by Edward Smith to Timothy Lynch, both of Chester, for five pounds sterling on March 8, 1768. This lot lies near the eastern tip of the island and is bounded on the west by Lot 18, the site of the Money Pit. It's not clear whether Smith was an original grantee of that part of the island or if he purchased it after 1759. But he may well have been the eponym of Smith's Cove, a name that was later applied to both the small inlet at the east end of the island and to the broader cove on the island's south side. (The eastern inlet has also been variously referred to on charts as Sheerdom Cove, Smuggler's Cove, and Pirate's Cove. Today the name Smith's Cove is the one most commonly used, as is the name South Shore Cove for the inlet on that side of the island.) Edward Smith was apparently unrelated to the John Smith who helped uncover the Money Pit, as the latter, according to DesBrisay, was born in Boston on August 20, 1775, and immigrated to the Chester area just prior to 1790.

Meanwhile, Anthony Vaughan, Sr., whose son was to be one of the Money Pit discoverers, had arrived from Massachusetts in 1772 and began farming a two-hundred-acre holding in what today is the town of Western Shore, directly opposite Oak Island on the mainland. Descendants of the Vaughan family still own much of that land. The origin and parentage of the initial discoverer, Daniel McGinnis, aren't known for certain. The only clue from DesBrisay is that among the early Chester settlers was a Daniel McInnis, a family name that was later changed to McGinnis.

From all available evidence, it would seem that the families of the three Money Pit discoverers had all emigrated from New England between 1770 and 1790 and that the three young men stumbled across Oak Island's mystery in the summer of 1795. The actual date was probably prior to June 26, 1795, because on that day John Smith purchased Lot 18, the site of the Money Pit. An extant deed records that it was sold to him by Casper Wollenhaupt of Lunenburg for seven pounds, ten shillings.

That summer Smith, who had married several years earlier, settled with his family on Oak Island, where he was to live on top of an enigma for the next sixty-two years.

CHAPTER TWO

The Mystery Deepens

FOLLOWING THEIR DISCOVERY AND EXCAVATION OF THE Money Pit down to thirty feet, McGinnis, Smith, and Vaughan finally told their mainland neighbors what they were up to and tried to enlist their help to continue the project. They were unsuccessful, partly because the hardworking farmers and fishermen of the area hadn't the time for the task, but also because of local superstition surrounding Oak Island. In the years preceding the discovery, inhabitants of Chester, four miles across the bay, had reported seeing "strange lights" burning at night on the island. Some speculated that the island was being used as an occasional base by murderous pirates, while others hinted at supernatural forces of evil lurking on the island. According to one legend, two Chester fishermen several years earlier had rowed out to investigate the nocturnal lights. The men were never seen again. Even today there are people in the area who regard Oak Island with superstitious dread, a feeling fueled by the complexity of the underground workings and the island's stubborn refusal to reveal its secret.

Nevertheless, John Smith remained convinced that the island had been selected by someone at some earlier time to bury a treasure. So he built his house and began farming the eastern end of the island with the intention of eventually solving the mystery that lay beneath his property. Over the next few years he acquired several more lots on the island's eastern end, while his fellow discoverer, Daniel McGinnis, took up farming on the island's southwest corner. They left the Money Pit untouched for several years, though according to some early chronicles the two men happened across additional evidence to indicate the place had been visited many years before. This included a copper coin dated 1713, a bosun's whistle, and an iron-ring bolt imbedded in a rock at Smith's Cove.

The mystery lay dormant until 1802, when Simeon Lynds, from the town of Onslow, at the head of Nova Scotia's Bay of Fundy, was in Chester on business and met Anthony Vaughan. Lynds heard the story of the 1795 discovery and was immediately caught up by the mystery. He returned home and formed a company financed by some thirty businessmen from Onslow and the nearby town of Truro to provide money and equipment to excavate the Money Pit.

The consortium, known as the Onslow Company, included the three discoverers, McGinnis, Smith, and Vaughan, then in their twenties. They began work in the spring of 1803, first digging out the Money Pit, which had partially caved in over the preceding eight years. They were soon down to thirty feet, and by midsummer had excavated the pit to ninety feet. As had been the case during the initial discovery, tightly fitted oak log platforms were found at exact intervals of ten feet. If puzzled by these platforms, the Onslow Company was also intrigued by layers of charcoal, putty, and a brown fibrous material that covered some of the wooden tiers. At that time they had no idea that the fiber was from husks of coconut; nor did they know that there was a lot more of it under this island that lies about 1,500 miles north of the nearest coconut tree.

The most mystifying clue awaited the workers at the ninety-foot level. Here, just before hitting another oak platform, they unearthed a large flat stone on which was engraved a strange inscription that none of them could decipher.

The story of this stone and its eventual fate is one of many frustrating footnotes to the Oak Island mystery. More than likely a stone with some sort of markings was found, for it is

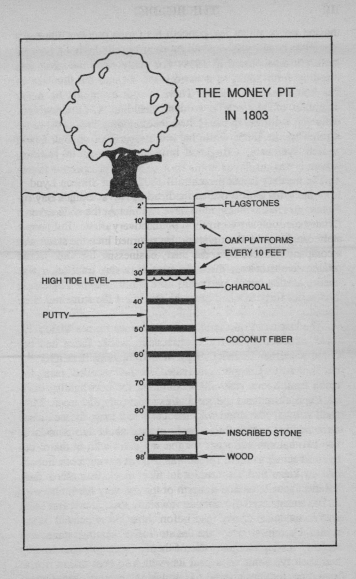

THE MONEY PIT
IN 1803

2' — FLAGSTONES

10' —

20' — OAK PLATFORMS
EVERY 10 FEET

30' —

HIGH TIDE LEVEL

40' — CHARCOAL

PUTTY —

50' — COCONUT FIBER

60' —

70' —

80' —

90' — INSCRIBED STONE

98' — WOOD

mentioned in all the early accounts of the Onslow Company's operations, and was reportedly seen by hundreds of persons before it disappeared in 1919. For many years the stone was used by John Smith as a curio piece set into the fireplace of his home on Oak Island. There it was examined by many members of later search groups, including A. O. Crieghton, who was a partner in the Halifax bookbinding firm of A. & H. Creighton. In 1865, while he was treasurer of an Oak Island search syndicate, Crieghton brought the stone to Halifax, where it was displayed at his shop to attract prospective investors in the Oak Island project.

About that time a professor of languages at Dalhousie University in Halifax claimed to have deciphered the code to read: "Forty feet below two million pounds are buried." But people were skeptical of this enticing translation, since the stone was being used to promote the sale of stock in the Oak Island search. Nonetheless, three decades after that translation was made, a later search party did bore through some interesting anomalies forty feet and more below where the stone had been found.

The last word on the stone itself comes from a March 27, 1935, affidavit by Harry W. Marshall, whose father had become a partner in the Creighton bookbinding firm after the death of A. O. Creighton in 1879. Marshall recalled seeing the stone from about 1890 till 1919 when the bookbinding business was closed and the stone was apparently discarded. Marshall stated: "The stone was about two feet long, fifteen inches wide and ten inches thick, and weighed about 175 pounds. It had two smooth surfaces, with rough sides with traces of cement attached to them (presumably from having been imbedded in John Smith's fireplace). The block resembled dark Swedish granite or fine-grained porphyry, very hard, and with an olive tinge, and did not resemble any local stone. But there was no evidence of any inscription either cut or painted on the stone. Creighton used the stone for a beating stone and weight." Other accounts state that the Creighton bookbinders had used the stone as a base on which to beat leather for at least three decades around the turn of the century. That fact, if true, would certainly have worn away the inscription.

INSCRIPTION ON THE STONE

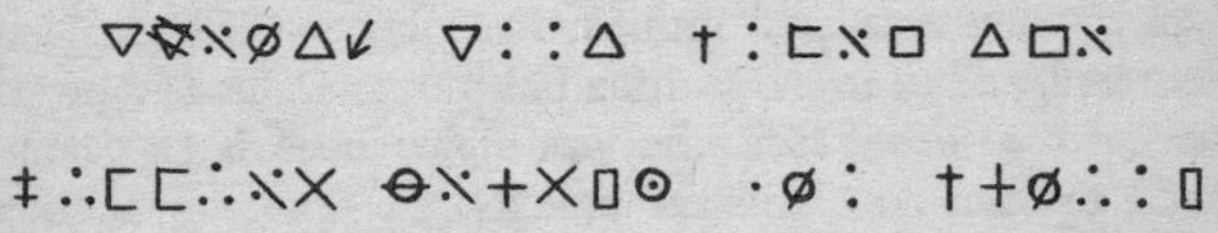

FOUND IN THE MONEY PIT IN 1803

If a photograph or rubbing of the inscription was ever made, it has never come to light. The most recent recording of the two-line, forty-character cipher by someone who apparently saw the inscription is contained in a 1909 letter by an elderly schoolteacher from the town of Mahone Bay. The glyphs, when translated into English plaintext letters, do indeed confirm the message reported by the Dalhousie professor. Yet the substitution letter-for-cipher code is so patently simple that one doubts its authenticity.

In September 1987, while having lunch with Joe Judge, senior associate editor of *National Geographic* magazine, I showed him a copy of the inscription. Intrigued, Judge took it back to his office. Within an hour he handed me his cryptanalysis of the message. His translation was identical to the one made by the Dalhousie professor.

More recently, Stephen M. Matyas of IBM's Crypto Competency Center in Manassas, Virginia, ran the inscription through the center's code-breaking computers. He concurred that the simplistic message is "most likely a fraud" and "cannot be trusted."

So while it is almost certain that an inscribed stone was found at ninety feet in the Money Pit in 1803, it's just as certain that the inscription as we know it today is a hoax, having been fabricated as investor bait in the 1860s. Nevertheless, many later searchers regarded the stone and its original cryptic message (whatever it was) as a key to the mystery of Oak Island. Whether that's true or not, the authentic inscription may at least have been a clue indicating how to get around the ingenious trap that lay below it.

After removing the stone and the wooden platform at ninety feet, the Onslow Company workers noticed that the earth was becoming soft and mushy. Yet they'd encountered no vein of sand or gravel that would indicate the possibility of a natural watercourse leading into the pit. According to the account in the *Colonist*: "At 93 feet [the water seepage] increased, and they had to take out one tub of water for two of earth. Still, they had no idea that anything was wrong." With night coming on, they probed the bottom of the pit to see if they could strike anything below, and at a depth of ninety-eight feet "they struck a hard impenetrable substance bound by the sides of the pit. Some supposed it was wood, and others called it a chest. They left for the night to resume operations in the morning, when they fully expected to solve the mystery."

But the next morning the diggers became the first to learn what the unknown engineer of Oak Island had in store for anyone who attempted to probe the depths of the Money Pit. The shaft, which during all those previous weeks of work had been dry, now contained about sixty feet of water. Discouraged but not defeated, they began bailing out the pit with buckets. Before long they realized their efforts were having no effect on the water level.

At this point the Onslow Company discontinued the project, as most of the workers had to return to their farms to bring in the autumn hay. But Simeon Lynds, convinced that the treasure lay just below the wooden obstruction that had been probed at ninety-eight feet, had every intention of returning the following spring with a new plan of attack.

The next year the Onslow Company was back, and again they confirmed the uselessness of trying to bail out the Money Pit. So they decided to circumvent the water by sinking a second shaft 14 feet southeast of the Money Pit and tunneling from there to the supposed cache. This shaft was dug to a depth of 114 feet with no water problems. "At this stage," said the *Colonist*, "they began to tunnel towards the old pit and got within two feet of it, having tunneled twelve, without encountering any hinderance. But at this time water oozed in upon them from the end of the tunnel and began to run in small streams. At length, the bank between the [Money] pit and tunnel giving away, they were obliged to effect an immediate retreat. And in less than two hours, water was standing in the new pit to the depth of 65 feet."

Again, bailing was futile, and this effectively put an end to the Onslow Company's Oak Island expedition. Another forty-five years were to pass before anyone would again make a serious attempt to reach the elusive treasure.

Most of the early reports don't indicate whether the 1803–04 searchers realized what they were up against in trying to drain or circumvent the water in the Money Pit. But the workers must surely have noticed, as did others who followed them, that the water was salty and that the level in the two pits rose and fell with the surrounding tide. Thus, their bailing efforts were tantamount to recycling the ocean. But how was seawater able to penetrate the island's hard-packed clay?

Without realizing it, the Onslow group had broken a primitive yet effective hydraulic seal when they removed the tightly fitted wooden platforms, particularly the one at ninety feet, just beneath the stone with its indecipherable message. It would later be established that the designer of the Money Pit had expected and wanted them to do precisely that. The Onslow Company had tripped a booby trap that had been set approximately two hundred years earlier.

CHAPTER THREE

The Trap Is Uncovered

AFTER THE ONSLOW GROUP'S FAILURE TO BRING UP ANY treasure, John Smith resumed farming his land on the eastern end of Oak Island, and at some point he filled in the two watery shafts. Much of the island was now being used by Smith and others as farm and grazing land as well as a source of timber. But the Money Pit and the frustrated attempts to reach its bottom became well known around Nova Scotia.

Not until 1849 was a new group formed to take another crack at recovering the treasure. This syndicate was known as the Truro Company, named after the hometown of most of its participants. Daniel McGinnis had died by this time, but Smith and Vaughan (both in their seventies) as well as Simeon Lynds were still around to point out the exact location of the Money Pit. The first task was to reexcavate the original shaft. This was accomplished in twelve days down to a depth of eighty-six feet, at which point water began entering and the workers were driven out. Once again, bailing proved useless and work was temporarily suspended.

Later that summer the Truro Company returned with a hand-operated pod auger of the type then used in prospecting for coal. The previously mentioned Jotham B. McCully was the drilling engineer. A platform was set up in the Money Pit at a depth of thirty feet, just above water level, and the inch-and-a-half diameter drill pipe lowered to the bottom of the shaft. The work involved screwing a chisel-tipped auger into the earth and then removing cores of drilled material.

The drilling program, which was to yield some interesting results, was recorded separately by McCully and another member of the Truro Company, and both versions generally corroborate one another. McCully, in a letter to a friend on June 2, 1862, and later in a report to another search syndicate says:

> We bored five holes, in the first of which we lost the only valve slugger we had. The second hole we bored struck the platform which the old [Onslow Company] diggers told us about—precisely at the depth they had told us they had struck it with a crowbar, 98 feet. After going through this platform, which was five inches thick and proved to be spruce, the auger dropped 12 inches and then went through four inches of oak; then it went through five inches of metal in pieces, but the auger failed to take any of it in except three links, resembling an ancient watch chain. It then went through eight inches of oak, which was thought to be the bottom of the first box and the top of the next; then 22 inches of [loose] metal, the same as before; then four inches of oak and six inches of spruce; then into clay seven feet without striking anything else. In the next [third] boring the platform was struck as before at 98 feet; passing through this the auger fell about 18 inches and came in contact with, as supposed, the side of a cask. On withdrawing the aguer, several splinters of oak, such as might come from the side of an oak stave, and a small quantity of a brown fibrous substance, closely resembling the husk of a coconut, were brought up. The distance between the upper and lower platforms was found to be six feet.

McCully described the chain that was brought up on the drill as "three small links which had apparently been forced from an epaulette. They were gold."

This was the first piece of tangible evidence that something of value was down in the Money Pit. Unfortunately, as McCully noted, the auger couldn't pick up any of the loose metal struck at two distinct levels. The final two holes were drilled near the inside walls of the pit. These only brought up further evidence of the platforms and loose earth without striking the metal, although James McNutt in his 1867 account states that "three pieces of wire which was copper were brought up by the auger" from the fifth hole.

If the workers couldn't physically get to the pit's watery bottom, they now had at least some idea of what was below the platform at ninety-eight feet: There appeared to be at least two large oaken chests filled with something metallic and laying one on top of the other at a depth of between 100 and 104 feet, after which there was another wooden platform spread across the pit at about the 105-foot level. Below that, in the seven additional feet they had drilled, the clay was loose, indicating that the Money Pit had originally been dug even deeper.

Shortly after these encouraging results, the Truro Company sank several more exploratory holes into the bottom of the Money Pit. The reported findings were basically the same as before. But now an element of intrigue comes into the story. John Pitbladdo, a mining engineer from Truro, was the foreman on this crew and was in charge of examining the drill-core samples that were brought to the surface. One day, John Gammell, a major shareholder in the Truro Company, happened to be on the site and saw Pitbladdo take something off the end of the drill, examine it closely, and then slip it into his pocket. Gammell later said he asked Pitbladdo what he had found, but was told he would have to wait until the next Truro Company board meeting when Pitbladdo would show it to all the directors.

Pitbladdo never showed up at that meeting; in fact, he was never seen on the island again. But he presumably had found something that convinced him there was treasure in the Money Pit. Nova Scotia provincial records show that on August 1, 1849, John Pitbladdo and an associate, Charles D. Archibald, who was manager of the Acadia Iron Works at Londonderry, Nova Scotia, applied to the lieutenant general of the province for a license to dig for treasure on Oak Island. They received permission several days later, but their license was limited to "ungranted and unoccupied lands on Oak Island." The two men then made a determined but unsuccessful attempt to purchase John Smith's land.

Nothing more came of Pitbladdo's scheme to get control of

the search area. Several years later Archibald moved to England and Pitbladdo was rumored to have died either in a gold mine or railway construction accident in the 1850s. However, in a second edition (1895) of DesBrisay's *History of the County of Lunenburg*, reference is made to a James Pitblado Sr., a mining engineer from Truro, who in 1875 was superintendent of a coal-prospecting venture in Chester. This could well have been John Pitbladdo, since in most written accounts of Oak Island he was incorrectly referred to as James Pitblado. In any case, no one, other than Archibald, ever learned what was brought up from the Money Pit on that summer day in 1849.

The next summer the Truro Company decided to sink another shaft about 10 feet northwest of the Money Pit. The intention again was to try to reach the treasure cache by lateral tunneling or, failing that, at least to use the new hole as a connecting pumping shaft to help lower the water level in the Money Pit. No water was encountered in this new shaft down to 109 feet, at which point the workers began tunneling toward the Money Pit. An account by Adams A. Tupper, one of the diggers in this operation, states: "Just before reaching that point [under the Money Pit], the water burst in and the workmen fled for their lives, and in 20 minutes there was 45 feet of water in the new pit." Two pumping gins, each powered by two horses, were set up over the Money Pit and the new shaft. According to Tupper, the pumping "was carried on night and day for about a week, but all in vain, the only difference being that with doubled appliances the water could be kept at a lower level than formerly."

It was now obvious that a huge volume of seawater was somehow entering the Money Pit at about the 100-foot level. Moreover, the flooding wasn't sporadic or accidental, since the two shafts that had been dug close to the Money Pit were in the same type of hard clay and went 100 feet deep without striking water. Only when they were connected to the Money Pit did they became flooded. And if the subterranean water channel that intersected the Money Pit was natural, then whoever originally dug the pit would have encountered it and been forced to abandon the project. Yet it was known that wooden

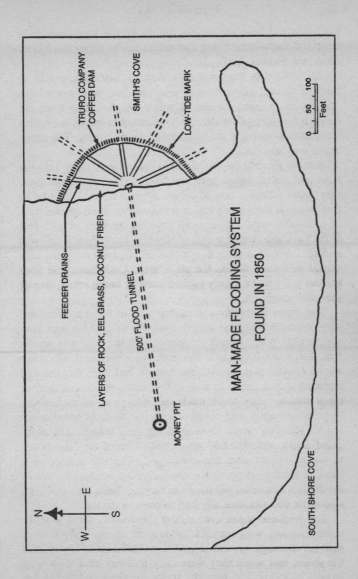

MAN-MADE FLOODING SYSTEM

FOUND IN 1850

TRURO COMPANY
COFFER DAM

SMITH'S COVE

LOW-TIDE MARK

FEEDER DRAINS

LAYERS OF ROCK, EEL GRASS, COCONUT FIBER

500' FLOOD TUNNEL

MONEY PIT

SOUTH SHORE COVE

0   50   100
Feet

N
W — E
S

platforms had been laid across the pit all the way down to at least 105 feet—something that could not possibly have been done in a flooded shaft.

At about this time someone noticed that at low tide in Smith's Cove, approximately five hundred feet east of the Money Pit, a small stream of water was trickling from the bank; it too was salt water. So a search was made of Smith's Cove beach, and this led to an amazing discovery. The entire beach was artificial!

Almost as soon as the workers started shoveling into the sand and gravel beach between the high and low tide lines, they came across a bed of brown fibrous material similar to that found in the Money Pit. It was coconut fiber; masses of it in a layer several inches deep covered an area of 145 feet along the shore from the high to low tide lines. Below this was another layer of four to five inches of decayed eel grass also spread uniformly across the same area. Underneath the fiber and eel grass was a tightly packed mass of beach rocks, free of sand and gravel.

The Truro Company's next step was to build a stone and clay cofferdam in order to hold back the tides. This took several weeks. When it was completed and the area was water-free, the rocks just inside the dam were removed. Here the workers found that the clay sea bottom had been dug out and replaced with a series of five well-constructed box drains, or catch basins. They were made of twin rows of rock about eight inches apart and covered with flat slabs of stone interspaced to allow water to seep along their length. The elongated drains were situated across the width of the false beach at the low-water line and converged, like the fingers of a hand, at a common point near the shore. An account by one of the diggers described the stones as having "been prepared with a hammer and mechanically laid to prevent caving."

The workers began dismantling the drains, starting at the cofferdam and working back toward the shore. They noticed that the drainage system sloped downward as it approached the shore, and when they were only halfway back they were already working five feet below the original beach. At this point, an Atlantic gale accompanied by unusually high tides washed away their cofferdam.

To rebuild it was considered too time-consuming and expensive, so a new plan was proposed. The Truro group had been able to expose only about half of the outer end of the drainage network and hadn't found the common point to which the drains apparently led. But they now had some indication of where the tunnel from the sea entered the island on its way to the Money Pit. Their plan therefore was to sink a shaft about one hundred feet inland from Smith's Cove in the hope of intersecting and plugging the flood tunnel.

This new shaft was dug to seventy-five feet before the workers realized that they must have missed the water tunnel. Moving about twelve feet to the south, another shaft was begun. This time, at a depth of thirty-five feet, they came to a large boulder. As soon as they started prying it out they encountered a rush of water. Within minutes the hole was flooded to sea level. They had found the tunnel. To block the drain, they partially refilled the shaft and drove wood pilings into its bottom. They were satisfied that they had short-circuited the trap that had prevented them from finding what was in the Money Pit.

They went back to bailing the Money Pit. With the pumping gins working continuously the water was lowered slightly, but it returned to sea level as soon as bailing ceased. Evidently, the tunnel from Smith's Cove hadn't been totally blocked. Or there was another possibility. According to McCully, the intersection of the flood tunnel near Smith's Cove had "slackened the flow of water into the old Money Pit, but did not stop it altogether, thereby inducing us to believe there might be another drain." McCully was beginning to comprehend the scope of the Oak Island workings, but he was still far from guessing the whole story.

McCully reported that in the fall of 1850 a new shaft was sunk 112 feet deep and slightly to the west of the Money Pit, to which it was connected by a tunnel. This shaft, too, was quickly flooded.

This setback effectively put an end to the Truro group's

work on the island. They tried the following spring (1851) to raise additional funds to continue operations. But the syndicate backers, discouraged by the obstacles encountered in the previous two years, weren't prepared to throw good money after bad, and the company was dissolved. Yet most of its members were certain that a great, if seemingly unattainable, treasure lay beneath the surface of Oak Island.

Despite their failure to recover the treasure, the Truro Company had learned a lot about the island that would be useful to later searchers. They had found evidence (which would later be confirmed) that someone had redesigned Smith's Cove into a gigantic feeder system capable of channeling the Atlantic Ocean at a rate of 600 gallons per minute into the Money Pit through a 500-foot-long stone-walled tunnel. The tunnel, which was 4 feet high and 2½ feet wide, sloped downhill on a 22 percent gradient from the shore to meet the Money Pit at a depth of 111 to 115 feet. Since the Smith's Cove catch basins lay between the high- and low-water marks, there was some tidal effect in the Money Pit and the surrounding shafts. The Truro workers observed a rise and fall of about 18 inches in the Money Pit water level, or a ratio of one-to-four to the normal six-foot tidal range of Mahone Bay. Moreover, the drains in the feeder system were cleverly prevented from silting up by a mammoth sponge filter composed of eel grass and coconut fiber.

The fiber, which occasionally is still dug up under the island's offshore silt, has indisputably been identified as coir, the material found between the nut and outer husk of the coconut. Botanists several times identified it as such in the 1800s. In 1916 a sample of it was submitted to the Smithsonian Institution in Washington, D.C., for analysis. The Smithsonian reported that the material is "undoubtedly from the fibrous husks surrounding a coconut" and added that "this fiber is especially resistant to the effects of sea water, and under the conditions in which it was found [in Smith's Cove] might have been there for several hundred years." The Smithsonian came up with the same result when more of the fiber was found in 1930. It has also been confirmed by analysis of samples uncovered in recent years.

While this use as a filtering agent seems unique, coconut fiber was commonly used during the sixteenth through nineteenth centuries as dunnage on sailing ships. It was laid on the bottom of the cargo holds as an absorption material to prevent water damage, and was also packed between casks and crates to inhibit shifting and breakage.

To build this elaborate water trap the unknown engineer of Oak Island would first have had to erect a cofferdam around Smith's Cove. (McCully mentions that "the remains of an old dam was seen outside of the place where we found the drain and tunnel to the shore." This indicates that the Truro Company's dam, even if it had held, probably wasn't built far enough out to encompass the whole drainage system.) Once the Money Pit, tunnel, drains, and rock-covered filter system were in place, the cofferdam was destroyed, thus setting the trap.

Clearly, the Money Pit with its wooden hydraulic seals worked on the same principle as a thumb-capped drinking straw dipped into a glass of water. Remove the thumb, and the water in the straw rises to the level in the jar. Such an elaborate system would have been constructed only to hide something of great value for a considerable length of time. But the full complexity of the system had yet to be discovered.

CHAPTER FOUR

The Money Pit Collapses

It was ten years after the dissolution of the Truro Company before another syndicate resumed the search. Meanwhile, John Smith's twenty-four-acre property (lots 15 through 20) on Oak Island's eastern end, which included the Money Pit and Smith's Cove, was acquired by Anthony Graves. That, together with other lots he'd previously purchased, made Graves the island's largest landowner. His farmhouse was on the north side of the island at Joudrey's Cove. (Its foundation can still be seen.) Other than receiving a lease fee for the use of his land, Graves wasn't involved with the 1860s treasure-hunting groups. But it was later rumored that he may have stumbled across something of value on his property prior to his death in 1888.

On April 3, 1861, the Oak Island Association was formed in Truro "for the purposes of making excavation on Oak Island in search of Hidden Treasures." The corporate secretary was Jotham McCully, who had been with the Truro syndicate of 1849–50. Some of the other backers also had participated in the Truro group. Under its charter the association had an issued capital of one hundred shares sold at $20 apiece, though this was added to several times in the next three years. Most of the funds were used for a large labor force, enticed to the island with the then-decent wage of $18 a month plus board and traveling expenses.

The first job was to clear out and recrib the Money Pit, which had partially caved in over the years. The water was bailed out easily and the pit reopened to 88 feet, though no deeper, as the muddy clay below that seemed to be effectively blocking any heavy flooding from Smith's Cove. Next, a new shaft was dug about 25 feet east of the Money Pit with the intention of intercepting the water tunnel. But it was abandoned at 120 feet after it had obviously missed the tunnel.

The workers then began another shaft about 18 feet west of the Money Pit and 118 feet deep. A tunnel four feet high by three feet wide was driven from its bottom to the Money Pit in the hope of striking the treasure vault.

McCully, in a letter written the following year, says this tunnel "entered the old Money Pit a little below the lower platform [the one bored through at 105 feet in 1849] where we found the soft clay spoken of in the [1849] boring. The tunnel was unwisely driven through the old [Money] pit until it nearly reached the east pipe, when the water started, apparently coming above on the east side." He then notes that three days of continuous bailing with a horse-operated pumping gin failed to reduce the water in the newly dug shaft. Moreover, water was again seeping up through the Money Pit itself.

A mammoth bailing operation was set up under the direction of George Mitchell, the superintendent of works. With a total of sixty-three men and thirty-three horses working in shifts, pumping gins were erected over the Money Pit and two other shafts. The bailing apparatus in each of the three holes consisted of four seventy-gallon casks that were continuously lowered, filled, raised, and dumped. This succeeded in almost draining the pits.

McCully writes that the workers "commenced bailing on Wednesday morning, continued constantly night and day until Friday morning when the tunnel leading from the West pit to the Money Pit, which was 17 ft. long, 4 ft. high and 3 ft. wide, became choked with clay, we sent two men down to clear it out. After they had gone about half way through [the tunnel] they heard a tremendous crash in the Money Pit and barely escaped being caught by the rush of mud which followed them into the West pit and filled it up 7 feet [of mud] in less than three minutes. In the meantime a stick of oak timber of considerable girth and 3½ feet in length was ejected with the mud."

Writing in the newspaper the *Nova Scotian* in September of that year, "the digger Patrick," who was at the scene of the collapse, recalled that "while the water [from the Money Pit] was hindered by this earth [in the tunnel] from coming through [to the westerly shaft] we took out part of the earth and wood. The wood was stained black with age; it was cut, hewn, chamfered, sawn and bored, according to the purpose for which it was needed. We also took out part of the bottom of a keg." An account by James McNutt in 1867 also mentions that a "piece of juniper with bark on [and] cut at each end with an edge tool" and "a spruce slab with a mining auger hole in it" were dug out of the mud that had gushed from the Money Pit into the west shaft.

These diggers would obviously have been able to tell the difference between timbers used in their own tunnel cribbing and wood that was far older. Consequently, they were presented with substantial proof that some sort of wood construction lay more than 100 feet down in the Money Pit. And the spruce slab with the auger hole through it may well have been part of one of the platforms drilled into at the 98- and 105-foot levels in 1849. Unfortunately, carbon-dating analysis hadn't yet been invented. A century would pass before this technique could be applied to original wood excavated from beneath the island. And the results date the original project to the late sixteenth century.

McCully reported that when some of the mud in the connecting tunnel between the west shaft and the Money Pit had been cleared, the west shaft again began to flood. So bailing was resumed and "continued until 3 o'clock P.M. of Saturday when, on clearing the tunnel [of mud] again, another crash was heard in the Money Pit which [we] supposed to be the upper platform [at 98 feet in the Money Pit] falling, and immediately the bottom of the Money Pit fell to about 102 feet measuring from the level of the ground to the top. It had been cleared out previously down [to] 88 feet. Immediately after, the cribbing [on the side of the walls] of the Money Pit, commencing at the bottom, fell in plank after plank until there was only about 30 feet of the upper cribbing left. On Monday the top fell in, leaving the old Money Pit a complete mass of ruins."

On that summer weekend of 1861, the Oak Island Association had undermined and inadvertently caused the collapse of the platforms and suspected chests of treasure that the Truro Company drillers had encountered between 98 and 105 feet back in 1849. But where had they fallen to? As McCully noted, the excavated bottom of the Money Pit dropped from 88 to 102 feet, or a total of 14 feet. This would suggest that the lower platform on which the chests rested was now at around 119 feet.

Much later, it was theorized that the platforms and other material had collapsed into a void 130 feet or more down in the pit. In fact, it would eventually be found that the Money Pit had been constructed far deeper than that, and that the 1861 group had probably tripped a booby trap that lay beneath one of the higher treasure vaults.

Samuel C. Fraser, a member of the Oak Island Association's executive committee and a participant in later search groups, outlined his theories about the collapse in an 1895 letter to A. S. Lowden, then manager of an Oak Island syndicate:

> As to the falling of the treasure, a man by the name of George Mitchell was then in charge. He finished the sinking of the 118-foot [westerly] shaft through which the water was taken away, while the Money Pit was to be cleaned out to the treasure. I was sent down to clean out the Money Pit, but before going into it I examined the 118-foot pit and tunnel which was then nearly finished. At the end of the tunnel I saw every sign of the cataclysm that was about to take place and refused to go into the Money Pit. . . . When the pit fell down I was there. . . . There went down 10,000 feet of lumber, the cribbing of the pit. Could these planks stop on their way down and turn into an 18-foot tunnel 3' by 4'? Would or could casks of treasure having 10,000 feet of lumber and

hundreds of tons of earth behind them turn into a 3' by 4' tunnel? And if they could perform the impossible, would an 18-foot tunnel, 3' by 4', hold all this material?

In his letter, Fraser theorized that the designer of the Money Pit "sank the shaft at first 155 feet deep, put part of the treasure there with a branch drain [flood tunnel] into it. Now, to dig into the Money Pit means to pull all those planks [from the 1861 collapse] out by the teeth. And to believe that they turned into that little 18-foot tunnel would require as much faith from me as that Halley's Comet went through it." Fraser then advised Lowden to "sink your pumping shaft deep— deep enough to drain the Money Pit at 155 feet, and you have the treasure."

What Fraser was getting at was that the collapse and disappearance of all that material indicated the presence of a large cavity deep in the Money Pit. In another letter to Lowden he stated that the top of the cavity would have to be below 120 feet or so, "because when I went into the tunnel [under the Money Pit] from the 118-foot pit, [the workers] were [digging] in disturbed earth." (This agrees with McCully's statements.) Fraser's theory was that whoever built the Money Pit "must have placed strong beams across the shaft [at or below the 120-foot level] and thrown in say ten or fifteen feet of earth on these under the upper treasure." Much of Fraser's hypothesis would be confirmed by later exploration.

Despite the devastating collapse of the Money Pit, the association was able to raise an additional $2,000 to continue work. That fall a cast-iron pump and steam engine were purchased in Halifax. Andrew Spedon reported that "in the fall of 1861, at great expense, pumps were erected to be driven by steam power; but scarcely had the work been commenced when the boiler burst, causing operations to be suspended until another season."

McCully and Spedon both fail to record the first death resulting from the Oak Island search. In an essay written in 1868, E. H. Owen of Lunenburg noted that in 1861 "the boiler of one company burst whereby one man was scalded to death and others injured." The island had claimed its first victim. Others would follow.

The association returned in the spring of 1862 and sank another hole 107 feet deep alongside and connected to the Money Pit. This was to serve as a pumping shaft for the steam-powered pump. The Money Pit was then cleared and recribbed to 103 feet, at which point the water seeping up from below exceeded the capacity of the pump.

McNutt said that while the mud was being cleared out of the Money Pit the workers came across some tools left by the 1849 Truro group at ninety feet, as well as tools belonging to the 1803 Onslow Company at one hundred feet. These presumably were found in recesses in the side of the pit, since they hadn't fallen with the other material when the pit collapsed the summer before. He also reports that the last tier of the Onslow group's vertical cribbing was found intact at ninety feet, thereby proving that the wood that had been recovered after the 1861 collapse was part of the pit's original construction.

The Oak Island Association was now broke but still determined to reach the elusive treasure. After raising a little money, they turned their attention to the drains at Smith's Cove. They couldn't afford to build a proper cofferdam, so work in the early spring of 1863 was limited to uncovering a section of the drains nearest the shore at low tide. Approximately forty feet of the drainage system was exposed and plugged tightly with clay. After allowing several weeks for the clay to compact and harden, the steam pumps were again started in the Money Pit and westerly shaft. Although the rate had diminished somewhat, seawater was still entering the pits, and eventually the tides washed the clay plugs away.

Work was suspended for about three months while the association endeavored to raise more money. On August 24, 1863, the *Nova Scotian* reported that operations had resumed and that "men and machinery are now at work pumping the water from the pits previously sunk, and it is said they are sanguine that before the lapse of the month they will strike the treasure."

Using pumps in various connected shafts, the water level in the Money Pit was held down to 108 feet, enabling the workers to crib the pit between 103 and 108 feet. They then dug a circular tunnel 95 feet down around the outside of the pit, intersecting a couple of earlier searchers' shafts in the process. Two other lateral tunnels were also dug, but their direction and depth were unrecorded. This mole labor continued sporadically into the following year, but it was generally found impossible to do any work below 110 feet in the immediate vicinity of the Money Pit without being flooded out. And the treasure, they knew, was now below that.

Sometime in 1864 the flood tunnel was struck at about the point where it entered the east side of the Money Pit. Samuel Fraser in his letter to A. S. Lowden in 1895 recalled: "As we entered the old place of the treasure [via a lateral tunnel at 110 feet] we cut off the mouth of the [flood] tunnel. As we opened it, the water hurled around rocks about twice the size of a man's head with many smaller, and drove the men back for protection. . . . The [flood] tunnel was found near the top of our tunnel."

They had found the man-made watercourse, but they were powerless to shut it off.

The association was now even deeper in the red and its backers were thoroughly discouraged. Moreover, the constant erosion of seawater was undermining the walls of the Money Pit, and some of the workers were refusing to enter it. The shaft was inspected by mining engineers who declared it unsafe and advised that it be condemned. That was it; the association was finished.

A new group calling itself the Oak Island Contract Company attempted to pick up where the Oak Island Association had left off. At their founding meeting in Halifax on March 29, 1865, the directors stated that 1,500 pounds at one pound per share (a total of about $6,000) would be solicited from the general public to continue the work. It was at this time that the inscribed rock found in the Money Pit in 1803 was removed from the Oak Island home of the late John Smith and brought to Halifax by the syndicate's treasurer, A. O. Creighton, as a lure for prospective shareholders. But the company never got off the ground (only six shares were subscribed for at the initial meeting), and no work was done on the island that year.

On May 3, 1866, the Oak Island Eldorado Company was incorporated with the same officers as those of the Oak Island Contract Company. This group successfully raised $4,000 in shares of $20 apiece and leased the eastern end of the island from Anthony Graves. According to a circular issued by the company, it proposed "to build a substantial wood and clay dam seaward [in Smith's Cove] to extend out and beyond the rock [drainage] work so as to encompass the whole within the dam, to pump out all the water within the area, and to break up the inlet from the sea; the cost of which [the directors] expect will not exceed 400 pounds." Shareholders were assured that "there cannot be any doubt but this mode of operation must succeed and will lead to the development of the hidden treasure so long sought for."

According to James McNutt, who worked on the island that year, the cofferdam was 375 feet long, 12 feet high, and was situated 120 feet below the high-water mark in the cove. But like the one in 1850, this dam was soon destroyed by Atlantic storms and abnormally high tides.

The Eldorado group then resorted to exploratory drilling to try to locate the treasure cache which was thought to have fallen in the collapse of the Money Pit in 1861. Three holes were drilled during a six-week period from November 26, 1866, to January 7, 1867. Significantly, the drill holes were cased inside a three-inch-diameter metal sleeve. This was the first time casing had been used, and it ensured that whatever material was brought up on the bit was found at the original level rather than something that may have fallen into the hole from higher up.

McNutt logged a day-to-day report on the drilling program. With the pumps holding the water at bay, the first hole was started from a platform on the bottom of the Money Pit at 108 feet. Measuring from ground level, spruce wood was struck at 110 feet, then several feet of coarse gravel, soft clay, and blue mud. Water mixed with chips of wood, coconut fiber, and charcoal were brought up from 128 feet. Water was struck again at about 140 feet, followed by soft clay and fine sand;

then more water at 150 feet. The next two or three feet yielded
a dry reddish soil that had never been disturbed.

The second hole was drilled from a platform at 78 feet and
was angled to the southeast; the third probe began at about 30
feet and slanted northeast. They were drilled to 103 feet and
160 feet respectively from the surface without striking anything of interest.

It's uncertain whether the Eldorado Company (which was
also known as the Halifax Company) did any additional work.
(They may have dug a shaft 175 feet southeast of the Money
Pit and run a series of tunnels toward the pit. There is no
original record of this work, although in the early 1940s tunnels were found that appeared to date from the 1860s.) By late
1867 the group had abandoned the search and the company
was dissolved.

By then the east end of Oak Island was a rabbit warren of
pits and tunnels. In the seventy-two years since the Money
Pit's discovery a total of eleven shafts (including the Money
Pit) had been dug, hundreds of feet of tunneling had been
excavated, and two cofferdams had been built. The search at
that point had taken one life and had eaten up an estimated $2
million at today's labor and material costs, and still no treasure had been brought up.

Both the mystery and the treasure appeared to be deeper
than ever, and twenty-six years would pass before another
serious effort was made to solve the riddle.

CHAPTER FIVE

The Kidd Connection

IN THOSE FIRST SEVENTY-TWO YEARS OF FRUITLESS SEARCHing, there was of course a lot of speculation as to who designed the project and for what purpose. Everyone associated with Oak Island assumed that no one would have dug and carefully refilled a pit more than one hundred feet deep except to hide some kind of treasure; and a treasure of great value, considering the work that went into protecting it with a tunnel to the sea. They also assumed the deposit was still down there. For, they argued, had the original digger returned to recover his loot, then the Money Pit or any access shaft leading to it would not have been refilled; no more than a departing house burglar would stop to repair a lock or replace a windowpane that he'd broken on his way in.

So those early searchers were confident that a rich hoard was still buried on Oak Island. And most of them were equally sure of the identity of the depositor: Captain William Kidd. From what is known today about Oak Island and Captain Kidd, the theory is untenable. Yet there are still some who believe it.

The origin and widespread acceptance of the Kidd theory by nineteenth-century Nova Scotians had much to do with the New England roots of the Mahone Bay area settlers. The 1759 founders of Chester had all heard accounts of Kidd's exploits from their parents or grandparents, who had lived in Kidd's time. In the ten years piror to his execution in 1701, Kidd—who had married a wealthy New York widow and owned property in what is now the financial district of Lower Manhattan—was well known for his daring seamanship as a commissioned privateer capturing French and other enemy ships for the British Crown. But in July 1699 he was arrested in Boston on charges of murder and conspiracy, and was shipped back to England where he was hanged on May 23, 1701.

Most historians who have researched Kidd's life have concluded that he was no more a pirate than other privateers of his time, and that he was made a political scapegoat in a scandal involving high British officials and East Indian trading interests. Nevertheless, his trial and execution stigmatized him as a notorious buccaneer, and he became a legend in England and the American colonies.

As was customary, Kidd and his crew were entitled to a share in the spoils obtained under their commissions as privateers. And no doubt Kidd and his contemporaries weren't above supplementing this share by concealing part of their captured booty before arriving back at their home ports. On his return to Boston in 1699, after three years roaming the Caribbean, the Indian Ocean, and the China Sea, Kidd had sixty pounds of gold, one hundred pounds of silver, and various other goods of value aboard his sloop *San Antonio*. Then, soon after his arrest, a party sent out by the Earl of Bellomont, governor of New York and Massachusetts Bay, found approximately 10,000 pounds sterling worth of gold, silver, and jewels that Kidd, on his way to Boston, had buried on Gardiner's Island in New York's Long Island Sound.

But many are still convinced that he must have stashed a lot more than that somewhere, and for over two centuries treasure hunters have sought the lost spoils of Captain Kidd. Legend places suspected Kidd caches in hundreds of coastal bays and islands along the Atlantic seaboard from South Carolina to Maine, as well as in the West Indies, the Bahamas, and the China Sea. Indeed, if every "authentic" Kidd map that has ever turned up represented an actual treasure location,

William Kidd and his crew would have spent more time digging than sailing and plundering.

Yet there is evidence that one Kidd treasure may still be awaiting its finder somewhere in the tropics. On May 12, 1701, after he had been sentenced to hang, Kidd made a desperate written appeal to the House of Commons offering to go as a prisoner aboard a government ship and lead the way to "goods and treasure to the value of one hundred thousand pounds" located somewhere in "the Indies." This was to be in exchange for a reprieve. The British government never took Kidd up on his offer, and there is still some debate over whether or not he was bluffing.

However, in the spring of 1699 Kidd had sailed from the East Indies around the Cape of Good Hope to the Caribbean aboard a captured Moorish ship, *Quedagh Merchant*. He left the vessel with some of his crew at Hispaniola and from there sailed home to New England aboard the *San Antonio*. An estimated 90,000 pounds sterling in booty was probably aboard the *Quedagh Merchant*, and that may have been the treasure Kidd attempted to trade for his life and freedom. What happened to the wealth aboard that ship isn't known, though many believe that a good part of it is buried on some unknown island in the West Indies.

The exaggerated stories of Kidd's piratical deeds and his hoards of buried loot were carried to Nova Scotia by the early New England émigrés. Small wonder, therefore, that he was given credit for the underground workings found on Oak Island. Kidd even had an influence on the early written records of the Oak Island search.

The accounts in the *Colonist* and the *Liverpool Transcript* in the 1860s, and later in the DesBrisay and Longworth essays, all begin with the statement that when the first settlers came to Chester they brought with them a widely publicized tale. Apparently, sometime in the mid-1700s an old sailor died somewhere in New England and on his deathbed confessed that he had been a member of Captain Kidd's crew. Moreover, he told his listeners that many years earlier he had assisted Kidd in burying some two million pounds sterling worth of treasure on an unknown island somewhere east of Boston. The

sailor had reportedly kept this secret until his death for fear of
being hanged as a pirate. These accounts suggest the possibility that the three 1795 Money Pit discoverers were aware of
this story.

With time, the story become more elaborate, to the point
where some believed that the discovery of the Money Pit was
no accident. In 1939 Gilbert Hedden, who was then involved
in the Oak Island search, tracked down and interviewed a
certain Captain Anthony Vaughan in New York City. Captain
Vaughan, who was ninety-nine at the time, said he was born
on the Vaughan farm in Western Shore and was a grandson of
the Anthony Vaughan who had helped discover the Money Pit.
He ran away to sea at the age of fifteen, taking with him a tale
he had heard in the family. Hedden, in a letter, gives the
following account of Captain Vaughan's statement:

> The Vaughans came to Nova Scotia by way of New England
> from Virginia. They were later followed by the McGinnises and
> Smiths. After having settled in the vicinity, some time in the 1790s
> two of the Smiths or McGinnises, or one of each family who were
> sailors, visited the [Smith or McGinnis] family after an extended
> voyage ending in England. While in England they had befriended
> an old sailor who said he was one of Kidd's crew, and in gratitude
> for their help and friendliness he had told them that Kidd did have
> a huge cache of valuable booty. He did not know exactly where it
> was except that it was somewhere in "New Anglia" and that it was
> on an island "covered with oaks." This information excited the
> local [Smith or McGinnis] family, knowing of Oak Island, and led
> them to carefully explore the island with the results that we know
> of.

Another version appears in Andrew Spedon's *Rambles
Among the Blue-Noses* (1863) in which the author introduces
his account of the Oak Island search with the fabricated tale of
a certain Lieutenant Lawrence, a member of Kidd's crew who
jumped overboard to escape hanging just before Kidd reached
Boston harbor. Lawrence is supposed to have sought refuge in
a Dutch settlement in Massachusetts Bay and died a few
weeks later. But on his deathbed he told his Dutch benefactors
that Kidd had deposited an immense treasure on the south

coast of Nova Scotia. A descendant of one of these benefactors was, according to Spedon, someone who eventually took up residence on Oak Island, presumably McGinnis or Smith.

Similar stories of this nature have cropped up over the years, all of them based on the revelations of a pirate who supposedly was once part of Kidd's crew. In one early account, even Simeon Lynds of the 1803–04 Onslow group was reported to have become involved with Oak Island after coming across a map drawn by this dying crew member.

It's very unlikely that Lynds or anyone else connected with the initial investigation of Oak Island had a map or other handed-down information that led them to the Money Pit. Such suggestions were probably added to the Oak Island story after the accidental discovery in order to lend credence to the notion that Kidd's treasure was at the bottom of the Money Pit. In *The Book of Buried Treasure* (1911), Ralph D. Paine points out that the dying sailor story was commonly associated with hunts for pirate treasure along the United States Atlantic coast during the nineteenth century. Such stories, he notes, are "strikingly alike in that the lone survivor of the red-handed crew . . . preserved a chart showing where the treasure had been hid. Unable to return to the place, he gave the parchment to some friend or shipmate, this dramatic transfer usually happening as a deathbed ceremony."

Dying sailor myths notwithstanding, it is difficult to understand how Oak Island chroniclers could seriously associate that particular project with William Kidd. Dunbar Hinrichs of St. Petersburg, Florida, spent much of his life researching and writing about Kidd and claims to be able to place Kidd almost daily during his years as a privateer from 1676 to 1701. In 1976 Hinrichs told me he has "never found a shred of evidence that William Kidd ever set foot on Oak Island in Mahone Bay or, for that matter, even knew this place existed." In addition, Kidd did not have the engineering ability to design something as elaborate as the Oak Island workings are known to be. Nevertheless, the Kidd–Oak Island connection would resurface in the 1930s under most peculiar circumstances.

Kidd is not the only pirate credited with being the genius

who designed the Oak Island workings. Over the years various theories have placed almost every well-known seventeenth-century buccaneer at the scene of the Money Pit's creation. These include William Phipps (1650–94), Henry Morgan (1635–88), William Dampier (1625–1715), and Edward (Blackbeard) Teach (?–1718). Yet, other than for Phipps, there is no record of these men ever having sailed near the coast of Acadia, as the province was known for more than one hundred years after its founding in 1604.

Phipps, born in Maine and initially a ship's carpenter, took to the sea in command of his own vessel in the 1680s. In 1686 he led an expedition to retrieve for the British Crown a sunken Spanish galleon off the coast of Hispaniola. He was successful and was knighted in 1687. As a privateer for the English he raided and looted the French settlement of Port Royal on Nova Scotia's Bay of Fundy in 1690. He is also reputed to have attacked other Acadian settlements on the south coast of the province. It is doubtful he ever took the time, as some have claimed, to stash his plunder on Oak Island. In 1692 he became the first royal governor of Massachusetts, a post he held until his death two years later.

As for Phipps's famous contemporaries, they were primarily operators in southern waters, particularly the West Indies, where they preyed upon the lucrative galleons and outposts of the Spanish New World empire. There seems little reason for any of them to have sailed 2,000 miles north to bury their swag when there were hundreds of uninhabited islands and coastal coves to choose from in their own backyard.

Many of those pirates used Port Royal, Jamaica, as their base—a city described as "the hellhole of the Caribbean" until it slid into the sea during an earthquake on June 17, 1692, taking with it the interred bones of Sir Henry Morgan. Some people have pointed to the fortifications of Port Royal as an example of the ability of pirates to join forces in order to construct something more elaborate than a ten-foot hole in the ground in which to place a chest of doubloons. But Port Royal, unlike the Oak Island project, was built in the open (using mostly slave labor) and posed no problem of pirates having to entrust one another with secrets of hidden wealth. The buccaneers made Port Royal their communal lair, but the location of their personal caches were usually known only to themselves. Had they not squandered their ill-gotten gains prior to their (often untimely) deaths, their secret was apt to die with them. As Blackbeard prior to his beheading in 1718 boasted: "I've buried my treasure where none but Satan and myself can find it."

One of the most insistent latter-day proponents of an Oak Island pirate connection was Johnny Goodman, an ex-machinist from Chicago who later settled in Liscomb Mills, a tiny fishing community 120 miles northeast of Oak Island. From 1968 until his death in 1985, Goodman spent most of his waking hours deciphering a myriad of codes that he claimed all related to the island. He got his information from the symbols found on the inscribed rock in the Money Pit in 1803, as well as from several other island markers and "pirate maps." (Most of his maps, found in books on Kidd and other pirates, have long been regarded as fakes.)

By using mathematical wizardry and by turning numbers into letters and vice versa, Goodman claimed to have pinpointed the locations of seven treasure caches with a total value of $210 million beneath Oak Island. Over the years he variously attributed the source of these treasures to Kidd, Dampier, and Morgan. However, his "evidence" tended to be either impossibly arcane or ridiculously simplistic.

I can recall one long session I spent with him in 1976 when he tried his best to convince me of the infallibility of his deductions. As an example of his investigative methods he showed me an ancient chart allegedly of Oak Island and bearing William Kidd's initials. But, Goodman explained, the map was actually drawn by William Dampier, and the proof was contained in a secret code on the map. As I stared blankly at the chart, Goodman drew my attention to a small flag drawn on one corner.

"How many letters in the word 'flag'?" he asked me.

"Four," I replied.

"Good. Now, what's the fourth letter of the alphabet?"

"D," I answered.

Goodman smiled triumphantly. "Correct; D for Dampier. It's just a matter of breaking the code."

And so the evening went. I drove home four hours later nursing a splitting headache.

Another of Goodman's clues lay in the numbers "44106818." By playing around with those figures he used them to confirm the location of one of Oak Island's treasure vaults. The numbers were supposedly on a card that Kidd slipped to his wife just before he was hanged in 1701. Although he refused to believe it, Goodman had been taken in by one of the more celebrated hoaxes in the history of pirate lore.

Briefly, the practical joke began in 1894 when a Chicago industrialist wrote a pamphlet describing a fanciful lawsuit being filed against descendants of the John Jacob Astor family of New York. The "suit" alleged that the Astor wealth originated from a Captain Kidd treasure that had been illegally removed from Deer Isle, Maine. (The invented number code applied to Deer Isle's approximate latitude and longitude: 44 degrees 10 minutes north; 68 degrees 18 minutes west.) The elaborate joke was taken seriously by some writers, and was often printed as fact in books and magazine articles during the early twentieth century.

In 1970, through dogged persistence, Goodman managed to persuade Triton Alliance, the current search group, to use a bulldozer to excavate several spots where he was sure there were tunnels leading to a pirate treasure cache. Nothing was found, and his agreement with Triton was terminated. But, explaining that he had miscalculated slightly in his chosen locations, he insisted on another chance. When Triton refused, he kept pestering them with registered letters, and even took his case to the Nova Scotia newspapers and radio.

In April 1973 Triton's president, David Tobias, sent him a terse letter asking him to "be good enough to stop all further correspondence and/or any communication" with members of Triton Alliance. But Goodman persevered for many years after, confident that only he had the answer to the Oak Island mystery.

When I last met him, in 1980, Goodman was still involved in his research and hoping to get back on the island to prove his theories. By then he had transferred all of his drawings of Oak Island's tunnels, treasure vaults, "death traps," and deciphered secret codes onto beautifully embroidered bed sheets. (When he wasn't pursuing his obsession with Oak Island, he was tinkering with inventions such as an automobile that he said ran "without gasoline, batteries, or even an engine." He'd also designed a "perpetual-motion machine," though he told me he hadn't yet figured out how to start it.)

Another code-breaker of pirate maps and inscribed rocks appeared on the island in 1985, trying to convince Triton that they were digging in the wrong spot. Vic Marcellus, a retired Milwaukee contractor, is convinced that Kidd buried the treasure and that it lies about 660 feet northeast of the Money Pit. Apart from the fact that Triton, for different reasons, had in 1974 sunk a 100-foot shaft in almost exactly the same location and had found nothing, the company studiously avoided Marcellus and his so-called proof.

As Dan Blankenship, Triton's field manager, explains, "If we carry on a dialogue with these people, and if anything is ever found, then they will step forward and make a claim on the treasure on the grounds that their information helped us to locate it."

One of the reasons Goodman was able to convince Triton Alliance to allow him to try his luck on the island was that until quite recently, even David Tobias believed that Caribbean buccaneers may have banded together to hide their stolen loot in a sort of communal bank under Oak Island.

According to this theory, the main shaft, or Money Pit, was first excavated. Then each group of pirates dug its own tunnel at a specific level and in a certain direction away from the Money Pit. A watertight vault was made at the end of each tunnel to contain the treasure. Only the pirate band using that particular tunnel would know the precise bearing and length of the corridor. Once they'd buried their separate caches, the pirates built the flood trap, filled in the Money Pit, and then opened up the drains at the water's edge. Neither the pirates nor any searcher who happened along would be able to get at the treasure vaults via the booby-trapped main shaft. But each group of buccaneers could come back anytime and retrieve its own loot simply by digging straight through virgin ground and into the vault, the depth and location of which would have been previously measured and recorded in relation to surface features on the island.

The theory is a good one from an engineering point of view. But considering the mistrust that pirates had of one another, it's difficult to conceive of them combining forces to hide their valuables. Even harder to imagine is the idea that pirates would ever spend the time and energy required for such a complex project. And then, if a large group of buccaneers was involved, surely some rumor of the operation would have later circulated through the bars and brothels of seaports around the world.

Tobias says pirate communal banks have been constructed elsewhere, such as Haiti and Madagascar. But there is no documented proof of this, at least not of a deep underground project similar to Oak Island's. And the Haitian bank to which he refers is probably a hoax, or at the very least greatly exaggerated.

In the late 1960s Tobias heard of Albert Lochard, a Haitian engineer who claimed to have uncovered a communal bank at a place he called Kavanach Hill in southern Haiti. Tobias sent Dan Blakenship to Haiti in 1970 to investigate the story. But he was unable to locate either the site or anyone who knew anything about the supposed discovery. Soon after, Blakenship and Tobias tracked Lochard down in New York, where he was living as a political refugee under an assumed name. Without asking for or receiving any remuneration, Lochard described his discovery of the communal bank. He said he found the workings in 1947 and secretly explored them for three years, removing about $50,000 worth of eighteenth-century coins from the site. He added that he fled Haiti in 1951 under "government pressure" before he could finish excavating the workings.

Lochard gave Tobias a diagram of the Haitian project. It included a dome-roofed chamber that extended from 140 to 180 feet underground and was 35 feet across. Five large tunnels led out from the chamber, and numerous smaller tunnels designed to channel underground watercourses into the vault were spaced at regular intervals. The flood tunnels were apparently plugged with clay, and Lochard said he was able to investigate the workings without being hampered by water. One interesting coincidence is that Lochard described a heart-shaped rock which he said he found in one of the tunnels. It was similar to a hand-chiseled rock that Blankenship had discovered (though Lochard didn't know it) under Smith's Cove in 1967.

The problem with Lochard's story is that there appears to be no one around who can verify it. During the 1970s some newspaper articles stated that the Smithsonian Institution had confirmed the existence of the Haitian communal bank. However, Mendel Peterson, the former curator of the Smithsonians' Historical Archaeology division, told me that he has seen no proof that workings similar to Oak Island exist in Haiti or anywhere else in the world. Peterson also expressed doubt that pirates would have gone to such elaborate lengths to bury their plunder.

In addition, several prominent persons who were in Haiti at the time of Lochard's alleged discovery express strong disbelief in the story. Paul Magloire was head of the Haitian army and minister of the interior from 1946 to 1950 and then president of Haiti from 1950 to 1956. (He was ousted by a coup in 1956, shortly before "Papa Doc" Duvalier came to power.) In 1977 Magloire, then living in exile in New York, assured me that he certainly would have known about it had someone fled Haiti in 1951 after finding a hidden treasure.

Max Bissainthe, who was head of Haiti's National Library from 1942 to 1956, also discounts the story as "legend, complete legend." In addition, several journalists who operated out of Haiti's capital, Port-au-Prince, in the late 1940s and 1950s say they never heard so much as a rumor of such a discovery.

If Lochard, who has long since disappeared, actually found underground workings, they probably weren't anywhere as elaborate as he'd led Tobias to believe.

Nevertheless, there *are* documented accounts of treasure

having been found on Haiti—not surprising considering that Haiti forms the western half of Hispaniola, a popular stopover for seventeenth-century pirates. But these have all been small deposits of French or Spanish coins, usually in chests or boxes buried no more than a few feet underground.

Nova Scotia too had yielded some deposits of treasure that can be traced back to the days of piracy. For, apart from Phipps, there were many lesser-known privateers and outright pirates who were active in these waters.

From 1604 to 1763 control over Nova Scotia swung back and forth between France and Britain. Both nations employed the services of commissioned privateers to raid Acadian settlements and shipping. Later, the Americans also used New England-based privateers to harass the British in Nova Scotia during the American Revolution of 1775 to 1783. (Similar raids were also carried out in Nova Scotia during the American-British War of 1812, though this, of course, was too late to have any bearing on the Oak Island project.)

In addition, freebooting pirates often attacked ports in Nova Scotia and Newfoundland in the seventeenth century. Although the pickings in terms of coin or other treasure were slim, these fishing communities supplied the pirates with provisions, shanghaied manpower, and additional sailing ships. So the early settlers of Nova Scotia weren't unfamiliar with piracy on their coasts. In fact, the name Mahone Bay is derived from the archaic French word *mahonne*, a low-lying sailing vessel that was popular with coastal pirates in the Mediterranean.

In the aftermath of all this larcenous activity, a number of pirate treasures have been uncovered in various parts of the province. In 1879, for example, William Moser, a farmer from Lunenburg (about ten miles from Oak Island) was digging up the floor of his barn when he encountered a cache of about two hundred French and Spanish gold coins dating from the mid to late 1700s. The barn had been built by his grandfather more than fifty years earlier, and presumably the coins had been buried long before that by unknown privateers or pirates. Similar accidental finds have been reported in other parts of the province.

But in all cases the treasures were relatively small and buried only a few feet underground. That a group of distrustful, undisciplined, hit-and-run sea thieves would take the time required for the immense amount of work that went into Oak Island is difficult to believe. Pirates were much more apt to dig a five- or ten-foot hole in the ground from which their treasure could be quickly retrieved at a later date.

Consequently, most serious investigators of Oak Island, including Tobias, today agree that those sixteenth- and seventeenth-century seafaring soldiers of fortune were not the architects of the Oak Island workings. As Tobias, quoting one of his Triton partners, said in January 1988, "It wasn't done by any dumb-ass pirates."

If pirates weren't responsible for what has been discovered on Oak Island, who was? As the exploration of the Money Pit and the adjacent workings progressed over the years, many whodunit theories would be advanced. And these range from the plausible to the incredibly bizarre. But first, there were many more strange pieces to be found and fitted into the puzzle.

CHAPTER SIX

A Vault Is Discovered

Not until the 1890s was any further attempt made to recover Oak Island's treasure. But in the quarter century that followed the frustrating failures of the 1860s search groups, the story, often a mixture of fact and folklore, spread to other parts of Canada and New England, and few tourists to the Chester area missed the opportunity to take a boat out to the island to peer into the water-filled pits.

Inevitably, there was some outside skepticism expressed over the possibility that someone could or would have hidden and so elaborately protected a treasure more than one hundred feet underground. An early example is found in the July 1870 issue of the *New Dominion Monthly*, a Canadian magazine published in Montreal. The author, J. A. Bell, declared it "incredible that persons possessed of common sense could be so deluded" as to invest time and money in the Oak Island search. The quest, he predicted, "will no doubt be referred to in future times as a remarkable chapter in the voluminous records of human folly."

But treasure hunters expect and are usually inured to such derision. In 1862 Jotham McCully had observed that "the public will judge [the Oak Island searchers] by the success we meet with. Should we be successful in getting a large amount of treasure, we will be considered a very sensible lot of fellows; and if we fail in finishing the work we will be set down as a set of phantom-following fools, fit for nothing but to be held up to public ridicule." McCully and his contemporaries did fail; yet not before making a stronger case than ever to prove that someone had constructed something most unusual beneath the island. It was only a matter of time before the bug that bit them would infect someone else.

In 1893 Frederick Leander Blair, a twenty-six-year-old insurance salesman living in Boston, developed an obsession with Oak Island that was to last until his death in 1951 at the age of eighty-three. He was originally from Amherst, Nova Scotia, and as a boy had heard detailed accounts of Oak Island from his uncle, Isaac Blair, who had taken part in the search during the 1860s.

Fred Blair was a conscientious researcher, and the first thing he did was amass whatever written documentation he could find relating to the work of searchers who had preceded him. He also interviewed everyone he could find who'd ever worked on the island. They included Adams A. Tupper, Jefferson McDonald, Robert Creelman, James McNutt, Jotham McCully, and Samuel Fraser, all veterans of the 1849–50 or 1861–67 Oak Island campaigns. In addition, some of them passed on to Blair information they had gotten directly from the three Money Pit discoverers, Smith, McGinnis, and Vaughan, and from Simeon Lynds, who led the 1803–04 group. Most of the material Blair collected survives to this day.

In the 1930s Gilbert Hedden, who headed a search group and was well acquainted with Blair, described him as "a man of very pleasing personality, extremely well preserved physically, possessing an accurate and exhaustive memory, and a man of sterling character. . . . His one possible fault seems to be his undying faith in the story of Oak Island." (Hedden, incidentally, also shared that faith until his own death.)

Under the direction of Blair, the Oak Island Treasure Company was incorporated in 1893. Most of its shareholders were Nova Scotians, though there were many from the Boston area and other parts of New England. In its original prospectus, which was written by Blair and Adams Tupper, the company briefly outlined the work that had been done on the island up to that time. The prospectus then stated:

> It can be proven:
>
> That a shaft about 13 feet in diameter and 100 feet deep was sunk on Oak Island in Mahone Bay, Nova Scotia, before the memory of any now living.
>
> That this shaft was connected by an underground tunnel with the open ocean, about 365 feet distant. [It's actually about 500 feet.]
>
> That at the bottom of this shaft were placed large wooden boxes in which were precious metals and jewels. [Presumably a reference to the loose metal struck by the 1849 drillers.]
>
> That many attempts have been made, without success, to obtain this treasure.
>
> That it is reasonably certain the treasure is large, because so great a trouble would never have been taken to conceal any small sum.
>
> That it is now entirely feasible to thoroughly explore this shaft and recover the treasure still located therein.

This last bold statement would be nullified by additional discoveries awaiting the new group of searchers. They would learn that Oak Island was a lot more complicated than their prospectus suggested.

The company planned to raise as much as $60,000 in shares of $5 apiece. Half of this was to be used to secure a three-year lease on the eastern end of the island as well as absolute rights to all treasure that might be recovered. The other $30,000 worth of shares would be kept in the company's treasury, to be sold as needed to pay for labor and materials. The company expected that only 1,000 of these shares would have to be sold to complete the work. With few exceptions, those who had sunk their money into previous searches took up stock in this new venture.

Outlining its plan of action, the Oak Island Treasure Company prospectus states:

> It is perfectly evident that the great mistake thus far has been in attempting to "bail out" the ocean through various pits. The present company intends to use the best modern appliances for

cutting off the flow of water through the tunnel, at some point near the shore, before attempting to pump out the water. It believes, from investigations already made, that such an attempt will be completely successful; and if it is, there can be no trouble in pumping out the Money Pit as dry as when the treasure was first placed there.

The company's optimistic plan was reported in several Nova Scotia and Boston newspapers, and the publicity helped attract new shareholders. By the end of the year the Oak Island Treasure Company had sold enough stock to begin work.

Blair and his group arrived on the island the following summer to carry out their announced plan of eliminating the water trap that had thwarted all the searchers before them. The spot selected for cutting off the flow from Smith's Cove was one that had been accidentally discovered sixteen years earlier by Sophia Sellers. She was Anthony Graves's daughter and was married to Henry Sellers; they'd inherited the eastern end of Oak Island from her father on his death in 1888.

One day in 1878 Sophia Sellers had been plowing with a team of oxen when the ground had suddenly caved in under the animals and they had dropped into a hole six to eight feet in diameter and more than ten feet deep. The oxen were extricated and the incident forgotten until many years later when Blair saw the hole and heard the story from Sellers. What interested Blair and his fellow searchers was that the hole, which they dubbed the "Cave-in Pit" was about 350 feet east of the Money Pit and directly over the suspected route of the flood tunnel from Smith's Cove.

Some investigators had previously suggested that a five-hundred-foot tunnel (from the Money Pit to Smith's Cove) couldn't have been built without having had at least one vertical shaft somewhere along its course. This would have provided an additional point from which the earth from the tunnel could be removed; more important, it would have served as an airshaft for those digging the tunnel. Blair and his associates also suspected that the creators of the Money Pit might have installed a valve or gate somewhere in the flood tunnel, to be used to shut off the water when they came back for their treasure.

So the first job was to excavate and explore the Cave-in Pit. At a depth of fifty-five feet, seawater began entering it. By the next day the water was at tide level (about fifteen feet below ground level at that spot) and it couldn't be lowered by bailing. That project was then abandoned. But the group was still convinced that the Cave-in Pit had been part of the original work. It showed clear indications of having been hand-dug at some earlier point, and there was no record of any previous searchers having put down a shaft in that particular area.

Many years later other searchers examined the same pit on the assumption that, if it wasn't an airshaft, it may have been designed as an access point to one or more subterranean treasure locations. They also assumed that the pit wasn't exactly in line with the watercourse, but was set off slightly to the side. For that reason, its collapse in 1878 hadn't diminished the flow of water to the Money Pit. It's not known why it caved in; perhaps an unrecorded branch tunnel dug by searchers in the 1860s had been driven under or near its base. Today the Cave-in Pit is a gaping circular crater one hundred feet deep and almost as many feet across. And the water in it still rises and falls with the tide.

In the fall of 1894 another shaft was dug thirty feet east of the Money Pit and eight feet north of the suspected line of the watercourse. Somehow, water started entering the shaft at forty-three feet, probably via an underground connection to a flooded tunnel dug by the previous searchers. Again, work had to be abandoned.

The Oak Island Treasure Company had gotten off to an inauspicious start. But now they decided to make a frontal attack on the Money Pit itself. An enticing find and a horrifying surprise lay ahead of them.

When the Oak Island Eldorado Company quit in 1867, they had refilled the top thirty feet of the Money Pit above the platform erected for their third exploratory drill probe. And either they or Anthony Graves had filled in some other shafts. Consequently, in the intervening quarter century, the eastern end of the island had lost many of its visible scars. The Oak Island Treasure Company began excavating the Money Pit during the summer of 1895, but they got down only fifty-five feet inside the old cribbing when once more water drove them out. At this point work was suspended until the latter part of 1896.

The company's $60,000 worth of stock was still far from being totally subscribed. Shareholder dissatisfaction over the lack of progress and dissension between the Bostonian and Nova Scotian leaders of the group over how operations should be conducted led to control of the project being placed in the hands of the Nova Scotian shareholders. They formed a new board of management. This included Fred Blair (who in 1895 moved from Boston to Amherst) as treasurer, and Captain John Welling as the on-site manager. T. Perley Putnam and William Chappel of Sydney, Nova Scotia, were also a part of the new management.

From the winter of 1896 through the spring of 1897 the workers again concentrated on the Money Pit. They were able to drain it with steam-powered pumps and clear it down to seventy feet before the water became excessive. But by putting a pump in the adjacent shaft they were able to further drain and excavate it to ninety-seven feet.

During this operation the island claimed its second victim. On March 26, 1897, Maynard Kaiser of nearby Gold River was being raised to the top of one of the pits when the rope slipped off the hoisting pulley and he fell to his death. Following the accident, most of his co-workers refused to go into the pits, forcing operations to be halted for about a week. Many of them were convinced that Kaiser's death was a warning and that some ghostly guardian of the buried treasure planned to kill anyone who tried to retrieve it. (If so, that "guardian" had an even more tragic warning in store for a future search expedition.)

The workers were eventually persuaded back, and the deepening of the Money Pit continued. Blair's notes show that on April 22, 1897, when they reached a depth of 110 feet, they came across one of the old Halifax Company tunnels entering at 108 feet and noticed that all the water flowing into the pit came from this tunnel. They explored it a short distance and came to an intersecting tunnel at the end of which was a large cribbed shaft extending up into the darkness as far as they could see.

According to Blair, "Water was boiling up through the bottom of this pit, and it proved to be the real Money Pit. The pit [we] had worked in all winter proved to be the old Tupper pit"—a shaft dug in 1850 to 109 feet and situated 10 feet northwest of the actual Money Pit. Several months and a lot of money had been wasted re-excavating the wrong pit.

Moving 10 feet to the southeast, the searchers broke through the topsoil and soon confirmed that they were now in the original Money Pit. On June 9, 1897, digging had progressed to 111 feet in the Money Pit when they came across an uncribbed tunnel 2½ feet wide on the east side of the pit. They dug down quickly, noticing that the opening was filled with smooth beach stones covered with a layer of gravel. And, as they dug, water gushed through at an ever-increasing rate. They had located the Smith's Cove flood tunnel, which, they recorded, was 2½ feet wide by about 4 feet high.

Blair recorded, "It entered the pit under great pressure and finally overcame the pumps; filled the pits [Money Pit and adjacent shaft] to tide level and brought operations to a standstill." It was obvious to Blair that it would be impossible to plug the flood tunnel in the Money Pit itself; the force and volume of water rushing down from Smith's Cove was too great. Work was then temporarily halted while the company's board of management met in Halifax to formulate a new plan.

The first thing that needed to be resolved was a legal position that for some time had been making the Oak Island Treasure Company's directors and investors somewhat nervous. Under a British law dating back to the thirteenth century, any treasure discovered in England or its colonies belonged to the Crown, and it was entirely up to the discretion of the Crown to decide what portion, if any, the finder could retain. The 1849–50 searchers, for example, had a "treasure trove license" that stipulated they were operating "by the right of Her Majesty [Queen Victoria] to whose liberality they were willing to submit to such salvage and reward as Her Majesty may graciously award them." Although in practice the British

Crown normally took only a small percentage of treasure recovered within its domain, the ambiguity of the wording of such licenses made it that much more difficult to raise venture capital.

Following the creation of the Dominion of Canada under the British North American Act of 1867, England assigned this right to the individual provinces of Canada. When the Oak Island Treasure Company was formed in 1893, it obtained a treasure trove license from the province of Nova Scotia. But this agreement also was noncommittal on what portion of any treasure would revert to the province. So in 1897 the company petitioned for and received a clear ruling stating that the Nova Scotia government would be entitled to no more than 2 percent of any treasure found on the island. (This royalty rate has been increased several times since. Today the province of Nova Scotia is entitled to the first 10 percent of anything found on Oak Island.)

Once they had clarified that issue, Blair and his company were able to sell additional shares to continue the dig. Having found the location of the flood tunnel in the summer of 1897, the company decided that the best place to cut off the flow was at Smith's Cove. Their plan was to set off underground charges of dynamite near the shore to demolish the flood tunnel for good.

Five holes, spaced fifteen feet apart, were bored in a line about fifty feet up from the high-water mark at the cove. All but the third hole were drilled to about ninety feet without encountering water. They were crammed with dynamite and filled with water, which served as a plug. When the charge was set off, the water spumed more than one hundred feet into the air.

The third hole was apparently bored into the flood tunnel. At eighty feet the auger struck rocks, and seawater immediately rose to tide level. This hole was filled with a huge 160-pound charge. According to Blair, when it was detonated the water in the Money Pit and the Cave-in Pit "boiled and foamed for a considerable time, and after the disturbance subsided, the oil in the dynamite showed on the water in both these pits."

The workers now assumed they'd finally choked off the water supply. Yet, when the pumps were subsequently run in the Money Pit, they were barely able to keep ahead of the incoming water. The blasting had had no appreciable effect on the flow from the sea. The answer to this puzzle would not be found until the following year.

With the pumps running night and day, the company was able to hold the water in the Money Pit, which had previously been excavated to 113 feet, down to about the 100-foot level. Under the direction of William Chappell, T. Perley Putnam, and Captain John Welling, the rest of the summer of 1897 was spent boring deep into the Money Pit from a platform set up at the 90-foot level. A full account of the drilling program and its tantalizing results is contained in notes prepared by Blair in 1900 and later in an affidavit sworn to by Chappell in 1929.

Several holes were bored with a 2½-inch drill through a 3-inch casing, usually in loose and apparently disturbed ground all the way down to 171 feet. Blue clay, which Chappel said had the "characteristics of puddled clay," was encountered between 130 and 151 feet and again between 160 and 171 feet. (Puddled clay is a hand-worked watertight preparation of clay, sand, and water, with a consistency similar to putty.)

The first hole was bored through several inches of wood at 122 feet, and at 126 feet the bit struck iron which it couldn't penetrate. So a 1½-inch drill was put down the same hole, and it was able to slip past the obstruction. It then went through puddled clay and, at 154 feet, struck what the drillers first thought was sandstone but was later found to be cement. The cement was 7 inches thick, and underneath it were 5 inches of solid oak, samples of which were brought to the surface.

At 155 feet the chisel-shaped drill bit struck what felt like soft metal. Chappel said it was found that this metal "could be moved slightly thereby forming a crevice of space into which the drill, when in alignment, would stick or wedge." This happened several times, and the chisel had to be continually pried loose. After spending two hours to get through four inches of this soft metal the boring became easier. But even then the drill would go down only by continuously twisting the rods and applying heavy pressure. And the workers noticed that the material would fill up the hole each time the drill was raised.

In his report, Blair said they "worked 5¼ hours getting down the two feet eight inches" of this material "and the chisel came up as sharp as [when] it went down." The drillers were certain this material was metal in small pieces, similar to that which had been struck in 1849 between 100 and 104 feet in the Money Pit, prior to its collapse. At 158 feet the drill hit the same sort of soft metal that had been found just under the oak wood. The chisel stuck fast and couldn't be turned or driven down, so the drill was withdrawn. An attempt to put casing further down in order to retrieve the loose metal proved useless as the casing pipe was repeatedly deflected into the side of the Money Pit by the iron obstruction at 126 feet.

The 3-inch casing was withdrawn and reset for a second hole a few feet away. The drill again hit wood at 122 feet, followed by puddled clay, then through 7 feet of cement between 154 and 161 feet. One side of the drill also encountered wood from about 154 to 158 feet. Below the cement the drill was driven through more puddled clay until it met what appeared to be an iron plate at 171 feet. Several attempts were made to penetrate the plate, but to no avail. Chappel reported that "a magnet was run through the material [on the end of the bit] and it loaded up with fine iron cuttings, thereby producing conclusive proof that it was iron we had been drilling on at 171 feet. No further attempt was made to go through this iron."

From their drill logs and the material salvaged from these two holes and others, the Oak Island Treasure Company profiled what they were certain was a large concrete vault deep in the Money Pit. All of the foreign material brought up on the auger was sent away for independent analysis, and this supported their discovery of a man-made chamber.

Geologists in Halifax declared that the puttylike clay found above and below the concrete chamber had been handworked. Interestingly, seventy years later (1967) an early drilling program by the current Triton group struck puddled clay at similar depths. Triton's consultants also declared it to be man-

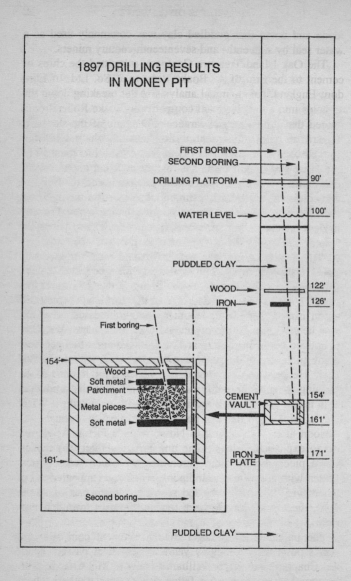

1897 DRILLING RESULTS
IN MONEY PIT

FIRST BORING
SECOND BORING
DRILLING PLATFORM — 90'
WATER LEVEL — 100'
PUDDLED CLAY
WOOD — 122'
IRON — 126'

First boring

154'
Wood
Soft metal
Parchment
Metal pieces
Soft metal

CEMENT
VAULT — 154'
161'

161'

IRON
PLATE — 171'

Second boring

PUDDLED CLAY

made and noted that puddled clay was commonly used as a water seal by sixteenth- and seventeenth-century miners.

The Oak Island Treasure Company submitted the chips of cement to the firm of A. Boake Roberts & Co. Ltd. of London, England, for chemical analysis. After breaking down the samples into their elemental components, Boake Roberts concluded that "from the appearance and nature of the samples, we are of the opinion that it is a cement which has been worked by man." (Analysis of cement drilled through by Triton Alliance in recent years has supported this opinion.)

Among the many bits of evidence discovered on Oak Island, one of the most interesting was included in the material brought up from the Oak Island Treasure Company's boring of the first hole just inside the cement vault at 155 feet. T. P. Putnam had personally cleaned the end of the auger when it was withdrawn from that depth, and the samples were never out of his possession until they were examined at the courthouse in Amherst several days later. On September 6, 1897, Dr. Andrew E. Porter, a local physician, conducted the examination in the presence of about a dozen witnesses. Most of what he saw consisted of pieces of wood and cement. But then he noticed something peculiar about what he first thought was a tiny piece of wood. It was a compact ball with a fibrous edge. He carefully untwisted it and flattened it out. After studying it under a strong magnifying glass he declared that "this is not wood and there is either paint or ink on it." He concluded it was a piece of parchment.

Soon after, it was sent to Nova Scotia's Pictou Academy and to experts in Boston. The unanimous verdict was that it was a piece of sheepskin parchment on which were letters written with a quill pen in India ink. The letters appeared to be either "vi," "ui," or "wi" and seemed to form part of some word, the sample having been torn by the drill from a larger piece.

The parchment, no larger than a five-cent coin, was in Blair's possession for many years. It was later passed on to Mel Chappell, the son of William Chappell. Mel Chappell, at the age of ten, was with his father, Blair, and the others when the vault was discovered in 1897. That discovery was to seduce him into a lifelong commitment to Oak Island until his death in 1980 at the age of ninety-three. The parchment is now owned by the Triton Alliance syndicate.

In that autumn of 1897 the directors of the Oak Island Treasure Company were more convinced than ever that a large and valuable deposit lay far down in the Money Pit. The results of their drilling program led them to believe that a cement-encased vault, perhaps seven feet high, had been built. They speculated that this chamber contained bars of a relatively soft metal such as gold or silver, wooden chests of coins and jewels, and even historical documents of some kind. Based on these findings, the company became almost a closed corporation, with existing shareholders readily advancing the necessary funds to continue operations. But their euphoria was short-lived.

In the late fall and winter of 1897 the company sank two new shafts 45 and 75 feet south of the Money Pit. Their intention was to go down about 180 feet and then tunnel laterally to the Money Pit below the iron plate that had halted their drilling progress. The first shaft was abandoned at 95 feet when water from a nearby 1860s searcher's tunnel burst through at the 70-foot level. The second pit got to 160 feet, when a large volume of water was suddenly encountered, driving the workers out. Pumping attempts failed, and this shaft too was abandoned.

The following spring Blair and his group decided to again try to plug the water entrance at Smith's Cove. In order to locate the position of the offshore drains, they poured concentrated red dye into the flooded Money Pit and an adjacent shaft and then pumped water from the shore into both pits. The idea was a good one. By filling the shafts above sea-level water table, they'd create a head of water that would backwash the system so that the telltale dye would show exactly where the drains originated out in Smith's Cove. But the experiment yielded an unexpected and horrifying result. The red-hued water was bubbling out not at Smith's Cove to the east, but at several locations beyond the low tide mark on the *south* side of the island.

The searchers now had two known flood tunnels to contend

with. The discovery helped explain why the dynamiting of Smith's Cove a year earlier had done little to check the flooding of the Money Pit. They didn't know at what depth this second tunnel entered the Money Pit area, put presumed it was somewhere around the 160-foot level where it had broken through their most recent shaft.

The Triton group has since established that there were indeed at least two man-made flood tunnels built to protect the interior of the Money Pit from inquisitive searchers. The first, a five-hundred foot tunnel from Smith's Cove has long since been destroyed. The existence of the second, a three-hundred foot tunnel from the South Shore Cove, was reestablished in the winter of 1981 when Triton was conducting pumping tests and discovered water bubbling through holes in the ice-covered bay at four distinct spots approximately seven-hundred feet off the south shore beach. Moreover, Triton's Dan Blankenship is convinced there are still several more independent flood traps waiting to be discovered.

Discouraged but not yet beaten, Blair and his associates spent the rest of that year and the summer of 1899 digging four more shafts with the hope of driving them deep enough to tunnel under the Money Pit. But each had to be abandoned because of excessive flooding. Moreover, as Blair and Chappell later observed, the water problem wasn't caused only by the two known flood tunnels. It was aggravated by some of their shafts striking lateral tunnels that had been made by searchers in the 1860s. These had created an uncharted labyrinth of underground streams through the eastern end of the island. Blair's group considered building a cofferdam at the South Shore Cove to enable them to dig up the water drains. But that was found to be prohibitively expensive, as the cove is about 1,600 feet across, considerably larger than the crescent-shaped Smith's Cove.

By 1900 the Oak Island Treasure Company was having trouble keeping its head above water in more ways than one, with some of the group's principal investors now close to personal bankruptcy. The company's prospectus was reissued, and a bit more capital was brought into the treasury. One more shaft (the twentieth since the discovery of the Money Pit) was dug, flooded, and abandoned, and a few more holes were drilled with no significant results.

That autumn the company was financially doomed. Creditors were moving in with liens on equipment, and the workers were demanding back wages. That brought to an end seven years of work by the Oak Island Treasure Company. Blair and his associates had been beaten, but they hadn't lost faith in the existence of the treasure. Their discovery of the concrete vault and of a second flooding system was seen as further proof that no ordinary treasure lay concealed deep beneath the island.

By the end of 1900 Fred Blair was on his own. He retained a lease on the Money Pit area from Sophia Sellers for $100 a year, as well as the treasure trove license from the Nova Scotia government. He then spent the next fifty years working in partnership with various search groups. And the first syndicate he lured to the island included among its members a future president of the United States.

CHAPTER SEVEN

The Search Continues

IN THE SPRING OF 1909, FRED BLAIR FOUND SOMEONE ANX-
ious to pick up where the Oak Island Treasure Company had
left off. Henry L. Bowdoin, a noted American adventurer and
engineer, had heard about the unsuccessful attempts to recover
the treasure. He was convinced that with the use of divers and
heavy machinery he could conquer the water trap that had
frustrated all of his predecessors. He stirred up public interest
in his plans through a series of interviews that appeared in
New York, Boston, and Nova Scotia newspapers, and in April
1909 he formed the Old Gold Salvage and Wrecking Company. The company, with offices at 44 Broadway, New York,
was potentially capitalized at $250,000 in shares of $1 apiece
being offered to the public.

Bowdoin's prospectus claimed that "a $10,000,000 treas-
ure" lay at the bottom of the Money Pit and that "with modern
methods and machinery, the recovery of the treasure is easy,
ridiculously easy." The estimate of the treasure's worth, a
conversion of pounds sterling to dollars, was based on the
supposed translation ("Forty feet below two million pounds
are buried") of the glyphs on the stone found in the Money
Pit.

The prospectus went on to say that Oak Island was just the

63

first of several treasure hunts the company planned to undertake, the others being shipwrecks that could be salvaged with the use of "Bowdoin's Air Lock Caisson." It further boasted that "the recovery of the [Oak Island] treasure would yield a dividend of 4,000 percent on the entire capital stock; and as operations should begin in May or June and be completed in three or four weeks, should be available this summer."

Despite his bombastic confidence, Bowdoin was able to sell only about 5,000 shares in his venture. Blair, in exchange for stock, gave the company the right to work on the island for two years. On August 18, 1909, Bowdoin and several associates sailed from New York to Halifax, where they purchased some additional equipment. On August 27 they arrived by schooner on Oak Island and set up their headquarters, which they dubbed "Camp Kidd."

Among those who purchased stock in Bowdoin's company was a man destined to become Oak Island's most distinguished treasure hunter—Franklin D. Roosevelt. At that time he was a twenty-seven-year-old law clerk with the Wall Street firm of Carter, Ledyard and Milburn. His interest in Oak Island originated from his boyhood years spent at his mother's summer home on Campobello Island in the Bay of Fundy. (FDR's treasure-hunting career seems to have begun in 1896, when, at the age of fourteen, he and a Groton prep-school roommate sailed from Campobello to the nearby island of Grand Manan. They spent four days on the island digging for a chest supposed to have been buried by Captain Kidd. All they found was an old plank on which some hoaxer had carved "W.K.")

Roosevelt had always been intrigued by the Oak Island story, which was widely known in the Bay of Fundy area, and in 1909 he saw an opportunity to take part in the search. That summer and autumn he and a few of his New York friends who were fellow investors made several brief visits to the island, where they worked with Bowdoin's crew.

After setting up their campsite, Bowdoin's men spent a short time trying to locate the flood-tunnel entrances at Smith's Cove and on the south shore. They couldn't find them, so they moved their equipment up to the Money Pit, which was filled to thirty feet from the surface with seawater. Because of their limited funds, a proposed 1,000-gallon-per-minute capacity pump hadn't been brought to the island and they were unable to lower the water level in the pit.

A diver dressed in a rubber suit and a brass deep-sea helmet was sent down to check on the pit's condition. He reported that it was clear down to 113 feet but that the cribbing was badly twisted and out of alignment. Bowdoin then decided to probe the pit's bottom with a drill, hoping that core samples would locate the treasure vault that had been struck in 1897. Once that was accomplished, he felt it would be an easy matter to raise additional funds to sink a watertight caisson into the vault.

First he dropped large charges of dynamite into the pit and cleared out much of the smashed timbering with a steam-powered bucket. That fall a total of twenty-eight holes were bored to between 155 and 171 feet from the surface. Bowdoin's drilling records stated that from 113 to 130 feet the drill encountered coarse gravel and sand; this was followed by about 16 feet of blue clay, small stones, and sand. He added that in several of the test holes "we struck cement six inches to ten inches thick at depths of 146 feet to 149 feet, but no traces of boxes, treasure, or anything of that kind."

At this point Bowdoin's funds ran out and he was unable to sell more shares in the Old Gold Salvage and Wrecking Company. So the equipment was put under wraps, and the expedition sailed back to New York on November 4. Bowdoin, who had been overconfident and undercapitalized, would later declare that Oak Island was nothing but a hoax.

His about-face followed an exchange of letters between him and Blair over the next year. Bowdoin wanted a new contract to resume the search, but Blair insisted that he first prove that he had sufficient funds to carry out the work. Bowdoin then threatened to issue a report that "would not help in getting further investments in Oak Island." Blair testily advised him to publish and be damned.

On August 19, 1911, an article entitled "Solving the Mystery of Oak Island" appeared under Bowdoin's name in *Collier's* magazine. In it the writer concluded, "My experience proved to me that there is not, and never was, a buried treasure on Oak Island. The Mystery is solved." The article, which distorted and omitted many known facts, refuted the authenticity of all the previous finds made on the island or else dismissed them as natural phenomena.

Bowdoin's sour-grapes conclusion did little to shake public belief in the treasure. Even Roosevelt continued to follow the mystery long after his own involvement with the island. His extant personal papers include correspondence on the subject dating as late as 1939, while he was in his second term as president of the United States. These letters between FDR and his fellow 1909 searchers and later investigators cover a thirty-year span and reveal his unabashed fascination with the mystery of Oak Island.

In the summer of 1912 Fred Blair entertained a new, though somewhat quixotic, proposal to recover the treasure. Professor S. A. Williams of Soldiers Grave, Wisconsin, organized the Oak Island Salvage Company, which planned to use something called the "Poetsch freezing process" to overcome the flooding problem. The company's prospectus said the process, whereby liquid calcium chloride at 35 degrees below zero would be injected into the ground around the Money Pit, had been successfully used in certain European mines where water or quicksand ruled out normal excavation methods.

But Professor Williams had even worse luck than Bowdoin in attracting shareholders. By the end of the year he hadn't sold enough shares to pay his passage to Oak Island, much less purchase any equipment. The company folded, and its agreement with Blair was canceled.

Over the next ten years a few more abortive attempts were made by Americans to solve the mystery. In 1916 a group headed by William S. Lozier, an engineer from Rochester, New York, surveyed the island and did some exploratory drilling without finding anything of consequence. Another effort was made in the summer of 1922 by Edward W. Bowne of Newark, New Jersey, who planned to sink a new shaft near the Money Pit. But after he'd been on the island two months without even beginning the shaft, his contract with Blair was terminated.

During this period Blair was approached by many people who, like Williams, had ideas and theories but who required stock promotions to finance the actual work. Blair realized that some of these individuals were hoping to milk the public by flogging the well-known history of Oak Island to raise funds that would line the promoters' pockets. He avoided these charlatans and sought out those who could finance their own ventures.

Blair took his search for a self-financed Oak Island partner to several U.S. and Canadian newspapers. On December 7, 1922, the following advertisement appeared on the front page of the New York City *Journal of Commerce*:

BURIED TREASURE

Speculative venture, partly proven, requires $50,000 for half interest. If successful, will produce millions within one year; otherwise possibly eighty percent loss. Satisfactory credentials, proofs partially successful efforts, will prove good sporting proposition for party financially able to take chance. Full frank details at interview. 228 F., Journal of Commerce.

Although the ad drew many inquiries, Blair didn't find his wealthy backer until 1931. And the investor, William Chappell of Sydney, Nova Scotia, was no stranger to the Oak Island mystery. Chappell had been on the drilling platform thirty-four years earlier when the samples of wood and cement and the piece of parchment had been recovered from more than 150 feet down in the Money Pit. Since then he had remained a firm believer in the existence of a large and valuable deposit somewhere in the vicinity of the 1897 drilling probe.

In the intervening years the family's contracting and lumber business had prospered. So Chappell decided to use some of the company's profits in another attempt to recover the treasure. He was joined in his venture by his brother Renwisk, his son Mel, and his nephew Claude. Blair also took part in the operation, and that spring he and the Chappells built a campsite on the island and lived there for the next six months.

Mel Chappell, who was a member of the Engineering Institute of Canada, consulted with several prominent mining engineers on the best type of shaft to use. The consensus was that an open-timbered pit would be the most practical. A centrifugal pump with a capacity of 450 gallons per minute was purchased to drain the shaft. It was powered by electricity, which was routed to the island through a submarine cable from the mainland. This marked the first time that electric power had been used in the search.

The plan was to sink a new shaft down into the chamber that had been drilled through in 1897. The first problem the workers faced was in determining exactly where to dig. No work of any consequence had been done on the island since 1909, the year in which Bowdoin dynamited and ripped out much of the cribbing in the Money Pit. Over the years, the pit had caved in, and by 1931 its location could only be estimated from memory and by the general depression of the earth in that area. They therefore decided to dig a relatively large pit (known as the Chappell shaft) twelve feet wide by fourteen feet long that would almost surely strike at least part of the center of the original Money Pit.

Shortly before his death in 1980, Claude Chappell told me: "When we first went [to the island] Uncle William staked out where we should put down the pit, and eventually we started it. Blair came out and said, 'You're about six feet from where you should be.' 'Well,' Uncle William said, 'we can't shift the head [of the shaft] now, but when we get down there we can look around.'"

Actually, the center of the Chappell pit was probably slightly southwest of the original Money Pit, with its northern end taking in one corner of the original pit. Most of the digging was done through previously worked soil. They encountered salt water, but the pit was kept dry with the large electric pump.

On their way down the workers came across tools and a lot of timber from earlier searchers' shafts. They also found an old anchor fluke at 120 feet, which, according to Mel Chappell, "was imbedded in the clay on the side [of the pit] and wasn't rusted." He said the anchor fluke was of an ancient design and that it may well have been an original artifact. (Blair had it in his home for many years, but it disappeared shortly after his death in 1951.)

Neither the Money Pit nor any immediately adjacent shaft had ever been excavated to more than 113 feet; so the old tools found below that depth in the Chappell shaft had somehow sunk from where they'd been left. But the question of what had happened to the metal, wood, and cement encountered between 126 and 171 feet by the drillers in 1897 remained unanswered. Apart from searchers' tools, the only interesting discoveries in the Chappell shaft were large chunks of what was believed to be either granite or concrete. Blair, in a report to William Chappell late that summer, offered the following explanation:

> I am convinced that down to 150 feet at least, one end of your pit was over the edge of what once was an open chamber. Due to the collapse of supports, etc. above, this chamber has been filled with broken ground or clay, through which the water being pumped has passed. Tons and tons of clay have passed out with the water this summer, and the gravel and other solids keep settling down to solid bottom as the work progresses. The wall of this chamber, undermined possibly by water, has broken down in the vicinity of our pit, and perhaps it is some of that [granite or concrete] wall we have taken out.

By that time Blair and William Chappell realized they were dealing with a dog's breakfast in the depths of the Money Pit area. This had been created by several collapses and reopenings of the Money Pit, the sinking of at least ten shafts within thirty-five feet of the pit, and lateral tunneling at several levels all around it. Add to that the effect of billions of gallons of water flowing into and being pumped out of the same area, and the total result could only be a confused subterranean soup stirred by a succession of searchers over those past 136 years.

On October 14 the Chappell shaft was down to 155 feet, deeper than any previous diggers had ever been. From there they drilled into the bottom and determined that the disturbed earth continued another 12 feet before they reached what felt like solid unworked clay. They also drilled horizontally through the sides of the pit at the 130-foot level. Several of the probes hit wood, but this was thought to have been timbers that had worked their way down from earlier shafts.

In order to further explore the surrounding area, a tunnel was driven from the bottom of the shaft through the north wall for about nine feet. A second tunnel was dug at the same level extending out from the eastern wall and then curving to the north, with the intention of joining it to the first tunnel. But before it could be reached, the soft earth began caving in, almost burying the foreman, George Stevenson, in the process. He was extricated in time by Mel Chappell. This was one of many mishaps encountered that summer. Two other workers suffered broken ribs in pit accidents, and severe storms knocked out the pump's electrical supply several times.

Claude Chappell recalled that when the shaft was down to 155 feet, "we came to a sort of shale rock and more water started coming in. It was coming in from three or four feet on one side; it wasn't just coming in from one little hole. It was a round, clearly defined tunnel." The diggers weren't sure, but this may have been the mouth of the suspected tunnel from the south shore. In any case, their pump contained the flow.

Apart from the work in the shaft, the Chappells drilled and dynamited several holes on the beach at Smith's Cove. But this failed to plug the flood tunnel. More coconut fiber was dug up on the beach and was authenticated by botanists in Halifax. In addition, Mel Chappell found a strange triangle of stones that his father and Blair had first seen on the south shore in 1897. On neither occasion was much significance given to the stone triangle. Its connection to the Oak Island puzzle would not be discovered for another six years.

On October 29, after they'd spent six months and about $40,000 on the island, the Chappells quit for the season, intending to resume the following spring. However, Sophia Sellers, who owned the eastern end of the island, died in 1931, and her twelve heirs wouldn't allow the Chappells to return without a substantial payment to each of them. The

Chappells declined to pay, but were determine to continue eventually the work they'd started.

Gilbert Hedden, who purchased that part of the island a few years later, interviewed William Chappell at length about his 1897 and 1931 operations. In a letter to President Roosevelt on September 1, 1937, Hedden said Chappell "maintained his belief and kept to the facts of his story under rigid cross-examination and averred that he would be at the site today if I had not purchased it when I did."

William Chappell died in 1946. His son Mel owned most of the island and controlled the search rights between 1950 and 1977. Shortly before his death in 1980, he assured me that he was "convinced that whatever Father drilled into [in 1897] is of immense value. I have no doubt about it. It's still down there; nobody has ever taken it out."

For some reason, the Sellers heirs allowed another searcher on their land in the summer of 1932. This was Mary B. Steward, a wealthy New York City dowager. Under an agreement with Blair she sent John Talbot, an engineer from Brooklyn, to the island. He spent two months drilling a hole a few feet away from the Chappell shaft and brought up a couple of chips of wood from between 113 and 150 feet. At that lower depth his drill pipe broke, and he abandoned the project.

The next searcher was Thomas Nixon of Victoria, British Columbia. In September 1933 he arranged with the Sellers heirs to dig on their property and also signed a contract with Blair, who still held the treasure trove rights. This agreement allowed Nixon to work on the island from April to November 1934, with Blair entitled to half of any treasure found.

Nixon had described himself as an engineer with enough financial backing to solve the problem within one summer. But his funding was in fact hypothetical and was based on what he hoped to raise through the sale of stock. As April drew closer, Blair began to have misgivings about the agreement. If Nixon didn't have the backing he claimed and didn't carry out his intended excavation, a season's work on the island would be lost. And Blair had meanwhile been approached by several other prospects. When the first of April arrived, Nixon wrote Blair asking for a month's extension, but he didn't arrive on Oak Island until early June. He spent the summer boring fourteen holes in the Money Pit area.

On September 28 Nixon wrote Blair:

> Drilled [hole] No. 13 and, on reaching a depth of 136 feet, drilled through what appeared to be a bulkhead, composed of oak and cement mixture about fourteen inches thick. On breaking through this, the tool dropped to 169 feet without touching anything; then I got mud and bits of old oak, which was in such a state of decay that you could rub the same into a powder in your fingers. This continued to 176 feet, where I struck a solid substance. I abandoned the hole and put another one, No. 14, down within a few feet of it and encountered the same as in No. 13, so undoubtedly that is the location of the Money Pit.

These holes presumably were somewhere north of the Chappell shaft. The report was accompanied by Nixon's promise that he would begin his planned excavation early the following year, and he therefore expected Blair to extend the agreement for another twelve months.

Nixon's drilling results were vaguely suggestive of the cement and wood-lined chamber that had been drilled into in 1897. But Blair was skeptical of Nixon's report, and on October 30 he informed him that their contract was terminated. Nixon threatened legal action to force an extension, but Blair held his ground and the matter was closed.

Apart from his annoyance over Nixon's lack of progress, Blair had another reason to sever the relationship. Waiting in the wings that autumn was Gilbert Hedden of Chatham, New Jersey—a man with the money and determination to take over the project and perhaps see it to its conclusion. His was to prove one of the more significant contributions to the Oak Island search.

CHAPTER EIGHT

New Theories Arise

THE EARLY-TWENTIETH-CENTURY OAK ISLAND INVESTIGA-
tors introduced not only new technology and approaches to
solving the mystery, but also new theories on the origin of the
underground workings. Although many still believed they
were in pursuit of buried pirate plunder, a wide variety of
possible alternatives were offered. Most of these suggestions
were historically linked to the province's early development.

Chronologically, the earliest people who've been considered the possible originators of the work are the Indians of
Nova Scotia. The Paleo-Indian tribes, which date back to
8600 B.C., comprise the oldest archaeologically established
evidence of a primitive culture in the region. But the Oak
Island project is unquestionably much more modern than the
Paleolithic or even early post-Paleolithic period. If it was done
by any aboriginal civilization, it would have to have been the
Micmac Indians. They apparently migrated overland to what
is now Nova Scotia from the northeastern United States between A.D. 700 and A.D. 1100 and were thinly spread out
across the province. In 1610, their total population was estimated by early French settlers at 3,000 to 3,500.

The Micmacs were a nomadic race, moving about the
province in tune with the seasons. Winter camps were situated

inland alongside rivers and lakes, and in the spring the camp-
sites were shifted by birchbark canoe to the coast, where fish,
scallops, clams, and sea mammals such as seals and walrus
were plentiful. Some of these coastal camps were on the
shores of Mahone Bay, and Oak Island may have been visited
on their fishing expeditions. But there is nothing in Micmac
culture to indicate they would have had any material or religious reason to construct the underground workings. In fact,
anthropologists are certain they never built anything more permanent than dwellings of fur and bark.

The first nonindigenous people to whom the work has
sometimes been credited are the Norsemen. It is now known
that Christopher Columbus was not the first European to discover America. The Norsemen visited North America
hundreds of years prior to 1492. (The Kensington Stone, unearthed in Minnesota in 1898, is but one example of such
evidence. Its runic inscription records the arrival of a group of
Norsemen there in 1362, although some people question its
authenticity.)

Norse sagas contain several accounts of the Vikings sailing
to and even forming small colonies in parts of what are now
Newfoundland, Labrador, and Nova Scotia. They had settled
Iceland in the late ninth century A.D. and the southwest coast
of Greenland one hundred years later. The next logical excur-
sion from there was to the northeastern regions of Canada. In
the year 1000 Leif Ericsson landed in an area he called Wine-
land, which many historians now believe to have been Nova
Scotia. Several years later Thorfinn Karlsefni set out from
Greenland with three shiploads of colonists to settle Wine-
land, which he renamed Markland. They spent three winters
there, according to records, though the location of their colonies hasn't been determined. The sagas also refer to other
Viking voyages to the North American continent.

Some have thought that Oak Island and the immediately
adjacent mainland had been the site of a Norse settlement and
that it may have thrived for many years before all or most of
its members were wiped out by epidemics or Indians. One
theory suggests the colonists at some point realized they
couldn't survive the hostile environment unless they strength-

ened their numbers. So those that were left spent their final months carefully hiding everything that was of value beneath the island—including, perhaps, runic stones bearing their mythology and a chronicle of the settlement's history. They then sailed off to Greenland or Scandinavia in hopes of eventually returning with others to resettle the area, but for some reason never did.

The problem with this hypothesis—and indeed with any pre-Columbian theory—is that wood samples that have been recovered from far below the island in recent years have been carbon dated to no earlier than 1500. And obviously the depositors brought, or at least had access to, tropical coconut fiber. Therefore the Norse connection with Oak Island is most unlikely.

Apart from the Norse, the first European awareness of Nova Scotia came with the voyage of John Cabot. On June 24, 1497, Cabot planted the English flag on Cape Breton Island, now part of Nova Scotia, claiming the new land (which he assumed was the eastern coast of Asia) in the name of Britain's Henry VIII. The next year he sailed down the province's Atlantic coast, and from there he crossed over to New England. (This, incidentally, made him the first non-Nordic European to land on the American continent proper.)

Cabot was followed to the Nova Scotia area by Basque and Breton fishermen, who discovered the rich Grand Banks fishing grounds off Newfoundland and who also landed on Cape Breton Island. Two unsuccessful attempts were then made to settle this new land, the first by Baron de Lery of France in 1518, and the second by the Italian explorer Giovanni da Verrazano in 1523. (Some accounts credit Verrazano with naming the area "Arcadia," and hence its original name of Acadia; but other historians say the name was derived from the Micmac word "acadie," meaning fertile land. The British changed the name to Nova Scotia in 1710.) As a result of these early expeditions, crude coastal charts of Nova Scotia were available to seventeenth-century explorers.

The territory appears to have been forgotten until 1604, when an expedition led by Sieur du Gua DeMonts and Samuel de Champlain established a temporary French colony at La

Have, about fifteen miles south of Oak Island. A year later
they created a permanent settlement at Port Royal, on the Bay
of Fundy, thereby giving France its first colonial foothold in
the province. But in 1621 the British Crown claimed ownership of the territory by virtue of the fact that Cabot had landed
there first in 1497. For the next 143 years France and England
hotly contested sovereignty over this part of the New World,
and the flag over Port Royal and other settlements changed
several times in the wake of the English-French skirmishes.
Both sides employed the Micmac Indians, who had previously
been a peaceful tribe, as mercenaries in their battles. Finally,
in 1763, Britain's rule over the entire province was confirmed.

   This period of Nova Scotia's early colonization and the
resulting French and English wars has been considered by
many people as the likely era in which the Oak Island project
was created. However, no evidence has been found in the
colonial documents of either country that the island was ever a
military installation or that it served any official purpose whatsoever. But one popular theory is that the island was used
secretively by the French as a temporary repository for royal
treasury funds that were used to pay troops and laborers involved in the construction of the great fort of Louisbourg, 240
miles northeast of Oak Island.

   When France lost the War of the Spanish Succession, she
was forced to sign the Treaty of Utrecht in 1713, whereby
England acquired most of the French colonies in Nova Scotia
and Newfoundland. France was left with only the islands of
Cape Breton, Prince Edward, and St. Pierre and Miquelon.
The French then spent almost thirty years and millions of dollars building a huge fortress at Louisbourg near the eastern tip
of Cape Breton. This supposedly impregnable fort was completed in 1744. But a year later the British led an army of New
Englanders against the French at Louisbourg, and the fort was
captured after a forty-nine day siege. It was handed back to
France by the Treaty of Aix-la-Chapelle in 1748, only to be
recaptured by the British in 1758. In 1760 the fortress was
demolished to ensure that the French would never again oc-
cupy it.

   The fifty acres of Louisbourg fortification had been built

by private contractors sent from France along with engineers and artisans. Most of the labor was supplied by the French troops garrisoned in the town that the fortress was designed to protect. Perhaps, because of the uneasy truce with England, the French government was wary of keeping the vast sums that went into building the fort in the town itself. It therefore may have sought a repository or "bank" that would be convenient to Louisbourg and yet be in an unlikely and isolated part of the province. So Oak Island might have been chosen, and the underground vault and flood tunnels constructed with professional engineers and military labor.

A related theory suggests that Oak Island wasn't a government project at all, but that some of the royal treasury funds shipped from Versailles to build the fort were siphoned off by a dishonest contractor or high-ranking French officer. With the aid of trusted cohorts, this person then designed and built the underground vault in which to hide the embezzled wealth, with the intention of returning to France a rich man.

Both these theories have also been applied to the period just after 1748 when France again shipped large sums to Louisbourg in order to rebuild those parts of the fort that had been destroyed in the British attack of 1745. It has also been rumored that the equivalent of about $10 million was spirited out of Louisbourg harbor on a French ship during the second British siege of 1758 and that the money was never heard of again. But there is no reliable historical record of this having happened. Three French frigates did escape the British blockade and several days later succeeded in making it up the St. Lawrence River to Quebec City, which was then still in French hands.

Similar arguments contend that an earlier French pay ship destined for Louisbourg may have foundered, by accident or design, near Oak Island. Its cargo of coin and bullion was then hidden, either for larcenous reasons or to keep it from falling into the hands of the British. But the only positive record of a richly laden French ship disappearing in that area occurred in August 1725 when the *Chameau* went down with all hands on a rocky reef just a few miles east of Louisbourg. She had 290,000 French livres (about $750,000) in cash aboard, part of which was recovered by divers in 1965.

Another suggestion links Oak Island to the ill-fated armada of the Duc d'Anville. In June of 1746 the French Crown, mortified by the fall of Louisbourg to the English the year before, assembled at Brest a fleet of sixty-five ships, and 3,150 troops to sail across the Atlantic and retake the fortress as well as the rest of the province. The fleet, under the command of the Duc d'Anville, was plagued with bad luck all the way to the New World. Even before reaching Nova Scotian waters, several vessels were lost in storms, and pestilence had broken out on many others. Then off the dreaded shoals of Sable Island (known as "the graveyard of the Atlantic") the armada ran into a violent tempest that claimed more ships and lives. On September 25 D'Anville's flagship and a few other vessels managed to make it to Chibucto Harbor (now Halifax Harbor), but most of the troops and sailors were dying of scurvy and other diseases. Two days later D'Anville himself died, reportedly of apoplexy, though it was rumored he had ended his problems with poison. The intended attack on Louisbourg was never carried out, for the armada had lost most of its ships and about 2,000 of its soldiers.

Theories have been advanced to the effect that one or more of the ships presumed lost in the storm off Sable Island may have actually escaped and sailed two hundred miles west into Mahone Bay. There is no record indicating that any of the ships in the fleet were carrying specie or bullion, but possibly some were. Had such a ship sought refuge in Mahone Bay, Oak Island may have been used as a temporary hiding place for this treasure.

This and other theories establishing a French connection to Oak Island, as either an official or unofficial deposit, conform with the necessary ingredient of secrecy. Until Halifax was settled and made the British headquarters in 1749, the southern coast of mainland Nova Scotia was virtually uninhabited. The principal settlement until then was at Port Royal on the northern side of the province, and most of the lesser settlements were in that same area. And prior to 1750 even the Micmacs appear to have made only sporadic visits to Mahone Bay. However, had the workings been secretly executed under the direction of the French government, some account of it would have turned up eventually in France. And if the work was done without the knowledge of the French Crown, surely some official mention would exist that a large amount of public money was unaccounted for about that time. No such records have ever been found.

But what if the project was a private French venture unrelated to Crown funds? Two such possibilities have been suggested: the Acadians and the Huguenots.

The sixty French families who formed Nova Scotia's first permanent settlement at Port Royal in 1605 were the province's original Acadians. For more than a hundred years they prospered, mainly by farming but also through fishing and commerce. Their villages and communities were for the most part situated along the shores of the Bay of Fundy and the adjoining Minas Basin. As early as 1632, however, a few Acadian families had settled in the communities of La Have and Merligueche, now known as Lunenburg.

The Acadians were peaceful and did their best to remain neutral during the French-English struggle for dominance in Nova Scotia. Yet they were not immune to raids on their villages by British and New England privateers, who sometimes seized their livestock, farm produce, and other possessions. When the Treaty of Utrecht ceded mainland Nova Scotia to England in 1713, the new rulers tried to force the Acadians to take an oath of allegiance to the British Crown, including the promise to bear arms against the French should France try again to assume control of the territory. The Acadians resisted for several years and then signed the oath only when a clause was inserted whereby they would remain militarily neutral in times of conflict.

Thus the situation remained until 1749, when Edward Cornwallis was appointed governor of Nova Scotia. By then there were an estimated 10,000 Acadians living on the mainland part of the province, and France had once again assumed control of Cape Breton Island and the Louisbourg fortress. Cornwallis saw himself faced with a dilemma. He felt threatened by the fact that so many French people, albeit neutral, lived in British-held Nova Scotia. But he knew if he forced the Acadians to leave, most of them would settle in Cape Breton, thereby greatly increasing the strength of the French in the nearby colony. So once again the Acadians were urged to take an unconditional oath of allegiance; and again they refused to relinquish their neutrality.

This uneasy state of affairs remained unresolved until 1755, when the British resorted to a heavy-handed solution. The Acadians were rounded up at gunpoint, stripped of their land and possessions, and herded aboard ships that carried them into exile. In 1755 alone some 6,000 Acadians were expelled, most of them dumped off at ports along the American coast from Maine to Georgia. Another 2,000 were rounded up and similarly deported in the next couple of years. (Some Acadians later drifted down to Louisiana, hence the origin of the name "Cajuns.") Not until after the Treaty of Paris in 1763 was the edict expelling the Acadians revoked. Many of them returned to Nova Scotia.

It has been theorized that sometime between 1749 and 1755 a group of Acadians, suspecting their eventual fate, may have designed the Oak Island project to protect their money and valuables from confiscation. They were certainly industrious and clever enough to have built something of that nature. There is one recorded instance of a group of eighty-six Acadians in 1755 digging a long tunnel through which they escaped from Fort Lawrence (near the Nova Scotia–New Brunswick border) where they were being held pending deportation.

However, it is doubtful that any Acadians ever amassed the kind of wealth suggested by the elaborateness of the Oak Island workings. Most of them were successful though not prosperous farmers. Some of them were involved in trading and even smuggling businesses, which would have brought them hard currency. They sold farm produce, meat, fish, and furs to the English garrisons on the mainland and to the French at Louisbourg. (This latter market was illegal under British rule and therefore involved smuggling.) In some instances they also sold supplies to coastal pirates in the Bay of Fundy, and they presumably received coins, jewels, and other plundered items in return. But nothing has been found in Acadian history that hints at the concealment of substantial wealth prior to their deportation. Moreover, no indications exist that a group of Acadians retrieved a deposit on Oak Island after they were allowed back in the province, and by that time the Mahone Bay area was becoming fairly well inhabited.

Another theory involving early settlers is more tenuous, but it contains an intriguing coincidence. While the majority of the Acadians were Catholic, there was a smaller group of Nova Scotia French colonists who were Protestant. These were the Huguenots, most of whom were drawn from the French nobility and affluent artisan class. The Huguenots were the principal victims of the religious wars of sixteenth-century France until the Edict of Nantes in 1598 assured their equal political rights with the Catholics. But on October 18, 1685, the edict was revoked and religious persecution was resumed. Consequently, despite the fact that their emigration was prohibited by law, some 50,000 Huguenot families fled to foreign countries, including parts of the New World.

In 1928, Dunbar Hinrichs, a historian and William Kidd biographer, was living in Chester, where he met a man who had come over from France to investigate a family legend. This Frenchman (whose name Hinrichs long since forgot) said one of his ancestors had been among a group of wealthy Huguenots who had escaped from France aboard two ships at about the time the Edict of Nantes was revoked. They reportedly took a great deal of money and jewelry with them. According to a story passed down through this Frenchman's family, the two vessels had sailed from La Rochelle across the Atlantic to Saint-Domingue (now Haiti). There, under the supervision of an engineer accompanying them, they constructed a complex underground vault complete with flood tunnels to guard it. A group of them deposited their personal fortunes in different sections of the vault and then sailed off on one of the ships to the British colony of New York, where they settled. (In fact, some Huguenots did sail into Long Island Sound in 1688 and established the town of New Rochelle.)

According to the legend, the second vessel headed for Nova Scotia with the rest of the Huguenots and their riches. The engineer who had designed the Haitian works was also aboard. The ship reportedly sailed into Mahone Bay, where an uninhabited island was selected for a project similar to that in Saint-Domingue. After storing their wealth these people then settled in the province. The Huguenots' intent was to prevent their fortunes from being confiscated or heavily taxed in the New World. The underground "banks," according to the story, had been constructed in such a way as to allow them to be reopened via a secret passage from the surface or else by the closing of a water gate somewhere in the flood tunnels. The funds could then be withdrawn as desired.

In a 1976 interview in St. Petersburg, Florida, Hinrichs recalled that he had found the Frenchman's story interesting but that he had never put too much stock in it. In fact, he had almost forgotten it until he saw an article about Oak Island that I'd written for *The Wall Street Journal* in August 1975. What caught his attention was the fact that (as the article explained) an underground project similar to Oak Island was said to exist in Haiti, and some investigators believed that both were designed by the same person. The curious part is that the Haitian workings weren't discovered until 1947, almost twenty years after Hinrich's conversation with the mysterious Frenchman. The Frenchman had been lured to Nova Scotia by publicity surrounding the Oak Island search, and he had seen a possible connection to the family legend. But he couldn't have known about the purported Haitian workings. Who this man was or what evidence he had to support the Huguenot connection will probably never be known.

Provincial records note the arrival of several prominent Huguenot families in Nova Scotia, though no conspicuous group appears around the year 1685. One of the earliest was the La Tour family, who came in the 1620s and founded a settlement (now Port La Tour) on the province's western tip. The majority of the Huguenots didn't arrive until around the time of the expulsion of the Acadians in 1755. They, as well as thousands of Germans and New Englanders, were enticed to the province with the promise of free land, much of which had been expropriated from the Acadians. (The Huguenots, being Protestant, were considered "safe" French settlers by the British.)

Any hypothesis that relates the Oak Island repository to eighteenth-century history suffers on two important grounds. First, recent carbon dating of wood found deep underground points to a period at least one hundred years earlier than that. Second, by the mid-1700s the Mahone Bay mainland was sufficiently populated to ensure that nothing of the magnitude of the Oak Island project could have been clandestinely carried out under the noses of the local settlers.

Nevertheless, one theory that has been seriously promoted by several investigators is that Oak Island was engineered and used by the British army during the War of American Independence from 1775 to 1783. Within the first year of the war, the British had good reason to fear that George Washington's troops would be the eventual victors. In March of 1776 the British forces evacuated Boston, and by mid-1778 their New York command post was under threat of attack by land and sea. This garrison contained an estimated several million dollars in funds used to pay troops and purchase supplies.

Suggestions have been made that the British relocated this treasury from New York to Halifax, their nearest secure base, so as to prevent its falling into the hands of the revolutionaries. Fearing a possible American attack on Halifax (which General Washington had in fact considered in 1775), a secret repository was built on Oak Island by British military engineers. The island was then used as a colonial treasury for the duration of the American Revolution. However, if such an operation had taken place, the funds stored on Oak Island must have later been recovered; had they not been, a major scandal would surely have erupted back in England. The immediate problem with this theory is that nothing has been found in British military records alluding to any such undertaking. Again, an operation like that would certainly have been observed and remarked upon by residents of the area.

Some who date the project this late argue that the eastern end of the island, the site of the Money Pit, is on the seaward side and therefore hidden from anyone directly across on the mainland. This, they add, would permit a secret venture to be carried out. The flaw here is that the island's eastern end is clearly visible from other nearby sections of the mainland north and south of the island as well as from several elevated spots in Chester itself. Also, the early settlers commonly traveled between Chester and Lunenburg by canoe or fishing boat, a route that would take them directly by the east end of Oak Island.

There have been other theories proposed in connection with the War of Independence. These range from American naval privateers using Oak Island as a base, to the island's being used as a weapons cache by New England settlers in the province who were sympathetic to their Yankee brethren and who hoped to expand the revolution to Nova Scotia. Some have even thought that a group of United Empire Loyalists (those Americans loyal to the British Crown who came to Nova Scotia by the thousands after the Revolution) may have secreted a personal treasure on the island. Again, the timing would render these explanations virtually impossible.

The common element in all of these suggestions is that they fit the known history of the province in the centuries prior to the discovery of the Money Pit. But as further investigation revealed the enormity and complexity of the underground workings, new theories were advanced to explain their origin. And some of these credited the work to people far removed from recorded Nova Scotian history.

In 1909, for instance, some of those associated with Henry Bowdoin's expedition believed they were on the trail of the crown jewels of France. The theory is historically untenable, yet it is one that is still espoused by some local Mahone Bay residents. The jewels were supposedly taken by Louis XVI and Marie Antoinette when they fled Paris on June 20, 1791, with the revolutionary mob at their heels. They were captured at Varennes a few days later and finally executed in 1793. According to legend, the crown jewels weren't found in their possession because they had been smuggled from Varennes to the fortress of Louisbourg in Nova Scotia by either a lady-in-waiting or an engineer reputed to be Mary Antoinette's lover. From this legend the suggestion was derived that the jewels were later buried on Oak Island.

The flaw in this enchanting story is that the jewels weren't brought to Varennes. In preparing for their escape, the King and Queen (no less farsighted despots than the modern-day Marcoses and Duvaliers) sent 1,500,000 livres (about $3,750,000) in cash and the royal diamonds by special messenger to Brussels. From there they were forwarded to a contact in Austria, where Louis and Marie had planned to seek eventual refuge. After the royal couple was captured, the money did in fact disappear. But it went into the pockets of various persons in Brussels and Austria. As for the jewels, they were eventually returned to the French government.

Other historically related theories were advanced in the 1930s linking Oak Island's secret to the vast fortunes in gold and silver ecclesiastical vessels, plate, and statues that disappeared from England and Scotland during the sixteenth-century Reformation and again in the seventeenth and eighteenth centuries. Fred Blair eventually became more partial to this theory than to his earlier belief in a pirate's cache. Writing in 1930 he stated: "One of the most reasonable explanations of the treasure is that it is the royal and church plate and valuables known to have been removed from England and hidden during the Protectorate of Cromwell [1653–1658] after the execution of Charles I [in 1649]. This treasure simply vanished from the face of the earth and has never been recovered. Very probably it now lies buried on Oak Island. If so, its value will far exceed, for archaeological and historical purposes, anything in the way of bullion or mere precious metal."

A similar hypothesis held that the Money Pit contained the lost treasure of St. Andrew's Cathedral in Scotland. The abbey's wealth is also thought to have included great spoils taken by the Scots from the British after the Battle of Bannockburn in 1314. In the late 1800s and early 1900s, several searches were made beneath the ruins of the cathedral itself, and a couple of secret underground passages were discovered and explored. No treasure vault was found, however, and it was speculated that the riches may have been taken out of Scotland and perhaps even abroad by the monks of the abbey.

Blair received several letters from people who were convinced that this legendary treasure had been transported to Nova Scotia. In February 1938, Oswald L. Holland, a Canadian then living in Britain's Channel Islands, offered to invest in the Oak Island search. He stated flatly: "Priests from the Abbey of St. Andrew's in Scotland took their gold plate and other treasures over to Oak Island in 1745 after the defeat of Prince Charlie at Bannockburn. [He presumably meant Culloden.] Nova Scotia was a wilderness then, of course. Do you know that I spent over three months at St. Andrew's years ago trying to find out what they had done with the stuff? Their journals were all written in old Latin and it was just fearful to make sense of it, but I got the hang of it at last. The lot that sailed away never got home, so the home lot never had a clue" as to where the treasure was taken. Gilbert Hedden, who was then in charge of the Oak Island project, discounted this theory as "a bit fantastic" and declined Holland's offer of financial assistance.

In addition to the whodunit theories, several maps allegedly connected with Oak Island were brought to Blair's attention during this period. But all of them had the common feature of no longer existing other than as legend or in the memories of their promoters. And in all cases their owners sought either financial compensation for remembered details of these "long-lost" charts, or else funds from Blair and others to underwrite a search expedition to the island. However, in the mid-1930s a map bearing an unmistakable connection to Oak Island would accidentally surface. Neither the origin nor the remarkable accuracy of this controversial document has yet been satisfactorily explained.

CHAPTER NINE

A Strange Map Is Found

In 1934 Gilbert Hedden of Chatham, New Jersey, decided to fulfill an ambition he'd had for six years—to go to Nova Scotia and solve the mystery of Oak Island. The bug had bitten him in the spring of 1928 while he was browsing through the magazine section of the Sunday *New York Times* and came across an article on the famous treasure hunt. He wasn't halfway through it before he became convinced that, given the time, the money, and some sound engineering principles, he could find out what lay at the bottom of the Money Pit. He was then a thirty-one-year-old vice president and general manager of his father's steel-fabricating business, Hedden Iron Construction Company of Hillside, New Jersey. Though not a certified engineer, he had studied civil engineering for two years at the Rensselaer Polytechnic Institute in Troy, New York.

In 1931 the family business was sold to Bethlehem Steel Company. Hedden became plant manager of that company's Hedden division. Within two years he left, sold life insurance for a while, and then established a Cadillac and Oldsmobile dealership in nearby Morristown, New Jersey. He also served as mayor of Chatham from 1934 to 1938.

The sale of his father's company had left Hedden fairly

well off, and in 1934 he found himself with the requisite capital and free time to pursue his Oak Island goal. That fall he traveled to Nova Scotia and met Blair. The latter was impressed with Hedden's sincerity, engineering background, and especially the fact that he was self-financed. Hedden assured Blair that he would solve the riddle within two years and that he was prepared to spend up to $100,000 to do it.

Hedden had hoped to begin work the following spring, but this schedule was upset by Blair's inability to secure the surface rights on the eastern end of the island. Blair had maintained his lease of the area for thirty years, until the death of the owner, Sophia Sellers, in 1931. The property was then jointly inherited by her three grown children and nine grandchildren. None of them were living on or farming the island in 1935, but they stubbornly refused to make any sort of lease arrangement with Blair or Hedden.

The reason was simple. Although Hedden had tried to keep a low profile, the word got out in the winter of 1934–35 that "a millionaire from the States" was coming to dig on the island. The Sellers heirs felt that their own potential Oak Island "treasure" lay in the sale of the property. So instead of leasing the Money Pit area, they offered to sell all of their island lots for $5,500. This was more than ten times the appraised value of the property. Blair declined to pay what he termed their "fancy price," and instead tried another approach.

In April 1935 he had a friend in the Nova Scotia provincial legislature introduce a bill seeking to place treasure trove licenses under the province's Mines Act. This in effect would allow someone holding such a license (as Blair did) to search for treasure on land that was owned by another party. Should the license-holder be unable to reach an agreement with the property owner, he could apply to the provincial secretary for an arbitration hearing on the matter. The secretary would have the power to allow the license-holder to proceed with the search and would also determine what compensation should be paid to the landowner.

After weeks of debate, the bill was voted down in committee (although it was eventually enacted in 1950), and Blair went back to negotiating with the Oak Island owners. But they were still interested only in selling, rather than leasing, the property. Hedden eventually gave in, and on July 26 he purchased the east end of the island for $5,000. The title was put under the name of George W. Grimm, a New Jersey lawyer acting as Hedden's trustee.

By then it was too late in the season to begin digging, so Hedden spent the remainder of the year getting ready for the following spring. A survey of the island was made by S. Edgar March, electricity was again brought to the island via an underwater cable, a wharf was built at Smith's Cove, and a house was erected several hundred feet north of the Money Pit.

Hedden was a conscientious researcher, and for over a year he had been collecting all the data he could find pertaining to Oak Island. Much of this he obtained from Blair's files and notes, but he also interviewed and corresponded with many others associated with previous search attempts. He compiled all of this information in a thirty-one page treatise entitled "Investigation of the Legend of Buried Treasure at Oak Island, Nova Scotia." He also collected old surveys and charts and even had aerial photographs taken of the island.

Hedden had originally intended to begin by driving a new shaft down in the Money Pit area. But after conferring with William Chappell in the spring of 1936, he decided first to drain the 1931 Chappell shaft and then use it to explore the adjacent ground by horizontal drilling at various depths. This way he hoped to relocate the exact position of the original Money Pit. Blair expressed disappointment over this approach, stating that "there does not appear to be anything very decisive about the work outlined; it being more along the lines of previous operations and open to failure without definite results."

But Hedden had made up his mind, and in April he hired a large drilling contract firm, Sprague & Henwood Inc. of Scranton, Pennsylvania, to carry out the work. Their engineering representative, Frederick R. Krupp, arrived a month later to take charge of operations. (He and his equipment were detained at the border for several days while Canadian customs officials pondered the rules related to an American firm digging for treasure in Canada.) Hedden also purchased a 1,000-gallon-per-minute turbine pump, the largest ever used on the island, to drain the pit. It was fed by 7,500 watts of electric power and proved more than adequate for the job.

Hedden kept a diary recording the summer's work. Some excerpts: "I arrived on Oak Island May 27, 1936. . . . Put in turbine pump. Ran the pump two hours and fifteen minutes and lowered the water seventy feet in the shaft, which would be one hundred feet below the deck head. I observed when the water was down to [that] level, an old shaft [the Cave-in Pit] was drained also, proving there is some clear passage between [the two]. . . . I also noticed that three other old pits are gradually becoming dried out since pumping operations [began]."

During the balance of the summer, the Chappell shaft was cleared and re-timbered to its original depth of 155 feet and then driven down to 160 feet. Some lateral probing was done at various levels, but the only discovery of any consequence was two large oak splinters found several feet to the east at a depth of 147 feet. From their state of decay and the location in which they were found, Hedden believed that "these splinters must be part of a box or an oak platform of logs which fell to that depth in the collapse" of the Money Pit in 1861. He concluded that the original Money Pit was probably slightly to the east of the Chappell shaft. He and his crew therefore left off work in September and planned to return the following spring to begin a new shaft in that location. This hole was to be large enough to allow pneumatic drills to be brought down and used for lateral drilling. The drill rods would extend out twenty feet in all directions from the shaft at vertical levels of two feet apart, beginning at the one-hundred-foot level and working as far down as necessary to locate the treasure.

Before leaving the island that summer, Hedden uncovered more coconut fiber six feet under the beach at Smith's Cove. He also made two other interesting discoveries.

One Saturday in July, while he was wandering along the beach at Joudrey's Cove on the island's north side, Hedden spotted a large granite rock half buried in the sand. He dug it out and discovered lettering etched into one of its flat surfaces. It bore the Roman numeral II and below that the letters

"GIN," which seemed to form only part of a word, as the rock had obviously been broken from a larger piece. He inquired around and from one of his local workers learned that a huge flat boulder bearing several inscriptions had been seen in the location sometime in the 1920s. It had been dynamited into many pieces and the ground under it excavated for a few feet in the hope that the rock covered a treasure deposit. Nothing had been found, and several of the inscribed pieces had been carried away by souvenir seekers. But Hedden's interest was particularly aroused when he was told that, although much of the inscription on the boulder had apparently been carved during the nineteenth century, one part of it had contained "strange symbols" which no one at the time could account for.

Hedden set his men to work exploring that part of the shoreline. In the next couple of days two more large rock pieces were discovered, one bearing the letter "W" and the other reading "S.S. Ross 1864." Hedden assumed Ross had been a worker with one of the search groups from the 1860s. (The "GIN" on the first piece may have been part of the name "McGinnis," as several generations of that family had lived on the island since 1795.) But then a fourth piece, weighing several hundred pounds, was found buried a few feet below the beach. On one of its flat sides was part of an inscription which was far more weathered than the others and totally unlike them.

These pieces were rafted around the island to the dock at Smith's Cove and then hauled by a team of horses up to Hedden's cabin. No two of the four slabs, all of which had irregular and jagged edges, fit together, and Hedden realized he was missing many pieces of the original boulder. His workers continued to search, but nothing more was found.

That the symbols predated the discovery of the Money Pit seemed quite possible. And perhaps people finding it later had dug up the boulder and on a whim had added their names to it. Neither Hedden nor anyone else could make any sense of the odd characters, and that piece of rock was left lying in front of his cabin. But in the 1970s these symbols would form part of some unusual theories about the origin of Oak Island.

Hedden's second discovery was less enigmatic, though its

true nature remained unclear to him. The remnants of the cofferdam built by searchers at Smith's Cove in 1866 were still visible at neap tides in 1936. One day Hedden noticed the ends of two large timbers protruding from the rocks inside the dam, and he had his men dig them out. His journal records: "They were about four feet apart, roughly parallel, and were buried under about four feet of sand. The timbers were about fifteen inches in diameter at the butt, and were notched for a quarter of the circumference at about every four feet. In each notch was inserted a rather heavy wooden pin. Beside one of them we also found several wooden cross members about four feet long. They had the appearance of having been used as a skid at one time, though nobody at the island had ever heard of them."

Hedden at first believed he'd found an old skidway used by the builders of the 1866 cofferdam. But the fact that wooden pins rather than iron spikes had been used in the construction led him to conclude later that it was much older, and that it may well have been part of the original Oak Island project. Hedden's workers dragged the timbers up on shore, where they were abandoned and forgotten. Had they been able to excavate past the low-tide mark, they would have realized that what they had found was only one part of a huge structure built by the island's unknown architects. The rest of the clue was to remain undiscovered under tons of silt until 1970.

After spending the winter with his wife, Marguerite, and their five children in New Jersey, Hedden returned to Oak Island in the spring of 1937. A large labor force was hired, and work began on a new shaft. This pit, known as the Hedden shaft, was the only one still open in the Money Pit area when Triton Alliance began its 1988 excavation. It was put down just east of the Chappell shaft and was twelve feet wide by twenty-four feet long—large enough to accommodate Hedden's lateral drilling program.

Between May and August it was excavated and strongly cribbed to 125 feet. All the way down it was evident from the disturbed condition of the soil that the workers were in an area that had long ago been dug up and refilled. But they weren't exactly in the Money Pit. (It was later determined that the center of the original Money Pit probably lay about 15 feet north of the north wall of the Chappell shaft and about ten feet west of the northwest corner of the Hedden shaft.)

On August 17, 1937, at a depth of 125 feet, work in the shaft was abruptly halted. Hedden had just seen dramatic proof of what some people still believe is the key to the riddle of Oak Island. And it had nothing at all to do with the shaft he'd spent all summer digging.

The events leading up to this discovery actually began two months earlier, when R. V. Harris, a Halifax lawyer who handled legal matters for both Blair and Hedden, showed the latter a map of an island in a book that had been published that year. It was *Captain Kidd and His Skeleton Island*, written by Harold T. Wilkins of London, England. Harris pointed out that the island depicted in the charts was similar in shape to Oak Island. Hedden picked up the strange trail from there.

According to Wilkins's book, the map and three others like it had been found separately hidden in false compartments of three sea chests and a desk. These items were alleged to have once been the property of William Kidd, and had been purchased in the early 1930s by Hubert Palmer, a British antiques dealer and collector of pirate relics. He in turn had shown the maps to Wilkins.

The chart in which Hedden was interested bore the legend "W.K. 1669" as well as a series of measurements and compass directions. The island shown had no name; nor were there any longitude and latitude reference points. The body of water around it was simply labeled "Mar Del" (sea of?). After close scrutiny Hedden detected many points of likeness between Oak Island and the Mar Del map. These included correct compass rose directions, similar shape and topographical features (Oak Island's two hills and the swamp are shown as "mountains" and a "lagoon"), and offshore soundings and reefs corresponding to those around Oak Island. He also noticed a circled dot in the general area of the Money Pit.

Hedden wrote to Wilkins, informing him of the similarities and asking for more information about the map. On July 7 Wilkins replied that his map was genuine, but that it hadn't the slightest connection with Oak Island. He said he knew the

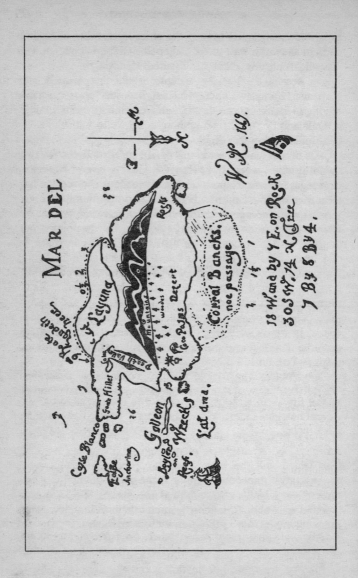

longitude and the latitude of the chart in question and that it was in an eastern sea, on the other side of the world from Oak Island. Moreover, Wilkins assured Hedden that Kidd had never been in the vicinity of Nova Scotia. In a second letter (August 13) Wilkins exhorted Hedden not to "waste any time trying to identify this eastern [hemisphere] island of Kidd with Oak Island."

But Hedden was unconvinced. He felt there were too many points of agreement between Oak Island and Wilkins's map to write it off as mere coincidence. He then turned his attention to the legend at the bottom of the Mar Del map:

18 W. and by 7 E. on Rock
30 SW. 14 N Tree
7 By 8 By 4

Hedden realized that if these directions were at all applicable to Oak Island, there must be some sort of markers that would tie in with them. He put this question to Blair, who told him about a triangle of stones that had been noticed by William Chappell and others near the south shore in 1897 and again in 1931. He also told Hedden that he'd once seen a granite boulder with a hole drilled into it somewhere north of the Money Pit.

On August 15 Hedden had his crew make a thorough search for these artifacts. The drilled rock was soon found about fifty feet north of the Money Pit. Then another one was found near the shore at Smith's Cove. In both cases the holes, two inches deep and just over an inch in diameter, were obviously artificially made.

Amos Nauss, one of Hedden's workers, was sent into the underbrush at the island's southeast end. Nauss, shortly before his death in 1981, told me that "Hedden gave me some idea that there was something down there at the beach that he wanted to find. So I explored around there with a hoe. I was clawing around and suddenly I hit one rock, then another and another, all in line with each other. So I decided there was something there, and I started clearing it and called Hedden over."

Nauss had found the triangle. It consisted of sixteen beach stones, each about the size of a man's head. The rocks were

covered with moss and other vegetation and were half buried
in the ground. As the undergrowth was cleared away, the triangle could be seen to be equilateral, ten feet long on each
side. Its southern base line was about forty feet up from and
roughly parallel to the beach. The triangle also had a medial
line consisting of eight rocks running from the northern apex
stone down through the southern side. It didn't bisect the side
but crossed it at a point four feet from the western angle and
six feet from the eastern angle. Below this base line was an
arc of six stones, which gave the whole thing the appearance
of a large sextant.

That evening Hedden called Charles Roper, a Halifax land
surveyor, and asked him to come out to the island. He and his
young assistant arrived the following afternoon. Roper, in an
interview, recalled that "Hedden showed us the triangle and
drilled rocks, but he didn't tell us what we were looking for.
He just told us to measure the distances and bearing between
those three things."

By the next day (August 17) the surveyors established what
Hedden already suspected. The drilled rocks ran on an east-
west line and were 415 feet, or almost 25 rods, apart. (One
rod equals 16.5 feet.) Using the directions on the Mar Del
map, Hedden had Roper establish a point along that line that
was 18 rods (300 feet) from the westerly drilled rock and 7
rods (115 feet) from the easterly rock. From that position,
which was close to the Cave-in Pit, Roper swung his transit 45
degrees, aiming it to the southwest. A distance of 30 rods
(495 feet) was chained off along that line. This brought them
just below the southerly base line of the stone triangle at a
point intersected by the triangle's medial line.

Roper then set up his transit on the medial line itself and
sighted along it over the center of the triangle's apex stone.
After making a quick calculation for magnetic variation,
Roper announced in astonishment that the line ran precisely
true north; that is, in line with the North Star. Moreover, the
extension of the line passed through Hedden's shaft and the
westerly drilled rock.

These findings amazed both Roper and Hedden. Three of
the directions on the chart, when interpreted as rods, connected the mysterious island markers. Moreover, the fact that
the line running through the triangle pointed to true north and
hit the Money Pit could not be dismissed as a coincidence.

However, the direction "14 N Tree" when measured out

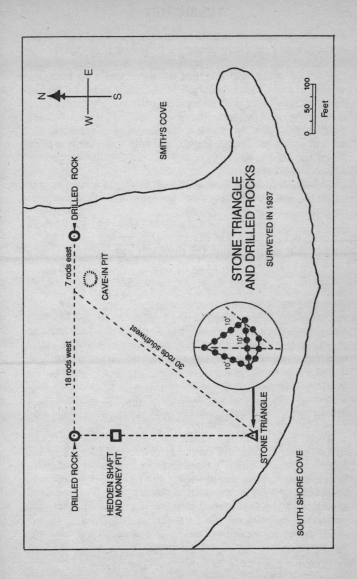

STONE TRIANGLE
AND DRILLED ROCKS

SURVEYED IN 1937

SMITH'S COVE

DRILLED ROCK

7 rods east

CAVE-IN PIT

18 rods west

30 rods southwest

10'
10'
10'
10'

STONE TRIANGLE

DRILLED ROCK

HEDDEN SHAFT
AND MONEY PIT

SOUTH SHORE COVE

N
W — E
S

0   50   100
Feet

97

from the triangle fell four rods short of the Money Pit. Also, nothing could be made of the legend's last line: "7 By 8 By 4." Even so, Hedden had seen enough to convince him that the drilled rocks and the triangle were part of the original work that had been done on the island. And it seemed that the Mar Del map had a definite connection to the project.

Writing to President Roosevelt on September 1, 1937, Hedden described his discovery of the map and the markers, as well as his previous research, and said these led him to the following conclusions:

> First, that a large amount of complicated and difficult engineering was done on the site for some purpose a long time ago, probably as early as 1640.
> Second, that Kidd knew of the site and of the work and probably who did it, but was not aware of its exact location.
> Third, that the early legends of the discovery of the shaft, the tunnels, the peculiar fiber, the mysterious stone with the inscription, the objects drilled through in 1850 and 1897, are to a large part true and can be, in a large part, substantiated today.

FDR sent Hedden a cordial reply, thanking him for the information and saying, "It vividly recalls to my mind our semi-serious, semi-pleasure efforts at Oak Island nearly thirty years ago. I can visualize the theories on which you are working. As I remember it, we also talked of sinking a new shaft on our main run out."

Hedden decided he had to meet Wilkins and see the original map owned by Hubert Palmer. He booked passage on the *Aquitania*, which was leaving New York on November 10, and wrote Palmer and Wilkins that he was coming to England.

He spent the intervening weeks at home in New Jersey poring over histories of Kidd and collecting old navigational charts of Nova Scotia waters. His studies yielded several interesting points of evidence. He found, for example, that most sixteenth- and seventeenth-century charts referred to the Atlantic Ocean as "Mar del Nort," and that the words "mar del" didn't appear on any sea in the Eastern Hemisphere. He also noticed that prior to 1675 (when the Greenwich Royal Observatory was built) longitude was shown as a meridian line measured from zero to 360 degrees east of the island of Ferro (now Hierro) in the Canary Islands. (Longitude today is measures from zero to 180 degrees east or west of Greenwich, England.) Thus, Oak Island's longitude on an ancient chart would be approximately 316 degrees East, instead of its current longitude of 64 degrees 18 minutes West. Hedden therefore wondered if Wilkins, who claimed to know the latitude and longitude of his "skeleton island," was confused as to its real location.

On October 27 Wilkins wrote to Hedden telling him that he'd be happy to see him but that it would be a waste of Hedden's time. He said, "When you see the actual Kidd charts, of which mine is an approximate copy, you will have realized that Oak Island and Kidd's island are not identical." This was the first time Wilkins had intimated that the chart in his book was less than authentic or exact. (Hedden should have realized that something was amiss from the fact that the legend and measurements reproduced in the text of Wilkins's book differ from those shown in the book's frontispiece.)

Hedden made the trip anyway. In a letter to his lawyer, R. V. Harris, on December 17, he reported the outcome of his investigation:

> Wilkins is a very peculiar character, and it is difficult to describe him adequately. I would say that in appearance and manner of speech he is every bit as crazy as his book would seem to make him.
>
> He almost immediately admitted that the chart as shown in the Kidd book is simply a figment of his imagination, and apologized sincerely for not being able to tell me [earlier] that it was. I am sure he is getting into a bit of hot water in that regard, as he has received many letters from all over the world in which the writer professes to identify the island and give its location. He admitted my claims by far surpassed any others he had received and agreed that his drawing was, according to the evidence, undoubtedly of Oak Island. When he submitted his book to the publishers, they demanded that he include some sort of map or chart. He put the request up to Palmer, who absolutely refused to permit any of the charts to be reproduced. Wilkins therefore drew the chart as shown, using symbols and marks shown on contemporary charts on file in the British Museum. The only actual marks [from the Palmer charts] were the valley and the lagoon, and he unconsciously made the general shape somewhat the same as the actual Kidd charts. The legend of the directing measurements simply

came out of his mind and had no basis in fact at all. Later, just before the book was published, it was necessary to make a frontispiece, and, not having the first drawing in his possession at the time, Wilkins reproduced it as well as he could from memory, which accounts for the difference between the chart in the book and the one on the front and last pages.

After I had convinced him that I had actually found markers at the points designated in his imaginary directions, he was amazed and went to great lengths to convince me that he had never been in America and had never seen an outline of Oak Island. As he became more and more convinced of the truth and sincerity of my story, Wilkins, and this may be a good commentary on his character and mental capacity, began to be convinced that he was a reincarnation of Kidd or some other pirate and had been selected to disclose the secrets of this long-hidden hoard to the modern world. By the time I left, he was completely certain of it.

Harris, who was horrified by this disclosure, wrote Hedden: "I have no language adequate to express my opinion of the faker Wilkins. His duplicity in advertising his book by a deliberate fraud should be exposed."

While in England, Hedden also met Palmer and saw the four original charts, which were drawn on old parchment. He noted that all were apparently of the same island; two were simple sketches, and the other two showed various landmarks and had inscriptions showing bearings and directions. These were quite different from the ones used by Wilkins and didn't tie in with the Oak Island markers. Palmer wouldn't allow Hedden to see the latitude and longitude on the charts, but Wilkins later gave the figures "from memory." These placed the island somewhere in the China Sea. Palmer then offered to sell the four maps for $12,000. Hedden, quite wisely, declined.

Although Hedden wrote Wilkins off as a fraud, he still believed that Palmer's charts were at least genuine and they may possibly have had some connection with Oak Island. Several later investigators also have sought to prove a link between those charts and Oak Island. The original parchment charts have long since dropped out of sight. Following Palmer's death in 1949, they were inherited by his nurse-companion, Mrs. Elizabeth Dick. She sold them sometime prior to her own death in 1965, and their whereabouts is now unknown.

But the authenticity of the Palmer charts has been questioned by several experts. In 1976, A. Stimson, curator of navigation in the Department of Navigation and Astronomy at the National Maritime Museum of England, informed me: "I think I should make it clear that I have no confidence in any of these charts being genuine, as they are all modeled on the chart drawn by R. L. Stevenson for his book *Treasure Island* and are part of the romantic pirate tradition. It seemed remarkable that five chests should turn up in the 1930s, some containing treasure charts, with Kidd's name engraved upon them. It is a well-known fact that a certain Eastbourne dealer at this time could supply 'relics' to order, and it was probably he who provided Mr. Palmer with his Kidd relics."

Nevertheless, there is still no satisfactory explanation for the similarities between Wilkins's map and Oak Island, especially the three measurements and directions that tied in with the drilled rocks and the triangle. Wilkins (who died in 1958) sent Hedden several rambling letters shortly after Hedden's unproductive trip to England. In those letters Wilkins saw himself as an "occult" messenger of Kidd. Alternatively, he suggested, "In some way I have had an involuntary and even subconscious backward glance at some event in the past, perhaps at an actual chart of Oak Island." While this is not entirely impossible (some people have been known to have had accurate flashbacks to periods long before their time) there are other explanations.

Wilkins, who spent most of his life tracking down and examining any treasure maps he heard of, may have at one time seen an ancient map that described but did not name Oak Island. The legend on it may have been unconsciously transferred from the storehouse of his mind to the Mar Del chart that he invented for the frontispiece of his book.

Then again, perhaps the whole thing was just an amazing coincidence. After all, only three of the seven measurements and bearings tied in with the markers on the island. And even the third, "30 SW," didn't quite hit the triangle but led to a point ten feet south of its base. (Though, curiously enough, a line drawn from the center of the Cave-in Pit to the point where the triangle's medial line meets its base is exactly thirty rods to the southwest.)

Of course, one could also argue that Wilkins's subconscious recollection wasn't perfect; that he actually did once see a map pertaining to Oak Island but erred in mentally transcribing some of its directions. For instance, one probable error on Wilkins's part appears in the notation "Lat d.md.," written on his chart. This perhaps should have read "Lat d.ms.," which was sometimes used on seventeenth-century charts to denote degrees and minutes of latitude.

In any case, the most important consequence of Hedden's experience with Wilkins and the Mar Del map was the discovery of the drilled rocks and the triangle. These markers are significant because they were probably made and left there by the designers of the Money Pit. And the fact that the triangle points to Polaris seems beyond accident, suggesting an advanced knowledge of navigation and/or astronomy on the part of the designers.

CHAPTER TEN

The Baconian
Connection

Hedden's search agreement with Blair, under which each was entitled to half of any treasure recovered, was scheduled to expire at the end of 1937. Before leaving for England to see Wilkins, Hedden assured Blair and their lawyer, R. V. Harris, that he planned to renew the contract and resume the following spring. But on March 25, 1938, Hedden wrote Harris to inform him that he was planning to expand his New Jersey automobile dealership and that consequently "I shall have to postpone my activities on the Oak Island adventure rather indefinitely." He asked Harris "to correspond with Blair and inform him of the present condition and of the fact that I will be unable to proceed any further this summer and possibly next."

Blair was shocked by the news. In the forty-five years he'd been involved with Oak Island, he believed no one had gotten closer to the solution than had Hedden. Blair was then seventy-one, and he was desperate to see the mystery solved. In an angry letter to Harris he said that Hedden's decision "is nothing more or less than a downright betrayal, and by a brother Mason at that." (Hedden, Blair, Harris, and several others who have been associated with Oak Island were high-ranking Masons.)

But Blair and Harris weren't aware at the time that Hedden, who had already spent $51,400 on his Oak Island search, was in dire financial straits. He was being sued by the United States Internal Revenue Service for back taxes related to the sale of his father's steel-fabricating business in 1931. Years of litigation followed, and by 1942 Hedden was virtually bankrupt, having been forced by the Treasury Department to sell most of his assets to pay the taxes. The IRS even considered putting Hedden's Oak Island property on the block. (Hedden had owned the island's eastern end since 1935 and had purchased eight other lots in 1937.) But for jurisdictional reasons and because of the property's limited real-estate value, the IRS dropped the idea.

Throughout the ordeal, Hedden remained hopeful that he would eventually return to Oak Island and finish the work he'd started. He visited the island briefly in the summers of 1938 and 1939 but was unable to return again until 1949. And in the following year he sold the property to another treasure hunter.

In any case, Hedden did not disassociate himself from the project. As owner of the Money Pit area until 1950 he had a pecuniary stake in anything that might be recovered. The normal arrangement was 40 percent to Blair (who still held the treasure trove licence), 30 percent to Hedden, and the remainder to whoever was conducting the actual search. Hedden retained his fervent interest in the mystery and continued to research and examine all possible reasons for the construction of the underground workings. Several widely circulated magazines such as the *Saturday Evening Post* and *Popular Science* published detailed articles on his 1935–37 operations. This publicity and the fact that he was the owner of the Money Pit for fifteen years brought him hundreds of letters from all over the world. Many of these were from people who had theories on how to recover the treasure or on the identity of who put it there in the first place. Hedden patiently answered all of the writers, even the obvious eccentrics, and he built up a voluminous file of correspondence, charts, old records, photographs, and folklore concerning Oak Island.

Of the many suggestions he received concerning the origin

of the project, probably the most fantastic was that the original manuscripts of William Shakespeare, as authored by Francis Bacon, lay beneath Oak Island. This extraordinary theory is worth some consideration.

The Bacon-wrote-Shakespeare controversy has been around for almost two hundred years, and approximately four hundred books have been written on the subject. Supporters of the Bacon theory include serious writers, critics, and statesmen: Samuel Taylor Coleridge, Benjamin Disraeli, Oliver Wendell Holmes, and Walt Whitman, to name but a few. They in turn have been vituperatively attacked by equally prominent pro-Shakespeareans.

The Baconians argue that Shakespeare (1564–1616), who left school at the age of thirteen to become a butcher's apprentice and later went on to be a two-bit stage actor, could not possibly have had the vocabulary, wit, and wisdom to write the plays and sonnets that are accredited to him. Nor could he have had the legal, medical, historic, geographic, and scientific knowledge so abundantly displayed in those works. Francis Bacon (1561–1626), on the other hand, was well versed in all of these fields. His books and essays show that he was a gifted writer, philosopher, linguist, lawyer, and scientist.

Bacon was appointed solicitor-general of the British Crown in 1607 and was made lord chancellor and keeper of the Great Seal ten years later. The Elizabethan court, as Bacon himself remarked, was one in which poetry and the theater were often scorned. Hence, it was not an uncommon practice for persons of noble rank to write poetry and plays under assumed names. Furthermore, these names were often "borrowed" from real people, such as insignificant writers or actors.

Thus, the Baconians claim that Bacon wrote all of the works attributed to Shakespeare and then published the folios under the latter's name. Moreover, some even credit Bacon with the authorship of the works of Edmund Spenser, Christopher Marlowe, Robert Burton, and several other less important writers of that era. A few Baconians have devoted their lives to detecting and pointing out similarities of thought, style, and actual lines in the works of all these writers, including Shakespeare. In addition, volumes have been written about Bacon's supposed use of complex word-ciphers in these pseudonymous works, whereby he "reveals" his true authorship.

One thing that Shakespeare and the other above-named authors have in common is that none of their manuscripts have ever been found. What happened to those original documents after they left the printers? Why so many manuscripts written in approximately the same period have all disappeared remains a mystery. (Original manuscripts of many other writers of that era are still extant in British museums.) In the case of Shakespeare, the most prolific writer in the history of the English language, the disappearance of all of his personally penned words defies the laws of probability. So, where *are* those handwritten works?

The Baconian answer to that question was summed up by Dr. Burrell F. Ruth in a lecture to a group of graduate students at Iowa State College on December 3, 1948:

> The person who kept these missing manuscripts, Francis Bacon, prized them very highly. And for good reason; he had written them. But there was an even better reason. Although he had published them either anonymously or under assumed names, he wanted the world someday, perhaps hundreds of years in the future, to recognize him as their author.
>
> Bacon envisioned a world of the future when mankind would have become good, wars a thing of the past, and scientific development brought to a height as he describes in his *New Atlantis*. Then, to this world of superhuman beings, he intended that someone should present, all at one time, the full documented positive proof that one single man—himself—had been responsible for that English renaissance of literature and philosophy we call the Golden Age of Elizabethan Literature. The proof was to have been a great collection of well-preserved manuscripts, just as they had been returned to him by the printer, together with an explanation as to just why he had concealed his abilities under pseudonyms and the names of people either absent from England, dead, or near death's door.

Bacon does make several references to the fact that he would be known for who he really was only long after his death. In his will, for example, he states, "For my name and memory, I leave it to men's charitable speeches, and to foreign nations, and to the next ages." (The reference to "foreign nations" is regarded by some Baconians as a clue that the manuscripts weren't hidden anywhere in England.) Following Bacon's death, his chaplain, William Rawley, also hinted that Bacon's greatness would be revealed at some future time.

Bacon's scientific tracts often dealt with the preservation of books, manuscripts, and other items of value, either by encasement, freezing, or by immersion in mercury. In his book of natural history, *Sylva Sylvarum*, Bacon writes of "bodies put into quick-silver. But then they must be thin; as a leafe, or a peece of Paper or Parchment." He cites many other examples of storing parchment in mercury. In *Sylva Sylvarum* Bacon also describes the procedure for constructing "artificial springs" using stone, sand, and ferns (a system similar to that found in Smith's Cove).

Baconians are convinced that somewhere there is a secret repository containing all of the missing Elizabethan-period manuscripts. In 1911, Dr. Orville Ward Owen, a prominent American Baconian from Detroit, headed an expedition to the mouth of the Wye River near Gloucester, England, in search of that literary cache. Owen had spent years deciphering codes he claimed to have found in Bacon's works, and it was these that led him to the Wye River. After following certain directions indicated in the codes, Owen and his group sank a caisson into the riverbed and excavated through the silt. They uncovered a room-sized vault made of stone and cement. It was empty, but Owen identified certain markings cut into the walls as having been put there by Bacon. Owen, who died in 1924, concluded that Bacon had intended to hide the priceless documents in that vault but that he had later changed his mind and sought a more distant and secure location.

In 1920, Burrell Ruth, then a student at Michigan State University, met Dr. Owen and soon became an avid Baconian. Years later, while he was a professor of chemical engineering at Iowa State, in Ames, Iowa, Ruth read about Oak Island and Gilbert Hedden's search in the October 14, 1939, issue of the *Saturday Evening Post*. From the complexity of the engineering work and the fact that a piece of parchment had been brought up from the Money Pit, Ruth concluded that here was the repository Baconians had spent years searching for.

He immediately wrote Hedden a thirty-page letter outlining his belief that below Oak Island was a vault containing the original manuscripts of works credited to Shakespeare and others, and that they were immersed in tons of mercury to protect them against the ravages of time. Hedden's initial reaction was that the idea was interesting but preposterous. Nevertheless, he was curious about a couple of things mentioned in Ruth's letter. In his reply he stated:

> Your prediction that the Money Pit contains mercury is one of the most amazing coincidences I have ever encountered. You can be certain that before sinking nearly a hundred thousand in this venture I explored it from every angle. One of these angles was the folklore, superstitions, and legends that have surrounded the pit since 1800. One of the most widespread and persistent of these legends, and one for which I was never able to find the least basis, was the curious belief that the Money Pit contained mercury. I never gave it any serious thought; it seemed too fantastic. But one point in favor of your theory is that there does exist an old dump on the island in which are the remains of thousands of broken pottery flasks. That this dump is very old is supported by the fact that we found nearby an old coin and an ivory boatswain's whistle which experts tell us date back to the Elizabethan period.

The old dump that Hedden referred to was found in 1937 near Joudrey's Cove on the island's north side while the searchers were looking for other markers that might tie in with the stone triangle and drilled rocks. In a 1976 interview, Amos Nauss, one of Hedden's workers, told me that a liquid residue discovered in some of the flasks was indeed mercury.

Ruth's theory was that Bacon, prior to his death in 1626, left instructions to his closest aides describing how and possibly where to conceal his "Shakespearean" and other original manuscripts. Then, perhaps years later, this group chartered a ship on which they loaded the cases of paper and parchment. They sailed first to Spain, where they purchased thousands of flasks of mercury, which would have been carefully crated and protected against breakage by the use of coconut fiber dunnage. From there they sailed to Nova Scotia and randomly selected Oak Island on which to make their deposit. A vault of oak timber and cement was constructed and placed deep in the Money Pit, cofferdams were erected at Smith's Cove and the South Shore Cove, and tunnels were driven from these points to the Money Pit. The chests of manuscripts were then placed in the vault and covered with liquid mercury. The vault was sealed, the Money Pit was refilled, and the cofferdams were destroyed in order to activate the flood trap.

Ruth surmised that the labor had been supplied by the ship's crew, who were paid well for their silence. In any case, they'd have had no need to know what was in the boxes they deposited in the vault, or exactly where they were in the New World.

There are a couple of historical factors that lend some circumstantial support to Ruth's amazing hypothesis. Bacon and his friends were certainly familiar with that part of the New World. Although there is no evidence that Bacon ever visited the region himself, in 1610 he was among a group of patentees granted colonial lands in Newfoundland by James I. Also, in 1621 the king doled out baronetcies in Nova Scotia to 140 English noblemen, some of whom undoubtedly were friends of Bacon's.

William Rawley, who besides being Bacon's chaplain was also his secretary and trusted friend, may have organized the transfer of manuscripts to Nova Scotia. He lived till about 1660 and held all of Bacon's original manuscripts, many of which he sent to the printer long after Bacon's death.

Another possible conspirator was Thomas Bushell, who as a young man assisted Bacon in his scientific experiments. He later became a mining engineer for the English Crown, and was know to be especially adept at recovering ore from flooded Cornish mines.

The Baconian connection to Oak Island might at least explain one part of the island's mystery. Many researchers have felt that whoever made the deposit didn't intend to retrieve it. Surely, so the argument goes, it could have been concealed quite safely for a few years at a more reasonable depth and without the added work of the flood tunnels. This water trap, as hundreds of searchers have found, has made recovery next to impossible. Clearly, the depositors weren't trying to get rid of whatever the treasure is; otherwise they'd have simply dumped it into the ocean. So it would seem they wanted it to be found eventually. Bacon, being a scientist, could foresee the day when modern technology could uncover the cache. In effect, a time capsule had been buried under Oak Island.

Hedden and Ruth continued to correspond, and Hedden gradually became more impressed with the merits of the Baconian theory. But as a result of his strange experience with the Mar Del map in 1937, Hedden still believed that William Kidd at least knew something about the Oak Island project. Ruth accepted that Kidd may well have been told something about it by a ship's crew member involved in the project, and that perhaps Kidd had drawn up a map based on what he'd heard. But he probably didn't know the exact location of the island or the nature of the deposit.

In the early 1940s Hedden also corresponded with and interviewed Orville Owen's daughter, Mrs. Gladys Stewart of Rochester, New York. She had carried on her father's work after his death, and she too became convinced that Oak Island was the site of the Baconian cache.

In the summer of 1952, Thomas P. Leary, a lawyer from Omaha, Nebraska, visited Oak Island while vacationing in Nova Scotia. He was fascinated by the history of the search, and, before returning home, he stopped off in New York, where he met Hedden. Leary recalls that he asked Hedden for his views on the origin of the underground workings. Among other possibilities, Hedden mentioned the Baconian theory. This fired Leary's imagination, and he was soon researching Bacon's life and corresponding with Ruth. He also attempted to establish a link between Bacon and the characters etched on the granite rock that Hedden had found in 1936, as well as the triangle that pointed to the Money Pit.

Leary and Ruth saw several interpretations that could be drawn from these markers, such as the triangle directly pointing toward the "truth" or "knowledge" that lay beneath the Money Pit. Yet nothing could be established that would conclusively identify Bacon as the designer of the project. In 1953 Leary wrote, hand-set, and printed one hundred copies of a thirty-six-page booklet entitled *The Oak Island Enigma*. In it he gave a short history of the Oak Island search and then offered his arguments for the possible Baconian connection.

Before his death in 1954, Ruth sent all of the particulars of the Oak Island story to the Francis Bacon Society in England. The society considered sponsoring its own exploration of Oak Island, but for various reasons this was never carried out.

Hedden, in his later years, accepted the Baconian theory as one of the more probable explanations for the Oak Island mystery. He hinted as much in a letter to Robert Gay, another Nova Scotia treasure hunter, on May 14, 1967. In it Hedden said, "I date the original work as about 1630, and I am convinced that the engineer who made the original layout had no intention of making a recovery in his lifetime, but intended to leave it for future generations."

Hedden's wife, Marguerite, informed me in 1977 that "Gilbert was willing to believe [the Bacon manuscripts] might well have been in the pit; he knew it had to be something precious because of the engineering job that was done there."

In September 1974 Hedden died without having learned the answer to the mystery he'd lived with for over forty years. But his discoveries on the island and his patient research provided significant contributions to later investigators who would apply Hedden's findings to their own Oak Island quests and theories.

CHAPTER ELEVEN

Exploring New Depths

THE NEXT PERSON TO TAKE OVER THE SEARCH WAS ERWIN H. Hamilton, a professor of mechanical engineering at New York University. He first approached Blair in 1935 but was informed that Hedden owned the Money Pit area and had exclusive digging rights under Blair's treasure trove license.

When Hedden was forced to drop out in the spring of 1938, Hamilton offered to take over his project. Hedden readily agreed and suggested a three-way split on any treasure recovered. Blair, who under his previous contract had been entitled to a one-half share, balked at this proposal and argued that Hamilton's cut should be taken out of Hedden's half. After a couple of months of negotiations, a compromise was reached entitling Hedden and Hamilton to 30 percent each and Blair the remaining 40 percent.

Hamilton spent the next five summers and $58,000 carrying out a two-pronged investigation of Oak Island. The first involved deepening and drilling into the sides of the Hedden shaft, and the second was locating, recribbing, and charting the maze of unrecorded tunnels that had been dug by searchers in the 1860s.

Hamilton hired Sprague & Henwood to continue the drilling program they'd started under Hedden. In the summer of

1938 a total of fifty-eight holes were bored horizontally from various levels in the Hedden shaft. Several of the probes from 119 feet encountered decayed oak just north of the Chappell shaft. They concluded that the wood was from the cribbing put down in the Money Pit by searchers in the mid-1800s. If so, this confirmed the location of the original pit.

The following summer Hamilton employed eleven men (at a wage of forty cents an hour) to retimber the Chappell shaft, which had settled and was twisted out of alignment. To further investigate the assumed center of the Money Pit, Hamilton drove a tunnel through the northeast corner of the Hedden shaft at a point 117 feet down. This 4-by-5½-foot tunnel ran westward for 21 feet and was then turned 90 degrees toward the north side of the Chappell shaft. After another 10 feet of digging, it was abandoned. The workers found nothing other than the fact that much of the tunnel ran through previously worked soil.

Over the next couple of summers, Hamilton's work included deepening a 6-by-6 foot portion of the west side of the Hedden shaft, which was 125 feet deep. This section went down to 155 feet, or the same depth as the Chappell pit. At that level the diggers encountered and explored the semicircular tunnel that Chappell had run from his shaft in 1931.

The Chappell shaft was then deepened to 167 feet, at which level the clay ended and a thick layer of limestone was found. From there, drill probes went through bedrock to below 200 feet. In a couple of instances chips of oak were brought up from below bedrock, the first time any evidence of previous work had been found that far down. And the work, as later drilling and analysis would show, was definitely original.

During these operations the large electric pump (which Hamilton had purchased from Hedden) was constantly running and was able to contain the heavy flow of seawater. In a letter to President Roosevelt on November 4, 1938, Hamilton stated that "our measurements this past summer show approximately 800 gallons per minute" entering the Hedden shaft.

Amos Nauss, who worked for both Hedden and Hamilton, recalled many years later that "when we were down there,

there was always salt water coming in. But we couldn't find where it was coming from. We never saw the flood tunnels. But some of it was coming in from somewhere further down from where we were" at 167 feet in the Chappell shaft.

Hamilton then conducted a dye test, similar to the one in 1898, in an attempt to trace the source of the flooding. As Nauss remembered it, the dye was put in both shafts "and it came out on the southeast side of the island, about one hundred yards out from the high tide. We took my boat out to it, and we could see the dye coming up from the bottom of the sea. So we knew there was a connection there with a water-way going through to the Money Pit area."

This indicated that at least one of the inlets to the flooding system was well offshore, even at low tide, and was under about fifteen feet of water. But Hamilton rightly concluded that this had not always been the case. Studies done earlier by Hedden and more recently by professional geologists have established that almost all of Oak Island's erosion has taken place on the south shore. The rate is estimated to be about two inches a year. Thus, over sixty feet of shoreline has been eaten away in the past four hundred years. Moreover, the sea level in that part of Nova Scotia has risen about four feet during the same period. Consequently, the geological conditions that existed when the island's workings were built were different from today's. This would explain how the original depositors were able to hold back the water with cofferdams and build flooding systems that extend well beyond the current low-tide mark.

Concurrent with his work in the Money Pit area, Hamilton also located and traced a network of tunnels beneath the island that had been dug by the searchers of the 1860s. It was basically a large triangular system running from the Money Pit to a shaft near Smith's Cove, southwest around the Cave-in Pit, and then back to the Money Pit. The cribbed tunnels were about one hundred feet deep near the Money Pit and eighty feet deep near Smith's Cove. He also located an old filled-in shaft near Smith's Cove and found three short tunnels leading from it at depths of between thirty-five and forty-five feet.

Hamilton's explorations ended in 1942, when, because of

the war, he found it next to impossible to hire labor. The following summer the shafts at the Money Pit and Smith's Cove were decked over and the equipment was transported to the mainland. Hamilton then went into the boat-building business with Amos Nauss at Marriott's Cove, and lived there until his death in 1969. According to Nauss, Hamilton remained convinced that a treasure had been buried somewhere under Oak Island, his favorite theory being that it consisted of gold from a French ship destined for Louisbourg.

Like Hedden, Hamilton kept President Roosevelt informed on the progress he was making on the island. And FDR appeared to be genuinely interested in those reports. On August 31, 1938, for example, Roosevelt wrote Hamilton: "Your note came while I was on my cruise in the Pacific. I wish much I could have gone up the coast this summer and visited Oak Island and seen the work you are doing—for I shall always be interested in that romantic spot. I hope that you will let me know how you have been getting on with modern methods— ours were, I fear, somewhat antiquated when we were there more than a quarter of a century ago."

The following August the president made tentative plans to visit the island while aboard a United States Navy cruiser that had stopped briefly in Halifax. However, according to a letter to his friend Duncan Harris on August 24, 1939, news of the imminent outbreak of war in Europe "made it impossible." (Hamilton had been eagerly looking forward to this visit and had even built a sedan chair to carry FDR from Smith's Cove dock to the digging site.)

The president wasn't the only head of state aware of Oak Island. Hedden, knowing that King George VI was scheduled to visit Canada and later confer with Roosevelt in June of 1939, had previously written His Majesty and filled him in on the history of the search. Hedden was thanked for this information by the king's secretary. (Hedden's idea, apparently, was to make sure King George wouldn't be at a loss for words should Roosevelt suddenly switch the conversation from the deteriorating European situation to Oak Island.) Hedden also corresponded with lesser luminaries such as Vincent Astor and Admiral Richard Byrd, both of whom were fascinated by the story of Oak Island and had considered taking part in the project.

In 1940 an approach was also made by the actor Errol Flynn to take over the search. Flynn had previously financed two unsuccessful treasure hunts in Alaska and the Caribbean, and he became interested in Oak Island after reading about Hedden's work. However, his enthusiasm waned when he learned that the search rights were already controlled by Hamilton.

In 1944 Blair's treasure trove license expired, but he was easily able to renew it with the Nova Scotia government for a further five years. That same year Hedden transferred his Oak Island property to his own name from that of his attorney, George Grimm, and began searching for someone who was willing to replace Hamilton on the site.

One prospect was Anthony Belfiglio, an engineer from Toronto who said he had backers willing to put $50,000 into the search. During his negotiations with Hedden in 1945–46 he offered to buy the land in the immediate Money Pit area for $15,000. But Hedden informed him that he would either have to purchase all of his Oak Island lots for $25,000 or else lease the property on an annual basis. The negotiations soon broke down.

In May 1946, Oak Island's briefest search attempt ever was made by Nathan Lindenbaum, a twenty-six-year-old G.I. from New York. He arrived unannounced with a pick and shovel and an "Oak Island treasure map" that he'd purchased for $125 at a New York City radio station auction. After scooping up a few shovelfuls of earth, he terminated his treasure-hunting career and went home.

Hedden was approached later that year by Edward Reichert, a Broadway stage singer who wanted to lease the east end of the island and conduct a search. He claimed to have no less than $150,000 in financial support from unnamed backers. Hedden tentatively agreed, and Reichert went to Nova Scotia the following May to meet with Blair and look over the island.

Reichert's plan was to use large steam shovels that would excavate a hole eighty feet in diameter and two hundred or more feet deep in the Money Pit area. While in Halifax he made arrangements to rent the required digging equipment at a cost of $4,500 a month. He estimated it would take him no more than ten months to complete the dig and that his approach would meet with "absolute success." But that summer, after he'd stirred up considerable newspaper interest in his proposed venture, Reichert vanished. Hedden spent several months trying to contact him and finally wrote him off as "just another crackpot." (It's an interesting coincidence that the dimensions of Reichert's proposed open pit almost exactly match those of the current Triton Alliance project.)

Hedden's next candidate was Colonel H. A. Gardner, a retired army officer from Arlington, Virginia. Gardner had visited the island briefly in the summer of 1947 and that September went to see Hedden with a unique proposal for locating the treasure. It involved using a portable radar scanner which had been developed during the war. His plan was to take it into the various shafts and tunnels under the island and use it to locate any original tunnels or chambers that might lie nearby. Hedden was impressed with the idea and was willing to lease the property to Gardner and claim only 10 percent of any treasure that might be found.

But when Gardner learned that Blair controlled the treasure trove license, he began to lose interest. The reason was that, ever since the end of the Hamilton expedition, Blair had been insisting on receiving a 50 percent share of the potential treasure. This was a sore point with Hedden, who felt that Blair's demand had been part of the reason why earlier applicants were unable to retain the support of their prospective backers. As Hedden put it: "The present status seems to be a stalemate situation. I own the property rights and Blair owns the treasure trove rights. Neither can proceed without the other, and Blair sticks to his 50 percent [demand], thereby scaring away all ventures of any kind."

Hedden and Gardner continued to negotiate, leaving Blair out of the picture. Eventually a solution of sorts was reached. Hedden decided to sell his Oak Island property to Gardner for a small down payment, with the balance to be paid over several years. Gardner then planned to go to the island and do some exploratory work with his radar equipment. He believed that if he located anything of interest, he'd be in a better position to reach an equitable agreement with Blair.

He made the trip in July 1948, but after several weeks of tests he found that the equipment wasn't working properly. He returned to Arlington, intending to adjust it and to try again the following summer.

Blair was furious when he learned that someone was conducting a search without his knowledge or permission. He got in touch with Gardner and was surprised to find out that he had purchased Hedden's land on Oak Island. Hedden had kept the transfer quiet, assuming that Gardner wanted it that way.

But the situation never came to a head, because Gardner died the following January and his widow canceled the purchase agreement. Hedden was again the owner of the Money Pit. However, within a few months he was approached by another prospective buyer, John Whitney Lewis, a sixty-year-old mining and petroleum consulting engineer from New York. On May 12, 1950, Lewis purchased Hedden's Oak Island lots for $6,000. He then flew up to Nova Scotia to prepare his planned assault on the island, unaware that Blair had little intention of allowing him to proceed.

When Lewis bought the property, Hedden informed him, quite correctly, that Blair's treasure trove license had expired on June 30, 1949, and that as far as he knew, it hadn't been renewed. Hedden suggested that Lewis apply for his own license, thereby avoiding the difficulties inherent in one person holding the license and another owning the land.

But on May 27, 1950, Lewis was advised by Blair's attorney, R. V. Harris, that Blair "has an agreement with the government for a period of five years, under which he may search for treasure on Oak Island." Harris and Blair were stretching things a bit, for Blair had only applied for, not received, a new license. This was granted to him on July 14, 1950, for a period of five years.

Blair had meanwhile contracted with sixty-three-year-old Mel Chappell of Sydney, Nova Scotia, to take over the search operations. Chappell, as a result of his own work on the island in 1931 and his father's findings in 1897, was determined to locate the elusive treasure. But he couldn't begin work until the Blair-Lewis conflict was resolved; Blair wouldn't allow Lewis to dig, and Lewis wouldn't allow Blair or his representatives to trespass on his property.

Lewis's fate was sealed by the enactment that year of a new Treasure Trove Act by the Nova Scotia legislature. It had been influenced in large part by the lobbying of Chappell and Blair, both of whom had close friends in the provincial cabinet. Under this act, holders of treasure trove licenses could apply for "special" licenses to be used in cases where the licensee was unable to secure permission to search on another person's property. The license granted its holder the right of trespass, providing the owner of the land was paid for any damages to his property. This in effect gave treasure hunters the same rights that mineral prospectors had under the province's Mines Act.

Lewis, claiming "misrepresentations" on the part of Blair and Harris, urgently appealed to the provincial secretary to block Blair's application for a special license. But the appeal was denied. Lewis was left with no recourse but to sell the Oak Island property, and he found a ready buyer in Mel Chappell. On November 27, 1950, the east end of Oak Island and eight other lots (a total of about fifty-six acres) passed into Chappell's hands. Lewis, a New Yorker who'd been snookered by the Nova Scotia old-boy network, was forced to sell it for the same $6,000 price he'd paid for it six months earlier.

Four months later, Frederick Blair died at the age of eighty-three. He had been closely associated with the Oak Island search for almost sixty years. But for him it was always more than just a treasure hunt. It had been an obsession with a riddle whose answer he had once said would be "equalled only by the discovery of King Tutankhamen's tomb."

Blair believed that money, or rather the lack of it, remained the only obstacle between the mystery and its solution. Writing to a prospective searcher in August 1947, he said: "Scientific engineering and modern equipment will do the work if properly financed. Previous failures, and there have been many, were due to lack of knowledge of conditions. In other words, they knew nothing of the original work, and in addition they lacked engineering skill and were short on the financial end. Today it is the financial backing we need, not a method of recovery. The latter will come with the former."

Blair's treasure trove license was immediately taken over by Mel Chappell. For the first time, both the license and the land were held by the same person. For the next thirty years, until his death in 1980, it was Chappell who determined who could dig for treasure on Oak Island.

CHAPTER TWELVE

Diviners, Psychics and Weirdos

IT IS NO SURPRISE THAT A MYSTERY AS PERPLEXING AND THEO-
retically speculative as that of Oak Island would elicit a good
deal of interest from investigators with unusual approaches to
the solution. And in the long history of the search these have
ranged from people with less than both oars in the water to
those who have made some uncanny connections to Oak Island.

One of the earliest of these bizarre solutions was proposed
in 1931 by John Wicks of Saginaw, Michigan, who told Fred
Blair that the Oak Island workings had been constructed by
the Incas of Tumbez, Peru, around the year 1530. Wicks, who
said the bulk of the treasure lay in a Gothic-domed chamber
175 feet below the Money Pit, also supplied a few details
concerning Oak Island that Blair knew he couldn't have gotten
from newspaper or magazine articles about the treasure hunt.

Blair was curious, especially since Wicks was wealthy and
offered to put $30,000 into the search to prove his theory. In
February 1932, Blair and Mel Chappell went to Saginaw to
hear more about the treasure of Tumbez. They were astounded
by Wicks's source of information.

The historical background to the theory is intriguing. Tumbez (now Tumbes) was an Inca city about six hundred miles

north of modern-day Lima. It was first visited by Europeans in 1527, when the Spanish conqueror Francisco Pizarro sailed down the Pacific coast from Panama with a small band of explorers. As Pizarro described it in his journal, they were amazed by what they saw: a fortified city where vessels of gold and silver were common utensils, emeralds as large as pigeon's eggs, a temple lined with plates of gold, and a palace filled with gold and silver ornaments.

Pizarro, in true conquistador style, coveted everything he saw and decided to return to Spain to raise a force large enough to loot Tumbez and the rest of the Inca empire. He left a few of his men in Tumbez and started the long journey home, his Inca hosts meanwhile believing that Pizarro had come in peace and would return in peace.

But it took some time for Pizarro to have his petition to return as conqueror of Peru approved by King Charles V and Spain's Council of the Indies. Finally, in the spring of 1531 Pizarro and a force of 180 soldiers arrived in Tumbez. There they found a city in ruins, completely ransacked of its fabulous wealth. And there was no sign of any of the Spaniards who had been left behind. Over the next few months, Pizarro led expeditions deep into the Peruvian jungles in search of the Tumbez treasure. The Incas, often under torture, told Pizarro that the city had been plundered during a battle between the armies of the Inca king Atahualpa and Huascar, his half brother and pretender to the throne. That may have been true, as an Inca civil war was indeed under way. But it was also suspected that the inhabitants of Tumbez, guessing Pizarro's plans, had stripped the city of its precious ornaments and hidden them. What actually happened is unknown, and the treasure has never been found.

Blair and Chappell were to hear an interesting sequel to this piece of Spanish New World history. On their visit to Saginaw, John Wicks told them he was an automatic writer, a psychic with an involuntary power to scribble down messages from the netherworld. He claimed he had been "contacted" by a Spanish priest by the name of Menzies who had remained in Tumbez when Pizarro left in 1527.

According to Menzies (using Wicks as his medium) he had

developed a respect for the Inca leaders after Pizarro's departure, and so told them of the conquistador's intentions and urged them to hide their valuables and religious ornaments as far away as they could. The city's riches were then carried overland to the Gulf of Darien in the Caribbean Sea, where the Incas built ships on which they loaded the treasure. With the seafaring and navigational aid of Menzies and other sympathetic Spaniards, they set out to find an uninhabited eastern Caribbean island to use as a repository. But they were driven northward by a series of violent storms, and weeks later landed in a desolate region (Nova Scotia) thousands of miles from home. They selected an island and built a complex underground vault to store their treasure. They eventually all perished on the island.

If Blair and Chappell found the story farfetched, they were nevertheless impressed by Wicks's automatic writing abilities. Through Wicks's hands, writing at incredible speed on rolls of paper, Menzies and an Inca priest, identified as Circle, repeated the tale to the two astonished observers. Most of the writing was in English, though some was in Spanish. In 1976 Chappell assured me that "there seemed to be some power behind it, because I know no one could by physical effort alone write as fast and as clear as [Wicks] did. It was amazing."

Chappell brought several rolls of the paper home with him, but unfortunately they were destroyed in a fire at his office ten years later. And Wicks, who wrote Gilbert Hedden in 1937 to warn him that "the time is not yet ripe" to recover the lost treasure of Tumbez, never did come to Oak Island.

In that same year Hedden had entertained a different yet equally strange approach to finding Oak Island's treasure. This was something called a "Mineral Wave Ray" that had been invented by Welsford R. Parker of Windsor, Nova Scotia, and was being promoted by a company called Avon Associated Enterprises. This miraculous machine was touted as being able to pinpoint gold and other valuables concealed anywhere from inches to hundreds of feet behind objects that the machine photographed. Fred Barton, one of the Avon principals, pestered Hedden for months to allow the machine to be brought to Oak Island to find the treasure. A dubious Hedden declined the offer. But then Hedden's lawyer, R. V. Harris, told him of a legal acquaintance who had seen a demonstration of the machine (finding the location of money hidden behind law books in his office) and had become a believer in the Mineral Wave Ray. (This lawyer, as it turned out, had formerly represented the Avon company.)

Hedden then became interested enough to arrange for a similar test of the machine. On Barton's instructions Hedden took a dozen photographs of a bookcase in his New Jersey home. There were at least four hundred books on the shelves, and before taking each photo Hedden placed $200 in cash behind one book and a gold bracelet behind another. The locations of the bill and bracelet were randomly changed before each shot, with Hedden keeping a record of their positions. He then mailed the twelve photos to Barton and waited for the results.

Months passed, and by the summer of 1938 Barton had sent back nothing other than excuses about the machine's temporary malfunction. Still, Hedden granted Avon the right to spend two weeks on the island that summer to test the apparatus on the site. The company spent one day there and then left, explaining that "further adjustments" were necessary. At that point Hedden wrote Avon and their machine off as "a complete and not very clever hoax."

Twelve years later Mel Chappell heard about the Parker Contract Company of Bellville, Ontario, which reportedly had had some success with a mineral-finding machine in the northern part of that province. The two principals of the company were Welsford Parker and Fred Barton. But Chappell was unaware at the time of Hedden's prior experience.

By 1950 the "Mineral Wave Ray" was a bit more sophisticated. It consisted of a black metal box about two feet long into which was crammed an assortment of wires, tubes, and batteries. A sort of camera lens protruded from one end of the box. To operate it, Parker would put a sample of the material he was looking for (gold, silver, uranium, etc.) inside the box, and a photograph of the area being investigated was placed in

Oak Island from the east. *(Nova Scotia Communications and Information Centre)*

The Oak Island Treasure Company at the Money Pit in 1897. *(Dodge Photo)*

1909 Search Group. Franklin D. Roosevelt is third from right; Captain Henry Bowdoin is at left foreground. *(Franklin D. Roosevelt Library)*

Frederick L. Blair. *(George H. Hill, Jr.)*

Gilbert Hedden. *(Courtesy of Marguerite Hedden)*

Hedden Shaft today. *(D'Arcy O'Connor)*

The Restall Family, 1964. *(Halifax Chronicle Herald)*

George Greene (with cigar).

Heart-shaped stone found at Smith's Cove in 1967. *(Courtesy of Triton Alliance Ltd.)*

Wrought-iron scissors found at Smith's Cove in 1967. *(Courtesy of Triton Alliance Ltd.)*

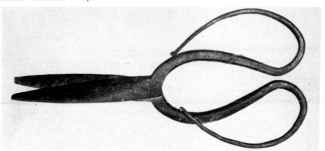

Small bits of metal brought up from a depth of approximately 200 feet in borehole #10. *(Courtesy of Triton Alliance Ltd.)*

Dan Blankenship on churn drill. *(D'Arcy O'Connor)*

Fred Nolan. *(Ty Grevatt)*

Borehole 10-X (150 feet deep). *(D'Arcy O'Connor)*

David Tobias.

Smith's Cove. *(D'Arcy O'Connor)*

front of the lens. Then he'd wander around the designated area with the box, waiting for it to emit a signal that would indicate a spot under which there supposedly would be more of whatever material had been placed in the machine.

Chappell decided to give it a try, and Parker arrived on the site in December 1950. Within a few days he located a spot about 150 feet north-northwest of the Money Pit and confidently stated that a large deposit of gold lay about 20 feet under the earth. A twenty-ton steam shovel was barged out to the island to excavate the area. But 200 yards off Smith's Cove the barge capsized. The shovel was eventually salvaged, and a pit 30 feet across and 50 feet deep was dug in the location indicated by Parker. Nothing was discovered other than the remains of an old shaft from a previous search group. In earlier 1951 Parker's machine "located" four more treasure deposits in the same general area. This time Chappell brought in a drilling contractor to probe the locations down to about 60 feet. Again the results were negative.

In those few months Chappell spent $35,000 to learn what Hedden had concluded back in 1938—the gold-finder was useless. "I fell for it," Chappell conceded years later. "It looked possible to me at the time, but it turned out there was nothing to it."

Parker died in 1976. His partner, Fred Barton, later told me that the machine's failure was due to the simple fact that there is no treasure on Oak Island. As for the fate of the gadget, he says it was "sold down the river" many years ago "because we were afraid of it. We discovered that we held the future of the world with that machine. It was too big for us so we got rid of it." Barton declined to elaborate on that cryptic remark.

Another man who claims he "had the only invention that could have unraveled the mystery" of Oak Island is L. J. Kennedy of Flin Flon, Manitoba. He wrote Chappell several times in the early 1970s seeking to use the device on the island. Chappell, wiser by twenty years and by his experience with Parker, politely declined. This detector consisted of large metal discs that supposedly could locate copper and gold. Kennedy said he would often mount the discs on the roof of his car and "pick up ore bodies at least ten miles away while driving down the highway at speeds of up to sixty miles an hour."

Alas, this wonderful machine no longer exists. Kennedy told me that "during my inventing years I had a complete neglect of God, to work for ego and money and buried treasure; the blood of others and the loss of my soul. On July 16 [1976] at seven in the morning I took my invention and everything pertaining to it to the town dump. I offered it up to God for His praise and glory and I was thanked through prophesy. It was not of Him, because there's no surer way of losing Him than to become rich. As I stood and watched the greatest invention go up in flames, I was proud of my offering; a supreme sort of feeling."

Another inventor in the late 1930s wrote Hedden stating that he owned a "treasure-smelling" machine that he carried in an airplane in order to detect veins of gold in the earth below. He reported that he had recently flown over Oak Island and that the delicate instrument had smashed itself to pieces when it sniffed an incredible hoard of gold in the depths of the island.

More orthodox metal detectors have been employed on the island. Their usefulness, however, is rather limited in the case of this particular search. They are normally capable of finding either small traces of metal no more than a few feet down or else ore anomalies such as a large mineral vein that may be far underground.

In addition, many attempts have been made to locate the island's flooding system, underground chambers, and even the treasure itself by the use of divining rods. The art of divining, or dowsing, goes back thousands of years and is even referred to in the Book of Genesis. It commonly requires the use of some sort of wand or rod, with hazel twigs giving way to metal rods in more recent times. It has been used to locate underground water, minerals, buried treasure, and even, according to some claims, buried bodies and escaped convicts.

Dowsing, because of the many instances of its proven success (particularly in locating water), cannot be dismissed as mere superstitious nonsense. But there is no commonly accepted scientific explanation as to how and why it works. It is a gift that only some people have, and the bending or jerking of the rod in their hands may be an involuntary muscle spasm induced by psychogenic forces. Whatever the cause, some particularly gifted dowsers have been employed by mining companies and oil and gas explorers, often to supplement geologic and seismic testing. Dowsing was also used by U.S. forces in Vietnam to locate Viet Cong underground bunkers and tunnels.

On Oak Island, Hedden occasionally amused himself by dowsing the subterranean water-filled tunnels with a supple twig from an apple or peach tree. The twig, held firmly in his hand, would invariably bend downward every time he crossed a tunnel, the position of which he would verify from his records.

Dan Blankenship, field manager for the current Triton group, also has dowsing abilities. He uses two welding rods held lightly between the thumb and forefinger of each hand and waits for them to be drawn together as if by magnetic attraction. Apart from getting readings over known tunnel locations, Blankenship says he has charted out an "immense" underground system of corridors and flood tunnels. "I wouldn't be surprised," he adds, "if there were a dozen separate flooding systems" feeding into the Money Pit area. Blankenship once showed one of his workers how to handle the rods, but didn't tell him the locations he himself had already pinpointed. In almost every case, the other man felt the rods twist in his hands over those exact same spots.

There can be no disputing the ability of certain individuals to dowse with remarkable accuracy over subterranean cavities or watercourses. But those who use the wand (often called a mineral rod) to locate metals in other than their natural state have a far less successful track record. And on Oak Island, where treasure has yet to be brought to the surface as a result of this or any other means, that record is total failure. Yet many have tried, and have claimed to have dowsed gold, silver, copper, and other minerals in various locations under the island. In the few cases where a pit has been dug on the basis of such findings and nothing has turned up, the diviner's usual defense is that the hole wasn't deep enough.

In 1974, E. J. Thurston, a mechanic from Sudbury, Ontario, who claimed to have had some previous success in locating ore bodies in western Canada, was brought out to dowse Oak Island. After spending several days divining, he mapped out his findings. These consisted of fourteen granite and copper-lined chambers far below the surface of the island's eastern end. He also said there were three levels of tunnels connecting these chambers. But nothing turned up in the few areas that were investigated by drilling.

Oak Island has also been visited by psychic investigators who go beyond the art of dowsing. One of the more recent was Ray Nutt, a construction worker from Huntsville, Texas. In the fall of 1976, he, his wife, and several associates spent a couple of months checking out certain portions of the island. They had been led there by psychic visions Nutt and his wife experienced earlier that year back in Texas. In these visions they took an eerie trip through tunnels and chambers far below the island where they saw part of a vast treasure and were face-to-face with some of the ghosts of Oak Island.

The workings, as Nutt described them to me, consist of a large cavern under the middle of the island, with several tunnels leading to it from the nearby swamp. One tunnel also leads southeast to the Money Pit, over eight hundred feet away. "I know for one thing," said Nutt, "there are going to be some bodies down there. In our visions there are two main exits from the cave, and there's a skeleton sitting at each one of them, like guards, and each skeleton has a sword beside it."

Nutt believes that passageways from the cave lead to "two main treasure chambers. And there will be things there that you cannot imagine. There is all kinds of religious material down there and all kinds of documents, too. There'll be a blue book found down there with a cross on its cover; I'm sure of that. There'll be chalices and statues, and possibly the Holy Grail. The dates of some of this stuff will go back three thousand years; things that were kept for centuries and then stolen from many parts of the world."

One recurrent apparition Nutt has seen is that of a monk or priest in the underground workings. "When I saw him, he had a hood on that was light tan. I saw him from the back, and he had his arms spread open. My wife has seen him too, only in her case the priest was talking to a pirate down in the cave." Through such mystical revelations Nutt has developed a theory that the Oak Island project was built and used over a period of twenty years or more, sometime between 1550 and 1750. "I think there was a city down there at some time—people living aboveground and doing their work underground. I'm reasonably sure there were probably as many as twenty or thirty ships there at one time, bringing in the treasures and being refitted."

Nutt also believes that the project was religiously inspired, planned by some sect that employed pirates to convey these worldwide treasures to the secret repository. Moreover, he's certain there is a "divine reason" why the treasure was deposited at Oak Island and that "it can and will be found only if it is to the benefit of mankind, and not just to make a few individuals rich."

During their stay in Nova Scotia, the Nutts and their associates spent every day prowling around the island looking for clues to confirm their psychic findings. Nutt concedes that they were "considered the local crackpots of Oak Island. But we don't care what others think. We can't expect everybody to understand the things we know." He claims their field work uncovered "a lot of evidence" supporting their theories, including "significant" rock markers, indicating that the swamp was once used as a dry dock with iron gates at either end of it, and, by dowsing, the existence of the tunnels and chambers that were revealed in their visions.

Triton Alliance, the current search group, barred him from doing any probing in the Money Pit area or any other lots then owned by Mel Chappell. His investigation was therefore limited to the middle portion of the island which is owned by Fred Nolan, an independent searcher. (This may have something to do with Nutt's conviction that all of Oak Island's treasure is in that general area and that the Money Pit is nothing but a decoy.) He tried to get Nolan to excavate the supposed location of the treasure vaults, but Nolan declined.

Some psychics who have never visited the site have disclosed certain things about Oak Island that are either known or at least suspected to be true. During the 1960s, Lavern Johnson, a continuing Oak Island investigator, showed a chart of the eastern end of the island to an elderly woman in western Canada who had a reputation as a clairvoyant. The woman drew a small circle with her finger on a section of the map and stated that a treasure was buried there. The circle centered exactly over the area in which Johnson, by his own calculations, is sure the treasure lies. The woman also described a small gnarled tree that she said grew in a particular spot. Her description of the tree and its location was exact. Johnson, who had approached the psychic experiment somewhat skeptically, is still baffled by the woman's findings. He notes that the details of Oak Island were obviously on his mind while he was with the woman, and wonders if perhaps her insight was the result of telepathic transference.

Oak Island has also been "read" from afar by map dowsers, those who claim to be able to locate buried items simply by concentrating on a chart or aerial photograph of the place in question. In January 1977 a large chart of the island was "pendulum dowsed" for me by Eugenia Macer-Story, a professional psychic now living in Woodstock, New York. She used a weight suspended from a string about three inches above the surface of the map. Over certain portions of the chart the pendulum swung in a circle. She then double-checked these areas by closing her eyes and slowly running her fingers over the map. In many of the same locations she felt a mild heat transferred from the map to her hand. These she marked as areas of "primary importance."

The chart I sent her was an accurately scaled outline of the island, with none of the established findings such as the Money Pit included on it. She pinpointed and circled some thirty locations, half of them described as "items of monetary value" and the others as "targets of whatever primary importance." Most of the locations were on the island itself, though a few were offshore. Many of the onshore targets she circled happen to be sites where previous digging or drilling has brought up some sign (traces of wood or metal) of original work. However, some key locations, including the Money Pit itself, were ignored by her pendulum. Offshore, strong responses were indicated in both Smith's Cove and the South Shore Cove, where two flood tunnels are known to exist. One such "target area," about seven hundred feet seaward of the South Shore Cove, she placed precisely on a spot where Triton Alliance has found almost conclusive evidence of a flood-tunnel inlet. Yet their discovery wasn't made until three years later, in February 1980. She also received strong readings from the swamp and Joudrey's Cove, where Nolan has found traces of early work.

Macer-Story makes no pretense at understanding what this power, which she has had since childhood, is all about. All she knows from years of experience is that she has it. "Pendulum dowsing," she said, "is a mental skill. I am not sure how or why the weight moves, but it does move independently of any physical impetus if you are doing the concentration correctly. The dowser must empty the mind of everything, including the question being asked the pendulum, and operate purely instinctively." (Macer-Story was one of several psychics employed by the New York City police department to track down the "Son of Sam" serial killer in 1977.)

When she dowsed my chart, Macer-Story didn't attempt to guess or divine what the treasure is or who put it there, but simply limited her investigation to the response she got from the pendulum and her own psychic hunches. Since then, through what she describes as a combination of "psi intuition and document dowsing" she has concluded that the Oak Island workings were built in two stages, perhaps 2,700 years apart. The first consists of underground water cisterns built by Mycenaean seafarers before 1100 B.C. The second she attributes to John Dee, a sixteenth-century navigator, astrologer, and mathematician who was an adviser to Elizabeth I. Dee believed the northern area of the New World to be ancient Atlantis (as did his contemporary, Francis Bacon). Macer-Story suggests that Dee's followers might have visited Oak Island while secretly exploring "Atlantis" in the 1580s, and that they constructed a subterranean outpost, utilizing the chambers and tunnels that had been dug long before their arrival.

I also sent a copy of the same chart of the island to another psychic, Paul Deardorff, a Detroit restaurateur who calls himself a "geopsychic," and claims to have successfully located oil and natural gas deposits in Texas by dowsing ordinary road maps with a pendulum. He says some of his findings were later verified by exploratory drilling. In the case of Oak Island, he "located" eight treasure vaults, all within a radius of 100 feet from the Money Pit and extending from 120 to 260 feet underground. (Some of his vaults can't possibly exist, as drilling and digging have penetrated many of the spots that he selected.)

But his "geopsychic analysis" goes much further than merely pinpointing the positions of the vaults. He says his "readings" show that four of the chambers contain gold and silver, three others are filled with gems and jewels, and the eighth contains documents and historical data. He adds that the total value of the treasure comes to $105 million. Moreover, Deardorff has psychically determined that the Oak Island project was designed by Prussian engineers and then built and used by the Portuguese and the Spaniards over a 150-year period from 1525 to 1675. He also claims that there is a secret room in El Escorial Castle near Madrid containing "all of the records of the engineering, wealth, and history of the Oak Island project."

Of course, the only sure way to establish the validity and accuracy of gold-finding devices, dowsers, or psychics is to excavate (usually at great expense) the areas in which they "locate" a treasure. In the few instances where this has been done, the mystical prognosis has proved to be wrong. But just as there are incompetent engineers, there are equally incompetent diviners, not to mention outright frauds. Perhaps some of the psychics, by accident or true ability, may yet be proven right.

Other investigators who confidently claim to have solved the riddle are those armed with maps or documents that reveal exactly what the treasure is and how to get it out. Throughout the history of the search, these individuals have popped out of the woodwork with some regularity, usually to offer their "priceless information" in exchange for a slice of the treasure and someone else financing the requisite dig.

Mel Chappell, during his thirty-year tenure as owner of the Money Pit area, received many such overtures. One of these was from George Wade, a farmer from Spearville, Kansas, who claimed to have inherited a map from his great-grandfather, "the only survivor of the pirate crew who buried the treasure on Oak Island." In the spring of 1954 he advised Chappell that he had a map and a four-hundred page manu-script (written in longhand) which showed what the treasure was and how to retrieve it. He said it consisted of coins and eight hundred pounds of jewels that were buried between 1778 and 1787 "on two different islands eleven leagues apart," one of which was Oak Island. The treasure, he stated, was worth some $30 million. As an added bonus he also promised to give Chappell "the location of the much-sought-after jewels of Marie Antoinette. The man who hid her jewels was a member of the Oak Island pirate band."

In another letter, Wade described the Oak Island cache and his proposed method of recovery:

> "In my opinion it will require 120 days and at least $200,000 [to bring up the treasure]. It will be necessary to built a shaft 56 feet in diameter, properly tubed to prevent collapse. When the treasure location was first discovered [in 1795] four men could have recovered it in about twenty-three days had they but looked around them and followed the diagram found in the keystone, which was very much in evidence at that time and plainly visible on the surface at a given distance from the original shaft. Now, after many attempts and great expense, all have proved futile and the location has been butchered and loblollied into a collapsible mess—the water still flows and will continue to do so until the system is understood and staunched. This system is composed of four 33-inch tunnels, each tunnel being 170 feet longer than its mate and each tunnel having five entrances 145 feet wide, each being covered by the sea at normal or high tide, and each having a reservoir 32 by 20 feet, 90 feet below the surface.

Chappell replied that he would be happy to allow the treasure to be recovered, providing Wade financed the venture. Wade, who figured that his knowledge (which seemed to be a compi-lation of facts from a 1954 *Saga* magazine article plus a few personal embellishments) entitled him to a free ride, quickly lost interest, and the matter was dropped.

Others who contacted Chappell had even grander visions of what their information was worth. One person flatly stated that he knew "who made the deposit, when it was made, where it came from, and how to recover it." And, "for 50 percent of what you recover I will give you the data and will be willing to oversee your work for $100 a day plus expenses." A more blatant approach came from someone who claimed to possess "a complete inventory of what is in Oak Island." The list of goodies was offered to Chappell for a mere $5,000.

In other instances Chappell was informed that anything found on the island was not his to keep. A man from New Zealand wrote to say that he and his family were the owners of all the gold buried on Oak Island and that they had "powerful connections in England" who would see to it that the treasure was returned to them. Also, a "Miss Kidd" from California wrote to point out that she was a direct descendant of William Kidd and warned that she would initiate legal proceedings against Chappell as soon as anything was found on the island. Chappell heard nothing more from her after he wrote back stating (incorrectly) that Captain Kidd never had any children.

Some of the most bizarre correspondence Chappell received came during the summer of 1954 from Charles B. Thomas, an eighty-year-old retired real estate salesman who was then living at the YMCA in Great Falls, Montana. When Thomas first read about Oak Island in the *Saturday Evening Post* in 1939, it was immediately clear to him what the mystery was all about. But he was forced by divine circumstances to wait fifteen years before revealing his information. He finally contacted Chappell on May 26, 1954:

> My object in writing to you is to inform you that I have a diagram that solves the mystery of Oak Island. Let me assure you that the treasure is not a hoard of pirate's gold, but a treasure of far greater value. I have not only the diagram, but the blueprint worked out, that shows the location of the rooms below where a sacred treasure is stored for safekeeping until the due time came for it to be recovered. And that time has come.

It is my belief, which is based on accurate knowledge of the divine plan of the ages, that the treasure will consist of a museum that will contain the sacred relics of the typical Kingdom of Israel, the gold and sacred things of the temple of Jerusalem, together with manuscripts and documentary evidence that will throw some light on human history and prevent a fourth [*sic*] world war.

Divine providence has them stored in the Money Pit for safekeeping until this symbolic four years—1954–1958—when the statesmanship of the world has failed to end the Cold War and make peace, and it will be this treasure that will turn the tide and show the way to peace and security for all nations.

Thomas told Chappell that if he was permitted to search on the island he would solve the mystery "within one hour." He also proposed that he and Chappell share these treasures on a fifty-fifty basis, though not as the owners but as "custodians" of the incredible secrets contained in the Money Pit.

In a follow-up letter Thomas explained that he'd previously spent forty years solving "the mystery of the Great Pyramid of Egypt" and it was that which led him to the solution of Oak Island. "The Master Mind that stored the treasure in the Money Pit was the agent for 'higher-ups' who know that the time would come when someone would solve the mystery of the Great Pyramid, and that in turn would solve the mystery of Oak Island and, I might add, every other problem. I am the one, and the Money Pit puts me on the spot."

Thomas urged Chappell to waste no time in signing an agreement to allow him to search. Chappell tentatively agreed to let him try, providing Thomas could prove he had the financial ability to carry out the project and that he state exactly what it was he was expected to find in the Money Pit. Thomas couldn't meet the first condition. And as for the second, he said it would "betray a sacred trust if I would divulge this secret without an agreement in order to avoid possible litigation after it is recovered."

Chappell had to wait three years before learning the nature of this remarkable repository. In the summer of 1957 he was in Winnipeg on business, and Thomas arranged to travel up from Montana and meet him there. In Chappell's hotel room Thomas finally disclosed his secret: Below Oak Island is an exact duplicate of the Great Pyramid of Egypt, but inverted, with its apex extending hundreds of feet into the ground. It contains large chambers filled with incredible wealth and documents explaining the origins of man. The pyramid had been placed there by Divine Providence to aid and enlighten mankind, and it was destined to be located in 1958. Chappell patiently pointed out that a good number of shafts and drill holes had been driven down almost two hundred feet all around the Money Pit area, and not once had any sign of a stone pyramid been encountered. But Thomas was fanatic in his insistence, and it was only with a good deal of effort that Chappell was finally able to get him out of the room.

Chappell received many other outlandish suggestions concerning who did what under Oak Island. And members of the contemporary Triton group have been offered equally bizarre solutions to the mystery. Dan Blankenship, for instance, once attended a séance in Florida in which a spirit identified as Nojean revealed that the project was built by the surviving "Sun People" of Atlantis following the destruction of their mythical continent.

There are also people who believe the Holy Grail will be found beneath the island, that Leonardo da Vinci designed the workings, that it is a seventeenth-century alchemistic chemical reactor, that is a subterranean UFO base, that it was built by Irish leprechauns, that it served as a holding pen for African slaves en route to the West Indies, or that it is simply a devilish hoax engineered by Satan to instill greed in men. The list of wacky theories is endless.

But as always, it is the persistent digging and drilling by searchers, and not armchair theorists, magic machines, or the prophesies of psychics, dowsers, and map owners, that has shed informative light on the ever-increasing complexities of Oak Island's secret.

CHAPTER THIRTEEN

Dying for Treasure

FOLLOWING HIS EXPERIENCE WITH THE PARKER METAL DE-
tector in 1950, Mel Chappell decided that he had sunk enough
of his own money into the search. As Fred Blair had done
before him, he sought others to invest the capital while he
provided access to the island and the exclusive use of his
treasure trove license. Any treasure found would be split
equally between Chappell and those financing and carrying
out the search.

In August 1955, Chappell was approached by George
Greene, a petroleum engineer who represented a group of oil-
men from Corpus Christi, Texas. They wanted to locate the
treasure vault by drilling, and in September a contract was
signed with Chappell. This was the first serious work to be
done on the island since Hamilton abandoned his search in
1942. Greene, a flamboyant cigar-chomping Texan, had previously made headlines in 1952 while on a geological survey
in Turkey. During an aerial reconnaissance over Mt. Ararat,
he photographed what he claimed were the remains of Noah's
Ark. But later expeditions to the reported site found nothing,
and many wrote off his photographs as a hoax.

In the fall of 1955, Greene, replete with Stetson hat and
cowboy boots, arrived on Oak Island and set up his drilling

equipment. Chappell showed him the approximate location of the original Money Pit as well as the drilling records from the 1897 expedition. Over the next three weeks Greene sank four holes with a four-inch core drill to a depth of over 180 feet. The holes were spaced several feet apart, and in all of them he struck wood (most likely earlier searchers' cribbing) at various levels down to 111 feet. After going through some limestone at about 140 feet, Greene said, "Below that there is nothing but cavity, the drills just dropped right through." The cavity extended for approximately 40 feet, after which the drill entered bedrock. He pumped 100,000 gallons of water into the void, but it ran out and there was no way of telling where it went.

When Greene left the island at the end of October, he stated: "We found enough information below the surface to know that something went on, and next May or June I'll be back to finish the job" with heavier equipment. However, the following year he was tied up with an oil-drilling contract in Louisiana, and his agreement with Chappell expired.

He kept in touch with Chappell, promising to return someday to solve the mystery. But he never made it back, and in December 1962 he was murdered while on a geological expedition in the jungles of British Guiana. Greene, incidentally, believed that any treasure under Oak Island was probably put there by the Spanish during their conquest of Central and South America in the sixteenth century. It's a theory that holds interesting possibilities.

Chappell's next application came in 1957 from William and Victor Harman, two brothers from northern Ontario who had previously been involved in gold-prospecting ventures. Their personal funds were limited, but they were in the process of organizing the Oak Island Exploration Co. Ltd., through which they proposed to issue one million shares at twenty-five cents apiece. A one-year agreement was signed with Chappell, and in May 1958 the brothers arrived on the island with drilling equipment and a professional driller. Like Greene, they believed the treasure consisted of a Spanish deposit, and they predicted they'd bring up as much as $200 million in gold by the end of the summer.

They spent a couple of months drilling in the vicinity of the Money Pit, with their deepest hole going down past bedrock to 212 feet. In late June the Harmans reported that they had brought up samples of oak and spruce, coconut fiber, and ship's caulking (probably puddled clay) from depths of 150 feet and more. They confidently stated that the treasure "is there for the taking and we're going to take it." At this point their money ran out, and the Ontario Securities Commission refused to allow them to launch a public-stock company unless they could first secure a guaranteed five-year lease on the island. Chappell was not about to tie up the property with a group that had no assurance of being able to sell enough shares to raise the required working capital. So the Harman brothers joined the long list of those who had been forced to give up because of insufficient finances.

However, Chappell soon found himself involved with several interrelated search groups that have provided some of the most significant developments in the long history of Oak Island. It was the start of a thirty-year era in which the search has continued uninterrupted to the present day.

But that era was to begin with a tragedy of immense proportions.

Bob and Mildred Restall met in England in 1931 while she was an aspiring seventeen-year-old ballerina and he was a daredevil motorcyclist from Toronto on tour with a circus. Within a year they were married. But they became partners in more ways than one. Bob had found someone with the nerve and coordination to help him create a spectacular new routine known as the Globe of Death. For the next two decades they toured circuses and carnivals throughout Europe and North America, thrilling audiences with an act that became legendary. It involved whipping around on high-powered motorcycles at speeds of up to sixty-five miles an hour inside a twenty-foot-diameter steel mesh sphere.

"It was a precision act with timing down to a split second," explains Mildred, a petite white-haired woman who is now in her seventies and still retains her Yorkshire accent. "I'd be riding around the globe horizontally while Bob was looping over the top. We did have a few accidents, of course. I broke my jaw once doing it in Germany, and Bob had his arm broken. But it was a good act, and we did pretty well with it."

In the early 1950s the couple settled in Hamilton, Ontario. They had three young children to raise and were tired of continually being on the road. Although they still occasionally spun around the Globe of Death (their last ride was in 1956), Bob also worked at various jobs in steel mills and contracting. Their life at last seemed to be settling into a mundane middle-class pattern, a situation not regretted by Mildred.

But a chance visit to Nova Scotia in the fall of 1955 would change all that. It was then that Bob first visited Oak Island, although he had read about it many years earlier. He met George Greene on the island and received a firsthand account of the problems presented by the baffling mystery. "After that," says Mildred, "it was all he could talk about."

Bob soon contacted Chappell and waited for an opportunity to take a turn at matching wits with the unknown designer of the booby-trapped treasure chamber. That chance came in 1959. Meanwhile, he had been busy reading everything he could find pertaining to the island's history. In 1958, R. V. Harris, Hedden and Blair's former lawyer, had published *The Oak Island Mystery*, a book that gave Restall a good idea of the frustrations he could expect in his search. Restall also stirred up interest among his friends in Hamilton, lining up prospective backing for the venture.

A contract was signed with Chappell, and in October 1959, Restall, then fifty-three, and his eighteen-year-old son, Bobbie, set up camp on the island. The following summer they were joined by Mildred and their youngest child, nine-year-old Ricky. (Their daughter, Lee, was then married and living in Oakville, Ontario.)

The Restalls were something of a Swiss Family Robinson. For more than five years they lived and worked on the otherwise uninhabited island, their only link to the mainland a sixteen-foot outboard motorboat. Life was Spartan and often lonely. Home consisted of two sixteen-by-sixteen-foot one-room shacks, one used as the kitchen and Bob and Mildred's bedroom, the other serving as the equipment shed and the boys' quarters. There was no indoor plumbing, running water, telephone, or (for the first three years) electricity, things they had always taken for granted. Warmth was provided by space heaters, which often proved inadequate during the severe winter storms, and Mildred did her cooking on a small propane stove.

"Primitive is the only way to describe it," says Mildred, for whom the isolated conditions were the hardest. Bob and Bobbie worked enthusiastically from dawn to dusk, certain that every shovelful of earth was bringing them that much closer to their El Dorado. For Ricky the island was one big playground all his own, especially during the long hot summer days when he'd fish, swim, and explore the fields and woods with Carnie, a Belgian sheepdog who never left his side.

Mildred maintained the house under these difficult conditions and helped Ricky with his correspondence schooling, but she never really had her heart on the treasure-hunting aspect of their life. "That was my husband's and Bobbie's dream. I wanted so much for them to find it. But I was never that sure there was any treasure there." What Mildred missed most was living in a city or town with other people she knew, having women friends, being able to talk about anything other than Oak Island and "the search." Always the search. In the summers, of course, there were tourists to talk to. But then they, too, were primarily interested in the search.

Yet in many ways the family was probably closer than they would have been back in Hamilton. Like castaways on a desert isle, they depended a great deal on one another emotionally, materially, and socially. They spent most evenings together in the main cabin, reading, playing chess, or discussing the future. Naturally, the conversation often turned to how they'd spend their wealth once the Money Pit coughed up what it owed them. Bob talked about yachts, Bobbie about racing cars, Mildred about long vacations in warm places where there were lots of people.

Bob put the treasure's value at $30 million. He based this on the legend ("Forty feet below two million pounds are buried") supposedly deciphered from the inscribed stone found in the Money Pit in 1803. He then converted pounds into dollars on an estimated rate for the early 1700s, when, in his opinion, the treasure had been buried. Restall believed the island may have been used as a long-term repository by English privateers during their raids on Spanish ships and settlements in the seventeenth-century. He thought, for instance, that part of the loot from the city of Panama may have found its way eventually to the island after the city was sacked by Henry Morgan in 1671.

Mildred, on the other hand, believed, as she still does, that any treasure on Oak Island was probably retrieved before the Money Pit was discovered in 1795. And her favorite theory is that the deposit was designed by a group of Acadians prior to their expulsion from the province in 1755.

Restall spent most of the first couple of years exploring the artificial drainage system at Smith's Cove. He had come to the island with only his life's savings of $8,500—hardly enough to purchase or rent heavy digging machinery. So it was basically a tedious pick-and-shovel operation. An old cofferdam (built in 1866) was still visible at low tide, and Restall and his son concentrated their search between the dam and the shoreline, a distance of about seventy feet. They dug some sixty-five holes, two to six feet deep, and uncovered sections of the five finger drains that had been first noticed in 1850. They also found layers of eel grass and coconut fiber anywhere from eight to twenty-four inches thick under parts of the false beach.

In his 1961 progress report, Restall said, "We now have a complete picture of the beach work, and it is incredible." He described it as being 243 feet across near the cofferdam, and composed of "paving stones" overlaid with eel grass, fiber, sand, and rocks. Much of it had previously been ripped up and destroyed by the 1850 searchers. Although Restall noticed that the drains all converged toward one main point near the shore, he wasn't able to find the main channel. Either the drains were no longer connected to it, or else it was far deeper than he was able to dig by hand.

Through a few of his Ontario friends, Restall was able to raise $11,000 to continue work. In 1961 he purchased the large pump that both Hedden and Hamilton had used on the island and set it up over the Hedden shaft. He explored and recribbed parts of both that shaft and the Chappell shaft and did some short tunneling work between the 100- and 120-foot levels. He also examined some of the 1860s searchers' tunnels, many of which were still in good condition.

By 1964 Restall had again turned his attention to the flood system at Smith's Cove. He poured cement into several of the exposed sections of the drain, but the water continued to flow into the Hedden shaft. He then began digging his own shaft on the beach at Smith's Cove on a line with the Cave-in Pit and the Money Pit. He was determined to locate and block the main feeder line from the cove to the treasure vault. This hole was abandoned at a depth of twenty-four feet, and a new shaft was started about thirty feet north on the beach.

All this time, Restall was worried about losing his hold on the island. His contract with Chappell was on an annual basis, and this made financing difficult, for it was always possible that Chappell at the end of any given year might decide to allow someone else to take over the site. "You have no idea what the pressure was like," recalls Mildred. "Chappell was always looking for a big fish" to take charge of the search. "He'd bring people over [to the island] and introduce them to my husband and son, and [the prospective searchers] would talk about their grand schemes to find the treasure. So we never knew from one year to the next if we'd be allowed to stay."

In order to resolve the uncertainty, Restall tried in late 1964 to raise money to buy the island. But Chappell wanted $100,000 for it, and the proposal eventually fell through. Still, Restall occasionally was able to sell shares in his venture and to continue working on a limited scale. One of his major investors was Montreal businessman David Tobias, who fronted Restall more than $20,000 to continue the search. That was Tobias's introduction to a treasure hunt that he has continued to pursue to this very day.

Another of his backers was Karl Graeser, a thirty-eight-year-old Long Island marina operator. Graeser was on the island the day Bob Restall's six-year treasure hunt ended.

That was on Tuesday, August 17, 1965, a humid, leaden day when the air hung oppressively heavy. Bob and his son had been working since six that morning down in the Hedden shaft. At two P.M. Bob came up to remind Mildred that he was going into town later and he'd be at the cabin in an hour to wash up and change his clothes. At about a quarter to three he walked down to Smith's Cove to check on a recently dug shaft. It was twenty-seven feet deep, and a pump was keeping the water down to about four feet from the bottom.

No one is quite sure what happened next. Restall was either descending the shaft or else peering into it when suddenly he was lying in the black stagnant water at the bottom. Bobbie, emerging from the Hedden shaft, saw that something was wrong. He ran to the cove, saw his father at the bottom of the pit, and scampered down the ladderway after him. Seconds later Karl Graeser arrived on the scene and saw both Restalls lying unconscious in the pit. He quickly climbed down to rescue them. Behind him was sixteen-year-old Cyril Hiltz, one of Restall's workers from nearby Martin's Point. Both he and Graeser toppled from the ladder before they reached the bottom. Another worker, Andy DeMont, seventeen, met the same fate.

By this time several tourists and a group of youngsters who were camping on the island had heard the calls for help and rushed to the pit. With them was Edward White, a vacationing fireman from Buffalo, New York. White's training led him to realize that there was some sort of deadly gas in the shaft. He quickly tied a rope around his waist and had others lower him down. He lashed another line to the unconscious DeMont and then desperately groped around in the murky water looking for a sign of the others. But he could feel nothing, and now he too was on the verge of passing out. He and DeMont were hauled out and given artificial respiration.

The bodies of Bob and Bobbie Restall, Karl Graeser, and Cyril Hiltz were eventually fished up from the bottom of the death pit. The Oak Island search, in its 170th year, had claimed four more victims.

There is some debate over what killed them. The autopsies found all four to have died by drowning. Yet no one is certain of the nature of the gas that caused them to plummet into the water. Some believe it was marsh gas (methane) that had seeped into the pit. But methane is colorless and odorless, and many of those at the scene said the gas had a definite stink to it. The more likely possibility is that carbon monoxide fumes from the pump's gasoline engine on the surface had accumulated in the depths of the shaft. Given the heat and humidity of that day, such an inversion could have occurred.

Following the tragedy, Mildred and Ricky moved to the village of Western Shore, only a mile from the island that had been their home those many years. Mildred, who retired a few years ago from an administrative job at a Chester medical center, still lives there. "It all seems so hard to believe," she says, "and one of the sad ironies is that Bob thought he was close, really close, to finding the treasure."

The aftermath of the accident is still very much a sore point with Mrs. Restall. She states that within days, "before my husband and son were even buried," she was being urged by Mel Chappell to go to Halifax to work out a legal transfer of the search rights to Bob Dunfield, a California geologist who wanted to take over Restall's operations. "Everybody was in such a hurry to keep the search going," she recalls. "And what good has it done them? Not a damn bit."

Dunfield, who had first heard about Oak Island as a young boy in Denver, saw it as a problem that could be solved by heavy digging equipment. In the fall of 1965 he brought in several wealthy backers from California to help him finance the project. Also in his group was Daniel Blankenship, a Miami contractor who was to become Oak Island's most obsessive searcher. Mrs. Restall was also given a small interest in the venture.

Dunfield's first move was to barge two bulldozers out to the island. They were used to clear away about twelve feet of overburden in the entire Money Pit area, exposing cribwork from several filled-in pits. One of these, fifteen feet north of the Chappell shaft and ten feet west of the north end of the Hedden shaft, appeared to be the original Money Pit. The bulldozers were also used to push hundreds of tons of earth and clay over the beach at Smith's Cove in an effort to permanently block the flooding system. This totally muddied the water in the cove, but when Dunfield pumped out the Hedden shaft, he found that the water entering it was clear. He was therefore confident that he had blocked the eastern tunnel. But obviously at least one other flood tunnel, probably from the south shore, was still operational.

Dunfield's next plan was to bring in even heavier machinery. He leased a 70-ton crane with a 90-foot boom and dragline bucket capable of digging a hole 200 feet deep and 100 feet across. But there was no possibility of getting this behemoth out to the island on a barge. On October 17, 1965, Oak Island ceased to be an island. That day bulldozers completed a 600 foot causeway linking the island's western end to the mainland. Dunfield got the crane across and was now ready for his major assault.

The machine was first put to work on the south shore to find and block the second flood tunnel. A trench about 15 feet deep and 80 feet long was dug along the beach. In one section of the trench they encountered a refilled shaft 8 feet in diameter. It had no cribbing in it, and there is no record of it in any of the previous search attempts, so Dunfield was certain it had been excavated prior to 1795. Significantly, the shaft was about 25 feet south of the mysterious triangle of stones. The shaft was followed to a depth of about 45 feet, which seemed to be the extent of the original digging, but its purpose was never discovered. The south shore trench didn't intersect the flood tunnel, nor did it decrease the flow of seawater into the Hedden shaft. Rather than deepen the hole, Dunfield decided to move the crane up to the Money Pit itself.

For the next two months Dunfield was plagued with mechanical failures and heavy rains. Digging the pit became a constant struggle, with the sides caving in and refilling the bottom portion. Each time work was halted for a day or more, as much as 20 feet of fill would slide into the hole, and it would take another couple of days just to reexcavate it. He eventually created a pit almost 140 feet deep and 100 feet across. In the course of digging it, he scooped out most of the timbers from early shafts, leaving only the Hedden shaft intact.

Dunfield later refilled the huge hole he had spent two months digging in order to gain a suitable surface from which to do some core drilling in the same spot. A series of six-inch-diameter holes were put down to almost 190 feet. In several he found the same cavity structure that George Greene encountered in 1955. Dunfield reported that it consisted of a 2-foot layer of limestone between 140 and 142 feet, followed by a 40-foot void that extended to about 182 feet. Below that was bedrock. Dunfield planned to use the crane to examine the cavity the next spring, when the ground would be drier and less susceptible to caving in.

Meanwhile, he excavated the Cave-in Pit to 108 feet, finding old timbers at 68 feet and again at 100 feet (perhaps part of the 1860 search tunnels). But once again heavy rain and mechanical failures halted the work, and the pit began caving in rapidly.

In April, Dunfield returned to California to dry out his clothes and count his losses. He and his partners had spent $131,000 during their seven months of investigation. He still hoped to reopen the Money Pit, but before proceeding any further he wanted to purchase the island from Chappell. However, the asking price of $100,000 was more than Dunfield could raise or wanted to pay, and he gradually lost interest.

Although his direct involvement in the search ended, Dunfield was an early shareholder in the current Triton Alliance group. He was convinced that a complex mystery remained to be solved under the island, but he knew it would take considerably more time and money to find the answer.

Dunfield spent his final years in Encino, California, running a gold- and silver-mining company. Before his death in 1980, he told me that "a preponderance of evidence suggests underground work done by men many years in the past" on Oak Island. In his opinion as a geologist, however, the so-called cement found underground at various times was "nothing more than limestone" forming part of the Windsor Formation in that part of Nova Scotia. As for the cavity he drilled into, Dunfield suggested it "could be a natural feature as found in limestone units throughout the world. Normally I would have considered this as a natural cavity, and I doubt that this geological concept could have been known by the depositors before burying anything of value." But he added, "If something is buried on Oak Island, the limestone could have been a surprise to any depositors and used to their advantage." He also noted that samples of wood and metal later found in and below the cavity by Triton "are man-made and foreign to glacial deposits."

Dunfield's heavy-equipment approach to finding the treasure evoked a lot of criticism among local people in the Mahone Bay area as well as from other investigators of the mystery. Some feel he contributed more than anyone to turning the east end of the island into a scarred mess of water-filled pits and mounds of earth. But that's an aesthetic complaint voiced by locals and tourists; the more significant damage was archaeological. A clam bucket capable of gobbling up more than sixty cubic feet of dirt in one bite can hardly be expected to distinguish between earth and underground artifacts. Dunfield did sift through material brought up from the lower depths, but some of those involved with him said the investigation was often cursory. The underground damage was probably limited to previous searchers' shafts, although that can't be known for certain.

But on the surface, the stone triangle, one of the island's most interesting landmarks, disappeared as a result of the trench Dunfield dug on the south shore. The triangle, which almost every investigator including Dunfield accepted as original and significant, fell into the eroding trench after he left the island. In addition, the drilled rock near Smith's Cove hasn't been found since Dunfield's time. The westerly drilled rock, however, was moved before the crane began excavating the Money Pit. Fortunately, the location of all those markers had been accurately plotted by Charles Roper in 1937 and again by Fred Nolan in 1959.

The local hostility toward Dunfield may also partially explain his many equipment breakdowns. Mel Chappell told me that some of the crane's broken cables had "the appearance of having been [previously] cut with a hacksaw or other tool." It was suspected that the saboteurs were local fishermen who strongly objected to Dunfield's causeway that forced them to detour around the seaward end of the island on their coastal runs.

If the search in the early 1960s was marked by futility, death, and destruction, the years that followed would provide some remarkable discoveries to establish beyond doubt the authenticity and complexity of the underground project.

CHAPTER FOURTEEN

The Ghosts of Oak Island

INEVITABLY, THE RESTALL TRAGEDY AROUSED A SHIVER OF superstitious gossip among the mainland inhabitants, many of whom wondered whether the deaths were really accidental. For it is believed by some that supernatural forces are at work on this strange island and that it is these, not the flood traps, that are the true guardians of the treasure. Could it be, some locals asked, that Restall was getting *too* close to the answer? And just what *was* the nature and source of that unidentified gas that sent him and three others hurtling to their death at the bottom of the pit? Even today there are people in the area who will shift uncomfortably and whisper conspiratorially when asked about the legendary custodians of Oak Island's secret.

An elderly descendant of Anthony Vaughan, one of the Money Pit's discoverers, recently assured me that, although he lives just across the mainland, he has never visited Oak Island and never will. When asked why not, he explained, "Weird as it may sound, I've seen people there; but not solid people. Ghosts. I've seen them from my property, from when I was a boy right up till now. They're ghosts, just wandering around, waiting for something . . . or for somebody."

This sense of foreboding even preceded the Money Pit's

discovery in 1795, which is partly why it took the three young men seven years to find anyone willing to join them in the search. And the continuing fear about the island, which feeds the endemic superstitions of many Nova Scotians, particularly among the old-timers, is enforced by a variety of myths and reported phenomena associated with Oak Island.

One legend that has been around for more than a hundred years is that of the "dog with the fiery eyes." According to some, this creature with bloodred eyes that glow like hot coals is nothing less than Satan's own watchdog. Others contend that it is the ghost of a ship's mascot left behind by the original depositors. Hannah Dauphinee, who lived on the island in the early 1930s, claimed to have seen it several times lurking around Smith's Cove. Another woman, a relative of Anthony Graves, once was startled by a dog "as big as a colt," which "disappeared into a wall" of solid stone on the north side of the island.

Harris Joudrey, who lived into his nineties at Martin's Point on the mainland, spent the first ten years of his life on Oak Island. Some years ago he told me that he saw the dog in the summer of 1900 when he was nine years old. As Joudrey recalled it, he and a couple of his friends were walking past the Money Pit one evening and "there was a dog sitting at the sill of the boilerhouse. He watched us till we were out of sight. It was a pretty big dog with some black and white on him, and we knew there was no such dog on the island. He was never seen before and we never saw it again after that. We were scared, I'll tell you."

A variation of the dog as the Money Pit's guardian is a long-standing belief that spirits of the depositors occasionally appear in the form of large crows or blackbirds to check on the progress of the search. But this belief isn't limited to Oak Island, as instances of these birds of omen are commonly found in Nova Scotia folklore. The origin of this superstition dates back to both the French Acadians and the Celtic settlers of the province. A few years ago a contemporary investigator of Oak Island pointed to a particular blackbird sitting on a tree branch on the island and stated, "It comes here every day around this time to watch what we're doing." His listener at first thought the person was joking, but then realized that he was dead serious.

Another Oak Island specter, this time in the form of an ancient man, was seen in the 1850s, by William Graves, a son of Anthony Graves. At the time, William was in his twenties and was dying of consumption. On his deathbed he is reported to have stated, "I am a dying man, and I would not tell a lie about it. I was out in my boat one evening spearing lobster on the north side of the island when I saw the figure of a man sitting beside twin trees [on the shore]. He had long white whiskers. He called to me saying, 'Come here and I will give you all the gold you can carry.' But I was so frightened that I rowed for home as fast as I could."

Other people claim to have heard unexplainable noises on the island, particularly at night. Thomas Nixon, who camped there during his search in the summer of 1934, was sitting in his tent with one of his workers one night when they heard a crash from the direction of the Money Pit. It sounded like planks being dropped, and they suspected someone might be stealing their lumber. Nixon said the two of them left the tent and circled around to opposite sides of the Money Pit. "Our idea was to hem in whoever was there. We each got to our place and waited, but there was nothing to see. But suddenly, right there between the drill and the forge, came the sound as if a man was dropping planks. We heard it again five times altogether that night." Several weeks later they heard the same thing, and again they investigated. But as before, the source of the sound could not be found; nothing existed that could be making it.

Mildred Restall acknowledges that the place did become eerie at times. "I was darn scared to go out of the cabin when it was dark. It was always spooky there at night, and when the fellows [her husband and two sons] left me at night to pull up the boat or something, I'd start to chew my fingernails if they weren't back in five minutes."

Mrs. Restall says many of the local mainland people could never understand how she and her family could live alone on the island. One man, Ronald Rafuse, "used to tell us about the strange lights he'd see on the island [from the mainland] when it was foggy. He used to say, 'I wouldn't spend a night on this island for all the treasure that's down there.' And he'd come out a couple of days after there'd been a heavy fog and ask, 'Did you see the lights the other night?' Then he'd describe them to us."

Several other people, including current treasure hunters Dan Blankenship and Fred Nolan, say they have occasionally heard strange rumblings beneath the island. The Restalls sometimes heard such sounds, though in one particular case they found an explanation. Mrs. Restall recalls, "We were sitting in the cabin one night and heard this *whumph* noise outside and everything shook. We went outside and found that part of an old tunnel had caved in and left a large depression in the ground."

The mystical oddities in Oak Island's history haven't been limited to reports of strange sights and sounds. There are several instances, for example, of persons having dreams that supposedly would lead them to the treasure. Amos Nauss of Marriott's Cove recalled one such incident:

The first time I had ever been to Oak Island was when I was fourteen years old [in 1911]. The people I was working for at the time, Scottish people, had a house down here. Colonel Miller was the name. They had an old woman who was their cook, and she was a superstitious sort. She had a dream that she knew where the money was buried. But the funny part was that she was never on the island. Yet she drew a map with a pencil showing where we were to land on the island, and the map showed we'd walk up and come to a fence after about 120 feet or something like that, and there'd be a gate in the fence. And we were to go through the gate where there'd be a bunch of scattered trees. Then we'd go down, come back toward the water, and there would be two mounds of earth about six feet apart.

Well, Ernest Miller, Mrs. Miller, her sister, and the old woman and I all went over there, and everything was where she said it would be. It was the same as if she had been there the day before she drew the map. I never got over to this day how she knew all that. She never left the house, and I knew and the Millers knew she was never over on the island.

Well, I was appointed to dig. It was one of those terrible hot days in July with lots of blackflies. I got down about three and half or four feet, and I was sweating. But I wasn't supposed to talk.

None of us could talk, according to the instructions from the old woman. But I forgot about that and I finally said. "Look, time for one of you to get down here and shovel." Well, the old woman got mad when I talked. She said, "Let's go home, let's go home; it's no use now." She figured the spell was broken by my talking.

The necessity of maintaining absolute silence while digging up a pirate's treasure is a common superstition. Pirates are traditionally thought to have decapitated or buried alive one of their comrades and left his ghost to protect the treasure. However, the ghost's malevolent power could be released only if someone in the search party broke the requisite silence. The spoken word was also believed to cause the treasure cache to sink farther into the ground and out of reach of the searchers.

Oak Island's folklore contains two suggestions for appeasing the wrath of the guardian ghost: Throw either a live baby or a black person into the Money Pit and the treasure will be found. There's no evidence that these grisly solutions were ever adopted, but they do crop up in local stories.

One concerns the Bogeyman of Lunenburg, and is recorded in an 1868 historical essay by E. H. Owen of that town:

> A few years ago while a company was at work on Oak Island, a man was seen wandering about Lunenburg. People said he was on the lookout for a baby to throw down the hole. Someone had dreamt that if a baby were put down the hole alive the treasure would be found. This man was engaged to get one and went about frightening all the little boys and girls wherever he went. A gentleman who was traveling alone through the woods some few miles from the town of Lunenburg met a boy with a fishing rod in his hand. On asking the boy, who seemed somewhat tired, if he would not like to get into his wagon and drive into town, the little fellow gave a yell, dropped his rod, and ran into the woods. The gentleman could not understand then, but afterwards found that the boy had taken him for the baby hunter and did not care about being carried away and thrown down a deep hole.

Another tale concerns Daniel Hirtle, who worked for a search group on Oak Island during the 1890s. His daughter, Amanda Hatt, of Western Shore, recalled a strange apparition her father described when she was a young girl:

One night he got home from working on the island, and he lay down and had a dream where he saw something coming in the sky wrapped up in a blanket that had just a head showing. This thing was hanging in the sky above where the causeway to the island is now. My father was excited. He couldn't get it out of his mind; it worried him.

In this dream he was rowing his dory and this thing came at him right straight through the air. It was a head that seemed to be wrapped up all in a blanket, and it followed him to shore. He thought there was something to it because he had the same dream three times the same night. The head in the sky told him he should dig in the [Oak Island] swamp; that there was money there, three chests of it. It wasn't where they had been digging [in the Money Pit area] at all. But according to the dream he had to leave one man in the hole and that was supposed to be the colored man, Sam Butler (a descendant of Samuel Ball, a freed slave), who was living on the island at the time. But father said he wouldn't think of leaving a man down in a hole like that. So he never tried to dig the treasure there.

Apart from nocturnal dreams, there are several instances of persons who've had Oak Island-inspired visions. One case occurred on a winter day in 1940. At that time Jack and Charlotte Adams and two of their children were the only inhabitants of the island, working as caretakers for Hedden and Hamilton. The incident, which involved their four-year-old daughter, Peggy, left a vivid impression on Mrs. Adams:

I was in the cabin making a fire on the stove and Peggy had gone out to play. After a while she came running in and she was crying. She was scared. She said, "Mommy there's three big men down there" at Smith's Cove. She said, "There's one sitting on the wharf down there that looks like Luthor," the big man in the Mandrake [the Magician] comic strip. And she said there's another one with funny-looking clothes and there's another one with a big patch on his eye. She said they were wearing pretty red jackets and had big yellow stripes down their pants.

About that time Jack came home and I said, "Jack, there's somebody on the island. Peggy says she's seen men coming up from the shore." There was snow on the ground. So he went down to the shore, but he saw nothing, not even any tracks. But Peggy still said she saw those men; she knew they were there.

Now, we had never mentioned anything about pirates or the treasure to Peggy, or even that everybody thought the island was haunted long ago. And she was never a child with a big imagination. Never in her life did she say anything like that; she didn't even say anything about any dreams. So it was unusual for her to say that.

The sequel to that story occurred many years later when Mrs. Adams was in Halifax and happened to visit the Citadel Museum. "I went into this one room and it came right to my mind that this was the kind of people Peggy saw that day. It was the same clothes she described." The room she was in contained effigies of eighteenth-century British militia in their red and yellow uniforms. Peggy, who now lives in nearby Bridgewater, still recalls the incident. "There's truth to it; I saw what I saw," she says. "I don't know what it means, but it was the only time something like that ever happened to me."

In 1977 a man associated with the search experienced something even more frightening. He was with another person on the island when he suddenly went into a sort of trance and, according to his companion, "started rolling around and screaming." After he had been calmed down and revived, the individual described how he had just gone through the death of a Spanish monk who had his throat cut and been entombed in a chamber far beneath the island. He was certain the killing took place and that the corpse is still down there.

Incidents such as these can't always be discarded as the product of an imaginative or overwrought mind, for there are many explainable instances of persons having the apparent ability to see backward or forward in time. In fact, second sight, or clairvoyance, is a prevalent belief in Nova Scotia, especially among the Cape Breton highlanders, for whom it is a part of their Celtic heritage.

One documented example of precognition occurred in 1877 at Mull River, in Cape Breton's Inverness County. It concerns a young man who was walking alone down a dirt road one night when he saw a large black object hurtling toward him. Its noise and the two streams of white light that radiated from its front terrified him, and he scurried into the brush at the side of the road. As the machine passed by him at great speed he noticed that the bright front lights had become two dim ones at the rear. He wrote an account of his experience and told others about it. But it wasn't until about thirty years later, when he encountered his first automobile, that he realized what he had seen.

Nova Scotia's most celebrated case of a past event being re-created involves the story of the *Young Teazer*, an American privateer vessel that harassed Nova Scotia shipping and coastal communities during the War of 1812. On the morning of June 27, 1813, the schooner was sighted on the open sea and pursued by five British warships, which chased her toward Lunenburg harbor. There the *Teazer* ran into heavy gunfire from shore batteries, and she altered her course into Mahone Bay, where she hoped to use the light winds, fog, and approaching dusk to her advantage and then hide among the islands. But two of the British ships, the *La Hogue* and the *Orpheus*, spotted her as she was crossing the bay and they began closing in. It was just a matter of time before the *Teazer* would have been outdistanced and captured.

But suddenly there was a terrific explosion, and the *Teazer* went up in a ball of flame. Of her crew of thirty-six only eight survived, and most of those were seriously burned. Frederick Johnson, the *Teazer*'s first lieutenant, had purposely set fire to the ship to prevent her falling into enemy hands. But the fire had apparently gone straight to the ship's powder magazine before the crew could launch the boats or jump overboard. This dramatic scene, which took place a couple of miles from Oak Island, was witnessed by many people along the shores of the bay. And the shock of the blast, which tore the schooner in two, was felt many miles inland.

Since that time, the *Young Teazer* has reappeared every so often in the form of a burning ghost ship slowly retracing her final voyage across Mahone Bay. The phenomenon has been observed and reported by hundreds of people living on the shores and islands of the bay. And always the fiery schooner is seen heading east from Lunenburg and then vanishing somewhere in the middle of the bay.

One such sighting occurred around 8:30 at night in September 1967. Two young cousins, Michael Slauenwhite and Wayne Boehner, were at the Martin's River home of Michael's grandmother, Pearl Boehner, when they both noticed a fiery glow out in Mahone Bay. Their grandparents and parents also observed it. Wayne describes what they saw: "It looked like a big ball of fire the size of a house; like it was a burning house on a raft. It was moving slowly toward Chester, and it was coming out from between Earnest and Kaulback islands when we first saw it. We called the rest of the family, and they all saw the same thing. We watched it for about ten minutes before it went out of sight. The next day other people around here said they'd seen it too. There was no report of a ship catching fire or anything that would explain it. It was some strange."

The boy's grandfather, Charles Boehner, told them he had seen it previously, many years earlier, and that he had known two men who had taken a small boat out into the bay for a closer look. They never came back, and their dory was never found.

There are many others in the area who similarly describe their own sightings of this Mahone Bay equivalent of the *Flying Dutchman*. In one case, a fishing vessel out of Lunenburg happened to be in the path of the phantom ship. The fishermen claim to have heard the screams of the *Teazer*'s crew as the burning schooner approached them. When they tried to dodge it, the privateer altered course and kept coming at them. Finally, just as the fishermen were certain they were going to be engulfed in the flames, the *Teazer* vanished into thin air.

Nova Scotia's folklore is rich with examples of the unexplainable, and Oak Island is therefore an apt setting for the world's greatest treasure mystery. Yet compared to other treasure islands, Oak Island is not an inherently forbidding place. It is not an isolated tropical isle infested with malaria, snakes, and wild animals, such as the famous Cocos Island treasure site 450 miles off the west coast of Costa Rica.

On a warm summer day Oak Island, or at least the three-quarters of it that hasn't been hacked apart by searchers, is an inviting picture of thick stands of evergreens and wild apple trees, fields of raspberry and blueberry bushes, and wildlife consisting of a large variety of birds, rabbits, and even occasional deer. And all of this is surrounded by the normally calm, blue-green waters of Mahone Bay.

But at night, or on those days when a thick fog rolls across the bay, or during a severe winter storm when the causeway is almost washed away and foaming breakers lash the shoreline, the island takes on a gloomy and desolate appearance. If one is alone on the island at such a time, he can be easily spooked by the knowledge that something very strange took place on this site several centuries ago; that persons unknown lived here, perhaps for several years, while they created a covert and complex project, the nature of which has still to be fathomed. And it is also very likely that there is not only treasure beneath the island, but also the bodies of workers killed to guarantee their silence about this secret place. Contemplating all of that while an Atlantic mist swirls through the evergreens and across the swamp can leave even a hardened realist with a chilling sense of Oak Island's haunting aura.

And of all the legends that have been generated by the two-hundred-year-old treasure hunt, one of the oldest and most persistent is that the quest will end only after all of the island's oak trees have died and the search has taken seven lives.

As I write this, there are three oak trees left on the island, and six men have been killed in search of the treasure.

CHAPTER FIFTEEN

The Mayor of Oak Island

IN JANUARY 1965, WHILE THE RESTALL FAMILY WAS STRUG-gling through its final frigid winter of isolation on Oak Island, a forty-two-year-old building contractor was sitting at his kitchen table in Miami reading a magazine article that was to change his life forever. It was a *Reader's Digest* feature about the Oak Island treasure hunt, and Dan Blankenship, fascinated by the complexity of the challenge, handed the magazine to his wife, Janie. "Take a look at this," he said. "I'll bet I could stop the water and find the treasure."

With those words Blankenship committed himself to a consuming obsession that today, nearly a quarter of a century later, finds him still on Oak Island, on the verge, he hopes, of winning that bet. But he has paid dearly for his quest: in money, in years of deprivation and frustration, and several times almost with his life.

Now in his mid-sixties, Blankenship, a stocky, muscular man whose leathery complexion testifies to years of outdoor physical work, tends to be philosophical about his continuing commitment to the search. As he explained it to me recently, "Who knows why I'm still here; maybe stupidity, stubbornness, who knows? I think the average person would shy away from being tagged as obsessed. But to go through what I've gone through these many years is, I guess, an obsession. But once you've seen the things I've seen, there's no way you can let go. No way."

To know Dan Blankenship is to know a man who will never let go. For, besides having the tenacity of a pit bull terrier, he is convinced that it is his destiny to bring the Oak Island search to its conclusion. His wife, Janie, often with nail-biting nervousness, has shared Dan's adventure. She acknowledges there are "certain aspects that sometimes make me regret our being here; the danger, the cost, the deprivation." And, she confesses, "Sometimes I regret that morning Dan saw the story in the *Digest*. I remember he showed it to me at breakfast. I should have torn up the article then and there."

But she didn't. Five months after reading the article Dan Blankenship went to Oak Island, where he worked first with Restall and then with Dunfield, investing $21,000 in the latter's venture. He wasn't overly impressed by the methods employed by either of those men, and he yearned for the opportunity to take a more direct role in the search. That chance came in the summer of 1966 when Dunfield's lease with Chappell expired.

For the first few years Blankenship bounced between Nova Scotia and Florida, spending summers in a Western Shore motel and winters at home with Janie and their three children. But as the treasure hunt became increasingly complex, they realized it was more of a full-time job than an avocation. So they sold their Miami home, gave up a successful $100,000-a-year contracting business, and moved to the Mahone Bay area, where they rented a house for a couple of years. In the fall of 1975, Dan built a comfortable two-bedroom bungalow on the southwest corner of Oak Island. It has been their home ever since.

Soon after they moved to Nova Scotia they were joined by their son, David, then in his mid-twenties. For several years, David, who shares his father's affable enthusiasm, worked on the search. He later married a local woman and moved to the mainland, where he became a construction steelworker, a career that was cut short in 1985 by a serious industrial accident that has left him partially disabled. However, he still assists in the dig and, like his father, is certain there is a vast treasure to be found under Oak Island.

Today Dan and Janie Blankenship are permanent residents of an island with a population of three: themselves and Dan Henskee, who for many years has been Blankenship's only full-time assistant in the day-to-day digging.

As a twenty-five-year-old farmer from Alden, in upstate New York, Henskee first visited Oak Island in the fall of 1965, lured by the same *Reader's Digest* article that Blankenship had read the previous January. He spent many of the following summers on the island, helping Blankenship with the dig and using his technical abilities to repair equipment and design gadgets used in the search. In 1982, after his mother died and the family farm was sold, the lanky, bearded Henskee, a pleasantly eccentric individual, moved to the island permanently.

Henskee has lived alone ever since with his cat Hoser in a junk-filled shack almost directly on top of the Money Pit. As he described it to me in the summer of 1987, "It's like living next door to a bank; you know the money's there, but you can't figure out how to get your hands on it." His years of monastic patience, for which he stands to receive about 4 percent of any treasure recovered, are, he says, "motivated by two things. First, I've got nothing better to do in the truest sense of that term; and secondly, I believe in [the search] enough that I'm sticking with it. Basically, I'm gambling a future on this being worth doing."

When the Blankenships moved to the island, they adjusted quickly to their radically changed environment. Unlike the Restalls, they have the conveniences of a modern home, and their neighbors and friends are only a short drive across the causeway. They are a popular couple around Mahone Bay. The mainlanders had often resented previous Americans, such as George Greene and Bob Dunfield, who'd arrived full of brashness and conviction that they'd show the local yokels how to scoop out the treasure in no time at all. But Dan and Janie are unassuming, low-key people with a sort of down-home folksiness. As one local acquaintance remarked,

"They're more like Nova Scotians than Americans." Consequently, they have made many close friends on the mainland,
even if some of those people believe that Dan or any other
Oak Island treasure hunter is living in a fool's paradise.

Their life, however, is centered on the island. Dan's idea of
relaxing after a long day at the Money Pit is to help Janie tend
a large garden behind their house. They are almost self-suffi-
cient in their produce needs, and what is not eaten in the
summer is canned and preserved for the long winter ahead.
Another of Dan's hobbies has been making wine, much of it
produced from the island's wild berries.

In the summers their island tranquility is disrupted by tourists who come from all parts of Canada and the United States
to visit the famous digging site. The tours, which previously
had been operated by the province, were taken over by Triton
Alliance in 1976. Janie manages a museum on the island's
west side, with hired guides escorting the curious to the
Money Pit on the eastern end. There, if they're lucky and Dan
isn't at the bottom of a deep shaft, the tourists get to meet
Canada's most famous treasure hunter. (The most illustrious
of these tourists was former Canadian Prime Minister Pierre
Trudeau, who in the summer of 1979 spent an afternoon with
his three sons on a Blankenship-guided tour of the island.)

If nothing else, Blankenship has achieved world-wide
notoriety. His years of patient exploration have been featured
in articles in *The Wall Street Journal*, *Newsweek*, *Life*, *Es-
quire*, *Smithsonian*, *Macleans*, and many other publications in
North America and abroad. Consequently, he receives a constant stream of letters from strangers offering encouragement,
derision, or suggestions on how to solve the mystery. One
such letter, from a group of Australian schoolchildren, was
simply addressed to: "The Mayor, Oak Island, Canada." It
reached him with no trouble at all. But Blankenship rarely
answers his fan mail. "If I did that," he explains, "I'd be
spending all day writing instead of digging."

IF DAN BLANKENSHIP IS THE ISLAND'S UNOFFICIAL MAYOR,
David Tobias is its absentee king and financial patron. Tobias,

a Montreal millionaire now in his early sixties, has owned
most of the island since 1977 and has personally sunk far
more money into the search (about $750,000) than anyone
else before him. Today, as the president and major shareholder
of the Triton Alliance syndicate, he is the controlling force
behind one of the world's biggest and potentially most lucrative archaeological digs. And Blankenship, as Triton's field
manager, secretary-treasurer, and second-largest shareholder,
is right there beside him.

However, it wasn't until 1967 that the two men teamed up.
Tobias first heard about Oak Island in 1943 as a young air
force pilot stationed at Maitland, Nova Scotia. He visited the
site while on leave, but, as he recalls, "It didn't impress me
that much. I figured that if there was something down there,
why didn't they just dig and get it out." Then in 1963 he read
about the Restall expedition and his interest was renewed
enough to invest about $20,000 in that search attempt.

Like Blankenship, Tobias was anxious to test his own
theories and methods on the island. In early 1976 he approached Mel Chappell, owner of the Money Pit and the treasure trove license, and told him about a company, Becker
Drilling Ltd. of Toronto, with a new type of drill that used
high-velocity air pressure to send up continuous core samples.
He offered to finance the drilling program (which cost
$130,000) in return for two-thirds of any treasure found.
Chappell readily agreed.

Coincidentally, Blankenship had by this time reached the
point where he was totally committed to the island but was
almost broke. And Tobias, who owned a packaging and label-
manufacturing company in Montreal, knew he could spend
only limited amounts of time in Nova Scotia. Therein was a
partnership born, with Tobias putting up the funds and
Blakenship managing the project.

"What I set out to establish with that drilling program,"
says Tobias today, "was proof that there were man-made
underground workings [in the Money Pit area]. I wasn't much
interested in anything found in the first 150 feet or so, since a
few [searchers'] shafts had been that deep before. I was interested only in hard, solid proof of *original* work." And, he

adds, "If I hadn't found it, seen it with my own eyes, I would have walked away from the whole thing then and there."

But find it they did. Between January and August 1967 the Becker Drilling contractors sunk some sixty five-inch-diameter holes in and around the Money Pit area. And it was that program that confirmed beyond doubt that all the previous searchers had been on the right track, but none of them had gone anywhere deep enough.

The boreholes determined that bedrock in that area begins about 160 feet down, though in places it varies 10 feet either way. The bedrock is mostly anhydrite, with some limestone and gypsum in the upper layer. By this time the surface of the Money Pit area was about 12 feet lower than its original elevation, as a result of the removal of much of the overburden by Dunfield in 1965. Thus, Becker's discoveries were recorded at depths a dozen feet closer to the surface than they would have been when the workings were originally built or when earlier searchers drilled into the same area.

Core samples from several of the holes around the Money Pit brought up pieces of china, oak buds, cement, wood, charcoal, and metal, anywhere from between 160 and 212 feet down. Some of the holes hit tunnels or chambers that appeared to have been cut through the bedrock. In these instances the drill went through 30 to 40 feet of rock, then hit several inches of wood, a thin layer of blue clay, a few more inches of wood, and then dropped into voids six to eight feet deep before again striking the bedrock floor. Samples of the wood were sent to Geochron Laboratories Inc. of Cambridge, Mass., for carbon-14 analysis.

The report dated the wood at A.D. 1575, plus or minus eighty-five years. Geochron also noted that the wood was definitely not part of a natural glacial deposit since that would have resulted in an age of 10,000 years or more. (Carbon dating involves measuring the amount of radioactive carbon-14 contained in organic matter such as wood. The isotope is absorbed by living organisms from atmospheric carbon dioxide at a fairly constant rate. After death, the isotope steadily decays and analysis can determine approximately how many years have elapsed since death. In the case of wood, this indicates the period at which the tree was cut down.)

Those findings convinced Tobias and Blankenship that there are man-made tunnels 200 feet and more below the island, perhaps with ceilings shored up with wooden planks or logs. Moreover, the approximate date of the project had now been established. The drillers also encountered the deep cavity that Dunfield had found two years earlier north of the Chappell shaft. In addition, they discovered a chamber extending from about 160 to 190 feet almost directly beneath the Hedden shaft. This cavern was about 30 feet in diameter and appeared to have been naturally or artificially cut out of bedrock. It was filled with a heavy, puttylike blue clay in which layers of small stones were found regularly spaced every eighteen inches.

A report later issued by Tobias on that finding states: "In the opinion of Major-General Colin Campbell, a leading mining engineer and consultant, this seems to indicate that the clay had been puddled on the surface and poured into the hole in layers. Under these circumstances the small stones present in the clay would sink to the bottom of each layer and produce the kind of stratification noted in the drill cores. General Campbell also pointed out that in the period before the development of concrete, clay was commonly used in underground workings as a water seal."

At 174 feet down in the clay-filled depression the drill chewed through metal and then brought up a piece of brass. This sample was submitted for spectrographic analysis. The results showed a high level of impurities, indicating that it had been smelted at an early but indeterminable date.

Samples of a bricklike material discovered at about 200 feet were tested by mineralogists and were found to have been exposed to heat at some former time. This is seen by some investigators as evidence that a primitive kiln may have once operated below the island's surface to make and repair iron tools. The charcoal might have been used as fuel to fire the kiln, or, as General Campbell suggested, may have been the residue of fires used to crack large boulders during the original excavation. A cementlike substance, analyzed by experts as being worked by man, was also brought up from cavities below bedrock.

One borehole in the Money Pit came to an abrupt halt at 198 feet. Blankenship and the professional driller operating the machine were positive, because of the high-pitched whining sound, that the drill was biting into hard metal. It required twenty-five minutes for the diamond drill to bore through a half inch of the material. But the core sample was lost just before it reached the surface.

Concurrent with the drilling program Blankenship explored other parts of the island. Here too he made some important discoveries. In 1966 he reopened and deepened the shaft that Dunfield had found the year before on the south shore. At about sixty feet Blankenship found an ancient hand-wrought nail and a kind of nut or washer. The hole was dug to about ninety feet, where he encountered a layer of round granite rocks, all about the size of a man's head, lying in a pool of black stagnant water. Blankenship was sure he had intersected a part of the south shore flood tunnel, and he spent several months trying to crib the shaft and evacuate deeper. But even wood and steel casing couldn't hold back the collapsing earth, and the hole was eventually abandoned.

The following year Blankenship dug up parts of the Smith's Cove beach. This yielded more coconut fiber. Tobias recalls that he was present when some of the material was found. "I remember picking it up and thinking maybe it was some sort of seaweed. But we sent a sample off to the National Research Council [in Ottawa], and sure enough, their botanists confirmed that it was coconut fiber. That was the first time I really believed there was coconut fiber under Oak Island."

Blankenship also uncovered the remains of the artificial drainage network under Smith's Cove. Beneath one of the stone drains he found a pair of wrought-iron scissors. These were submitted to the Smithsonian Institution in Washington, which found them to be Spanish-American in origin, probably made in Mexico. They were examined by Mendel Peterson, former curator of the Smithsonian's Historical Archaeology division, and he said the scissors were of a type that was being made 300 years ago or earlier in Mexico. Other artifacts found beneath the beach included an ancient set square, which metallurgists dated to sometime before 1783, and a heart-shaped stone. Peterson, who examined the stone, concluded that it had been chiseled with some sort of tool at an early though undeterminable date.

Those discoveries, along with the startling drill results, convinced the searchers that there was no question that someone had visited this island hundreds of years earlier and had dug a maze of tunnels deep in its interior. But Tobias knew that it would require far more money than even he had to get to the bottom of the mystery. So through his business connections, some twenty new shareholders were brought into the search in April 1969 with the formation of Triton Alliance Ltd. (Considering the island's flood traps, the name Triton— the Greek demigod who was half man and half fish—was well chosen.)

Those early Triton partners, who initially invested about $500,000 in the project, are, significantly, not the sort of men to be taken in by get-rich-quick schemes. They include heads of large Canadian and U.S. companies, lawyers, and scientists: men like George Jennison, a past president of the Toronto Stock Exchange; Charles Brown III, a wealthy Boston real-estate investor; Donald Webster, a Toronto financier; Bill Sobey, honorary chairman of one of Canada's biggest supermarket chains; and Gordon Coles, Nova Scotia's former deputy attorney-general. Mel Chappell, the island's former owner, was also a major shareholder and member of Triton's board of directors until his death in 1980.

Many of the original participants are still active in the company, contributing additional capital over the years despite the fact that none has yet received a dime of return on his investment. In most cases their allegiance has as much to do with their faith in Tobias and Blankenship as it does with their curiosity about Oak Island.

Bill Sobey, currently a Triton director with a 10 percent equity interest, has spent his entire life in Nova Scotia. As he told me in July 1987, "I remember as a bug-eyed kid fifty years ago hearing stories about Oak Island. So I grew up with the mystery. But I'm also enormously impressed with Dan and David; the way their enthusiasm never wanes. Dan takes great physical risks down in those holes, and it never seems to faze him. And David I know has put a great deal of money into that island, but he never seems to waver from his belief. So one becomes somewhat enthused by the devotion of those two people."

With the creation of Triton and its injection of new capital, Blankenship spent much of the summer of 1970 using bulldozers to construct a four-hundred-foot earth and rock cofferdam around the perimeter of Smith's Cove. It extended about fifty feet seaward of the dams that had been built by searchers in 1850 and 1866 and was therefore well outside the low-tide mark.

This cofferdam, like the others before it, was eventually destroyed by Atlantic storms. But during its construction a large U-shaped structure was found buried below the silt beyond the low-tide line. It consisted of several huge logs about two feet thick and from thirty to sixty-five feet long. They were notched exactly every four feet along their length, and beside each notch was carved a Roman numeral, each number different from the others. The notched surfaces had been bored, and some contained the remains of two-inch-thick wooden dowels. These presumably had been used to fasten crosspieces to the logs. In fact, several crosspieces and some hand-sawed boards were found buried in the mud in the same area. They had uncovered an extension of the same wooden formation that Gilbert Hedden had first noticed in 1936.

Experts were brought in to examine the structure, and they suggested it was an ancient wharf or slipway, or perhaps even the remains of the original cofferdam built to contain the sea while the flood tunnel was driven to the Money Pit. One of the investigators, Dr. H. B. S. Cooke, a geologist from Dalhousie University in Halifax, stated, "I have no doubt whatsoever that it was an artificial structure, probably a cofferdam, with a well-built wall."

Blankenship believes that it was more likely a wharf built by the original depositors, though it may have been a combination wharf and cofferdam that was purposely destroyed after the Money Pit and flood tunnels were completed. Triton had samples of the wood carbon-dated, and it was found to date back 250 years or more.

Prior to that discovery, Blankenship had found two other crudely built wooden structures beneath the beach of the island's western end. These appeared to have been slipways used to haul out boats. Handmade wrought-iron nails and metal straps were also found in these areas, and laboratory analysis determined the metal to have been forged sometime before 1790.

Blankenship has unearthed other strange artifacts scattered around the island. These include a pair of old leather shoes nine feet below the island's western beach, and three drilled rocks north of the Money Pit that are similar to the two found by Hedden. He also discovered several rock piles under which were mounds of gray ash. The ash was later analyzed and found to be the remains of burned bones; how it got there isn't known.

In order to confirm its earlier drilling results, Triton hired Golder & Associates of Toronto, a leading geotechnical engineering firm, to conduct the most complete study ever done beneath the island. In the summer and fall of 1970, Golder drilled a series of deep holes all around the island's east end, analyzed core samples, and ran seismic and other tests to measure the exact nature and porosity of the soil and the underlying bedrock. They also determined that the water under the Money Pit area was coming in at a rate of 600 to 650 gallons per minute. Based on this data, pumping holes were put down in spots where they would be most effective in holding the water below the bedrock level.

The Golder project, which cost Triton over $100,000, produced detailed charts and cross-sectional drawings of the island's interior, with the engineers mapping out a combination of natural and man-made formations below bedrock. Based on those and later findings made by Triton and its consultants, engineers have estimated that, given sixteenth- or seventeenth-century tools and technology, approximately 100,000 man-hours went into the original project. If, for argument's sake, the labor force consisted of forty men, the operation may have taken a year to complete. And, as the current dig continues, the original design may turn out to be far bigger than that.

Golder's work also indirectly led to one of Triton's most dramatic discoveries. It was during a piezometer test (used to determine the flow and pressure of water) in a hole labeled Borehole 10-X, 180 feet northeast of the Money Pit. And it was a hole in which Blankenship, six years later, would come within a few seconds of terminating his search.

CHAPTER SIXTEEN

Is There a Treasure?

DESPITE THE MANY PUZZLING ANOMALIES THAT HAVE BEEN found on and beneath Oak Island, particularly since the arrival of Triton with its systematic analysis of recovered artifacts, there are still those who doubt that the underground workings are man-made, and even some who suspect that Triton and its predecessors may be victims of an ancient hoax.

It has been suggested that the original Money Pit might have been a natural sinkhole caused by an underlying geological fault. According to this line of reasoning, the sinkhole occurred decades or even centuries prior to the Money Pit's discovery, and in the intervening years the surrounding earth slumped into it, taking with it such vegetation as fallen trees. So in 1795 the boys found a depressed area in the ground, which, when excavated, had the appearance of a refilled shaft containing log platforms.

Some support for this argument was accidentally discovered in 1949 at Mader's Cove, five miles south of Oak Island on the shore of Mahone Bay. In 1976 the owner of the property, Dr. G. D. Donaldson, told me that he had hired workers to dig a well, and a spot was selected where the earth was relatively soft. At about two feet down a layer of fieldstone was struck. Then logs of spruce and oak were unearthed at irregular intervals, and some of the wood was charred. The immediate suspicion was that another Money Pit had been found. Researchers from Dalhousie University in Halifax rushed out to Mader's Cove to take part in the excavation and to examine the material. The hole was dug to eighty-five feet, at which point fresh water started seeping in.

Donaldson said the project was abandoned when the experts concluded that the pit "was nothing more than a natural sinkhole that had occurred hundreds or even thousands of years earlier." Over those centuries the original hole, which may have been more than one hundred feet deep, had been gradually refilled with washed-in earth. And at various periods the surrounding trees, some of them killed by lightning or forest fires, had fallen into the pit.

Geologically, a similar sinkhole could have occurred on Oak Island. Some people think the so-called Cave-in Pit, for example, may have been just such a case. Others believe that it was an airshaft dug by the original depositors when driving their flood tunnel to Smith's Cove. Perhaps both explanations are wrong. The collapse may have been simply the delayed result of the ground under the pit being undermined by a section of tunnels dug by searchers near that area in the 1860s.

But any theory that seeks to explain the Money Pit as a sinkhole is untenable. For that would mean that the accounts of the wooden platforms embedded into the clay walls and evenly spaced every ten feet were either gross exaggerations or outright lies. The same assumption would have to be made for the accounts of pick marks found in the walls of the pit, as well as the putty, charcoal, coconut fiber, and the inscribed rock discovered at ninety feet. One would have to assume that two of the discoverers, Smith and Vaughan, as well as Lynds and others in 1803–04 group, took part on the next search of 1849 knowing full well that the earlier "evidence" was inflated or nonexistent.

It is a significant point that from 1795 to the present day there has always been an overlapping of investors and searchers from one group to the next, each of them interviewing those who preceded them. So the idea of successive treasure hunters being lured into the search by exaggerated "discoveries" hardly seems possible. Similarly, any suggestion that those three boys or their immediate successors launched a two-hundred-year-old hoax is equally ridiculous, even without the evidence of Triton's deep borehole discoveries.

As for the origin of the flood tunnels, it has occasionally been proposed that they are natural water-bearing fissures running through the soluble anhydrite and limestone known to exist anywhere from 150 to over 200 feet down in the Money Pit area. This would be geologically possible under certain conditions. But it doesn't explain the flooding that was encountered at about 100 feet in the Money Pit when the surrounding soil was all hard, unworked clay. Nor does it explain the drainage system that was found at Smith's Cove in 1850 and re-examined since that time, or the stone-walled tunnel that entered the Money Pit at 111 feet.

The best guess, and one frequently advanced by geologists, is that the flooding is due to a combination of natural and man-made systems. That is, the tunnels from the sea were artificially designed, but once the seawater was channeled into the east end of the island, it may have created other watercourses through gravel fills and soluble bedrock. Moreover, the various tunnels dug by searchers over the years have undoubtedly added new branches to these underground streams above bedrock.

Given all the evidence, it is safe to say that it was the ingenuity and labor of men, not nature, that constructed the Money Pit, the Smith's Cove drains, and other works known to exist on the island.

One thing that Oak Island cynics have never been able to explain is the discovery of huge quantities of coconut fiber beneath the beach at Smith's Cove. It is still being found today.

There have been suggestions in the past that the material is something other than coconut fiber. In 1937 the Botanical Museum of Harvard examined a sample and suspected that it was "manila hemp fibers" that may have come from "the partially disintegrated remains of some ship's cables or hawsers." But considering the amount that was found, this is most unlikely. In the early 1940s Erwin Hamilton theorized that it was hemlock bark, which may have been dumped on the shore by either the original depositors or the 1803–04 search group after they had stripped the logs that were used for cribbing. The problem with this suggestion is that hemlock bark would deteriorate rapidly in salt water, and also that the fiber is found in short pieces of six inches or less; hardly the way in which someone would debark a tree.

In point of fact, there should be no doubt the material is coconut fiber. As already noted, it was analyzed and declared as such by the Smithsonian Institution in 1916 and 1930, with their conclusion supported by Canadian botanists in more recent years.

There is no way to explain its presence on the island other than that it was brought by ship from some tropical locale. One Oak Island debunker, in an article in the *Atlantic Advocate* magazine of October 1965, claimed that the fiber could have drifted north from the Caribbean via the Gulf Stream and been deposited by storms on the shores of Smith's Cove. But the article fails to note that the Gulf Stream cuts to the east a good three hundred miles south of Nova Scotia. More important, we are given no explanation as to why one island out of some 350 in Mahone Bay (not to mention the province's hundreds of miles of southern coastline) is the only known beneficiary of this freak of nature.

Actually, there are reports of coconut fiber having been found on the shores of Sable Island, two hundred miles east of Oak Island. This is not surprising, since Sable Island is the site of some 250 shipwrecks, and, as stated earlier, the fiber was often carried aboard as dunnage to protect cargo. But any suggestion that a similar dunnage-laden ship was long ago wrecked in Smith's Cove still doesn't explain the rest of the stone drainage system or how the coconut fiber found its way into the Money Pit.

Among the island's other mysterious features are the stone triangle and the drilled rocks. There is no way to prove that the triangle was laid out by the original depositors, but no other explanation makes much sense. The record shows that it was first seen by Blair, Welling, and William Chappell in 1897. None of them had previously heard of its existence, even though they interviewed members of search groups from 1850 on, and those people had in turn interviewed the searchers before them.

Since the triangle's medial line pointed toward the Money Pit, some have speculated that it may have been put there by an early search group after they abandoned their attempt, and that it was meant as a guide to relocating the Money Pit at some future date. But then why place it so far from the pit? Why would it have to be laid out exactly on a true-north line? And why not simply plant stakes or other markers directly on or beside the pit?

Another guess is that the triangle was put down as a reference point by Charles Morris when he first surveyed the island and divided it into thirty-two lots in 1762. The fact that it pointed to the yet undiscovered Money Pit would then have to be considered an amazing coincidence. The parallel lot lines run approximately 30 degrees east of true north. But they evidently do so because that was the most logical way to divide the island into equal four-acre tracts, each with its own water frontage. Morris or any other surveyor could have easily ascertained that without needing to know where true north lay.

Charles Roper, who worked with Hedden in 1937 to establish the still unexplained relationship between the Mar Del map and the triangle, was a surveyor for most of his life. He is certain that the triangle was laid down by whoever built the Money Pit, and has assured me that he never heard of anything like it being used for surveying purposes. This opinion is shared by other Nova Scotian surveyors who examined the triangle and tried to fathom its purpose.

Then there are the drilled rocks—the two that Hedden found, and others discovered by Blankenship. Here again, no conclusive proof exists that they were a part of the original work, although most investigators believe they were. Contemporary surveyors discount the possibility that they were used by early Nova Scotian surveyors as markers or as foundations for sight-line poles. Why go to the trouble of hand-drilling a hole in granite when you could get someone to hold the pole or else drive the pole into the ground?

Another possibility is that the holes were drilled by early farmers on the island. In eighteenth-century New England rocks were sometimes split by using an auger to drill a hole into which a wooden plug was tightly inserted. Water was poured over the plug, and, with luck, the plug would expand enough to crack the rock apart, usually leaving two flat surfaces. This method was used to break boulders that were too large to haul off a field or where the flat surfaces were required for construction purposes, such as barn or house foundations. This might suggest that the drilled rocks found on Oak Island had been bored by early settlers (most of whom were New Englanders) in order to split them; the water-dampened plug hadn't worked, and the rocks were left lying where they were found, the wood by then having rotted away. Of course, there too, the builders of the Money Pit and artificial drains could have drilled the rocks for that same purpose.

In any case, the triangle and the drilled rocks are real and cannot be dismissed as a hoax or practical joke left behind by members of earlier search groups. They are too elaborate and subtle for that. However, many of the inscribed boulders that have been found occasionally on the island may be regarded with suspicion. It was common practice among workers with various search groups to amuse themselves by carving their initials or even cryptic dates and names on rock surfaces.

For instance, Amos Nauss recalled that during Hedden's time there was a large flat rock on the island on which someone had carved "Capt Kidd 1671." Nauss said that at the end of the Hamilton expedition in 1943, "I took the rock over to the South Shore Cove and buried it under the bank near a tree, thinking that the next guy that came along looking for the treasure would go crazy when he found it." (Apparently it still awaits discovery by some unsuspecting searcher.)

Oak Island's false clues haven't been limited to pirate messages carved on stone. There are several instances of workers salting shafts with artifacts in order to temporarily excite their fellow searchers. According to Nauss, "Some of those guys used to bring stuff like old chains and broadaxes down into the pit where they were working and would send it up in the buckets. They'd always make sure that guys like Hedden and Hamilton were around to see it come up. It would stir up a little commotion every time."

But such mischief occasionally served a more practical purpose. Early search operations sometimes employed as many as sixty local men to help with the digging, and, when the fishing was bad, this was about the only other available work in the area. The treasure hunt also provided additional income for local merchants who supplied the operators with food, lumber, and digging equipment. Consequently, it's rumored that on more than one occasion a company would "accidentally" strike something of interest just about the time that its backers were becoming discouraged and preparing to give up the search. The new discovery would then keep operations going for a bit longer.

For example, one version of the discovery of the three links of gold chain brought up on the end of a drill from the Money Pit in 1849 is that one of the men operating the auger overheard a director of the Truro Company state that if nothing significant was found by the end of the week, the company would be pulling out. The next day the gold links appeared on the drill bit. But in all the excitement no one noticed that the driller's watch chain was exactly three links shorter.

In other instances, earlier searchers may have had their hopes raised not by hoaxes but by their own false assumptions. During the 1849 and 1897 drilling programs the drillers said they felt the bit "going through metal in pieces." Since none of this material (thought to be coins) was ever brought up, we are left with only the faith these drillers had in their ability to distinguish between loose metal and gravel. Could these drillers also have been sure of the difference between the feel of a "metal plate" and an extremely hard rock? And could they have been sure that the wood they brought up with their augers was original rather than timber from an earlier group's shaft?

In fact, only Triton's drilling has ever brought any metal to the surface. And it, together with the wood they've recovered, has come from depths and parts of the island where no previous search work was ever done. That fact, supported by scientific analysis of the samples, conclusively establishes that the project is by no means a natural phenomenon, hoax, or mere wishful thinking on the part of its investigators.

Yet if there's ample evidence that the project is real and ingeniously designed, what proof is there that it was built for the purpose of concealing treasure? So far this question can be answered only by deductive reasoning, and a treasure cache is the most logical explanation. Nonetheless, a few other possibilities have been advanced.

Some have speculated that the workings were either underground living quarters built by a Micmac Indian band, or else a mining operation dating back to the original French colonists. But both these theories may be quickly discarded. Micmac history has been well researched by anthropologists, and there isn't the slightest indication of their having the ability or the reason to attempt such a project. As for a mine, the island contains no minerals of value.

Nevertheless, one current investigator, David Hanson of Santa Clara, California, is convinced the island was originally a mine site. "Without question, I think the workings are an abandoned gold mine worked in 1577 and 1578 by as many as two hundred Cornish tin miners," the sixty-one-year-old oil and gas wildcatter told me in January 1988. Hanson has spent years investigating Elizabethan history and the voyages of Martin Frobisher and Francis Drake in the latter part of the sixteenth century. Through his research and "by playing around with the early charts of Frobisher in a rather allegorical way" he believes that Frobisher landed on Oak Island by happenstance in 1575 and discovered what he believed was gold. "But in fact," says Hanson, "it was pyrite [or fool's gold, which does exist on the island] that he brought back."

According to Hanson's theory, Frobisher and his backers soon realized this, but in order to finance further exploratory voyages they conned the Elizabethan Crown into believing they had found gold in the New World. Under the direction of Thomas Bushell (a sixteenth-century mining engineer who has been linked to Francis Bacon's possible connection to Oak Island) the Cornish miners were sent to Nova Scotia, where they spent two years tunneling beneath the island and the surrounding ocean, bringing back thirty-six shiploads of unrefined pyrite ore. When the fraud was discovered, says Hanson, it was of such immense proportions that all direct records of it were destroyed.

Hanson even goes so far as to speculate that this crooked mining venture may later have been used to serve another, more incredible, purpose—to store the original manuscripts of the plays and sonnets attributed to William Shakespeare. As outlined earlier in this book, that extraordinary suggestion is not a new one. However, Hanson believes it was not Francis Bacon but rather Edward de Vere, the seventeenth Earl of Oxford, who penned that great body of literature. De Vere, he says, was one of the backers of Frobisher's voyages and was a participant in the mining scam. Hanson offers detailed circumstantial evidence to make a case for de Vere's authorship of the Shakespearean works, and then theorizes that the manuscripts were later hidden in the abandoned pyrite shafts of Oak Island, along with Plantagenet plate and even the interred bones of the Earl of Oxford himself.

Hanson, who was a close friend of Bob Dunfield, the 1965–66 Oak Island explorer, tried to get the Triton group interested in his theory in 1983. But, he says, "Tobias was then involved with litigation [over ownership of Oak Island] so we weren't able to negotiate a joint venture agreement." Hanson today admits that his answer "is all theory and speculation. But, based on what I've read and studied, it seems right. And it makes a lot more sense than those preposterous pirate theories."

In 1970 another theorist, Edward Parker of Philadelphia, suggested that the Money Pit was designed as an "an ancient maritime water purification system used to replenish the water casks of ships." Basically, his idea was that seawater would flow to the bottom of the Money Pit from Smith's Cove and then rise to sea level (about thirty feet from the top of the pit) through a series of filters consisting of loose metal, layers of wood, coconut fiber, and charcoal. At that point, according to his theory, the water would be potable. Apart from the fact that desalinated water couldn't be produced that way, digging freshwater wells on the island (as the early settlers did) or else taking it from streams and rivers on the nearby mainland would have been a good deal easier.

A more reasonable non-treasure theory is that the workings comprise an ancient dry dock, secretly built by the French government while they were in control of Acadia in the late seventeenth century. This hypothesis was formulated some years ago by George Bates, a Halifax surveyor and cartographer. His first involvement with Oak Island was in 1937, when, as a young apprentice to Charles Roper, he helped check the measurements between the drilled rocks and the stone triangle. Ever since, he says, "I had always asked myself, 'If it's not treasure down there, what else could it be?' Then one day it hit me—the first shipyard in North America, maybe a dry dock or ship-repair base."

The shipyard, according to Bates, consisted of a large dry dock made of wood and earth at Smith's Cove. Once a vessel entered it, the seaward end of the dock would be closed and a floodgate was opened to allow the water within the dock to flow down a tunnel and into a chamber (the Money Pit). The ship was now high and dry and could be replanked, caulked, or whatever was needed (with a lot of coconut fiber dunnage in the hold being removed in the process). As soon as the work was done, the seaward gate was reopened and the ship refloated.

But in order to repeat the process for the next damaged vessel, the chamber beneath the "Money Pit" first had to be emptied. Here Bates believes that the pit was in fact a large pumping shaft operated by either a windlass or windmill power from the surface. The water would be pumped up and allowed to run downhill toward the south shore. The oak platforms found every ten feet in the Money Pit, he suggests, were actually the horizontal support structure for the pump casing.

The theory is interesting, but it contains serious flaws. First, there is nothing in recorded French or British Acadian history to suggest that such an elaborate dry dock was ever built. Second, its construction, even if technically possible, would have been very expensive and time-consuming. Surely careening would have been a simpler method. In fact, some of the best careening ground in the world exists near Port Royal in Nova Scotia's Bay of Fundy, where tides (which have as much as a fifty-foot rise and fall at the head of the bay) can easily leave any ship high and dry for six hours or more. And with enough manpower a sailing vessel could be rolled a short distance on logs to put it out of reach of the next high tide.

Bates's proposal also runs contrary to the fact that whatever was done on Oak Island is one of the best-kept secrets known to man. We can assume that such a project didn't involve something that would have been known to hundreds of sailors or to the large military force that presumably would have built the dry dock.

(Bates was not the first to suspect that Oak Island was a ship-refitting base. In the winter of 1941, while the Adams family were the caretakers on the island, seven heavily armed Canadian Navy Intelligence officers suddenly arrived and insisted on inspecting the Hedden and Chappell shafts. They had received a tip that German U-boats were using the island for a supply and refueling station, a rumor that apparently began when a local fisherman spotted a moose swimming from the mainland to the island and mistook it for a submarine. The searchers, according to Charlotte Adams, spent several hours examining the pits, storehouses, and other parts of the island before satisfying themselves that the underground workings hadn't been converted into a submarine pen.)

Accepting the weight of evidence and logic that Oak Island was designed as a repository for something of great value still leaves the question: Is the treasure still there?

For more than a hundred years there have been rumors that some or all the booty may have been secretly found and removed since 1795. This is an opinion shared by many in the Mahone Bay area, though there are no facts to substantiate such stories. Some of the locals are convinced that the three discoverers of the Money Pit found a small treasure a few feet down and that John Smith then encouraged the later search groups to dig even farther, his motive being to lease his property and sell lumber for the shafts. Others will tell you that the loot was removed by one or another of the nineteenth-century search parties, and that they purposely kept quiet about it in order to avoid paying the compulsory royalty to the Nova Scotia government.

One long-standing legend concerns Anthony Graves, who purchased much of the island after John Smith's death in 1857. Graves built his house at Joudrey's Cove and lived there until he died in 1888. Graves is rumored to have occasionally purchased supplies on the mainland with Spanish coins of gold or silver. In 1930 a silver Spanish coin dated 1785 was found near the foundation of his house. Another coin, a Spanish *maravedi* said to be dated 1598, was supposedly found in 1965 near Joudrey's Cove, though the coin's authenticity is suspect.

The Graves story would seem to be nothing more than gossip, since his own family wasn't aware of it. Graves's granddaughter, Florence Eisenhauer, told Mel Chappell in 1955 that she hadn't heard of any discovery of treasure by her grandfather. But she did say that her aunt, Sophia Sellers (Graves's eldest daughter) "believed that if any treasure were buried on Oak Island, it was carried away, because she remembered a vessel coming into the cove one evening and it disappeared or departed before morning, and there were marks in the sand on the shore like a barrel having been rolled out."

Edward Vaughan of Western Shore is another whose name often comes up in local speculation about who made off with the island's treasure. His father, George (a grandson of Anthony Vaughan), is rumored to have found a chest on the island in the late 1930s. He died in 1941, and some say he left one of his two sons, Edward, an inheritance consisting of several gold ingots. Edward disappeared shortly thereafter, leaving his wife and children behind. He surfaced in Ontario many years later and died in 1968.

If Vaughan or anybody else did find something on the island, Fred Nolan, the current owner of several Oak Island lots, would not be surprised. He is certain no less than eleven separate caches have been carted away "in the past eighty years or so." He bases that claim on his discovery in recent years of several previously dug holes, none of them more than four feet deep, and most of them in the island's swamp area.

Nolan believes that there are "many more treasure locations" still to be discovered on the island.

An interesting counterpoint to Nolan's unsubstantiated claim is an equally unprovable charge by competing treasure hunter Dan Blankenship, who recently told me, "Nolan has found some treasure on his lots; I'm sure of it. But he's keeping it a secret." Nolan laughs off the charge as "an example of Dan's paranoia."

Stories of people with Spanish coins, unaccountable inheritances, or leaving mysterious holes in the ground make for fun tavern gossip, but they offer no proof that a single coin of Oak Island's treasure has been removed. Until such evidence is forthcoming, it's safe to assume that any treasure left unclaimed by the depositors is still there.

But that, of course, raises the more relevant question of whether the treasure was ever reclaimed by those who put it there. Why would someone have gone to all that trouble to bury something and yet not have come back to retrieve it? If in fact the treasure is still there, we can assume the depositors died before they could return to the island or before they could pass on the secret to someone else.

Obviously, searchers who have spent huge sums and many years on Oak Island have had reason to believe there was gold at the end of the rainbow. The basic argument used to support this belief is that there is not, and apparently never was, any indication to the contrary. That is, there has been no physical evidence that the treasure was removed prior to the Money Pit's discovery in 1795.

Some investigators believe that access to the treasure was through the Money Pit. Others theorize that the pit was intended to be entered via a secret tunnel from some other part of the island. Still other state that the treasure was never in the Money Pit but in chambers at the ends of tunnels that radiated out from the pit. But whichever theory is accepted, the depositor would have had either to open the Money Pit or dig a hole somewhere else to reclaim his wealth. Had he done this, so the argument goes, why would he have refilled the pit or any other access shaft?

According to the records, all that was found in 1795 was

the depression indicating the location of the Money Pit. That same year Smith and McGinnis took up farming on the island, and within a couple of decades many others followed them. If any of the settlers on this relatively small island had seen surface evidence of another shaft, it surely would have been remarked upon and investigated, considering the interest aroused by the Money Pit.

Dan Blankenship, like many before him, has thoroughly explored the island looking for signs of an access shaft. He insists that the treasure is still there, "because I haven't seen any physical evidence of anything having been taken out of the ground. And I believe that if they took anything out, they wouldn't have been careful about concealing it. Why should you cover up your tracks once you've taken something out?"

Lavern Johnson, a former searcher and continuing investigator, agrees with that argument. "If the depositor had returned and retrieved his cache, he would have left open the recovery shaft and departed in haste. The remains would have been visible to early settlers and searchers, and it would have been examined and explored. There are no reports of anything like that having happened."

Triton's David Tobias is not so certain. Depending on his level of optimism when he's asked to guess, he puts the odds of the treasure still being down there at anywhere from 25 to 50 percent. But, he added, "our chances are nine out of ten of finding something of significant archaeological and historical value" in terms of establishing who built the project and why.

Another factor to consider is that the project dates back to well over a hundred years prior to the discovery of the Money Pit. Suppose the depositor had returned within a few years, dug a small access shaft that led to the treasure vault or entrance tunnel, removed the treasure, and sailed off. The shaft could have been almost anywhere on the island and needn't have been more than ten or twenty feet deep if the tunnel that led to it sloped upward from the Money Pit. After more than a century of natural erosion, the access shaft could have filled itself in and been completely covered by the island's vegetation.

Alternatively, what if the repository was intended to be

used more than once? The builder may have retrieved his original cache, carefully refilled and concealed the entrance, but then for some reason never came back to reuse it.

For that matter, who's to say the depositor didn't have a weird sense of humor that prompted him to refill the access shaft (a relatively quick and easy task) and leave for good, knowing that perhaps he might be responsible for someday totally befuddling anyone who tried to understand what had happened on Oak Island? I advance this possibility only half-seriously; but were it true, the depositor's joke has obviously exceeded his wildest expectations.

In any case, the most enticing aspect of Oak Island is the proven existence of the deep underground workings. Even if the depositors did return for their wealth, they left behind an enigma. And from an archaeological point of view, the value of the solution could be far more important than chests of gold and silver. If Triton's current dig is successful, the searchers will be presented with a secret chapter from history that has gone unrecorded for hundreds of years. The solution, says Tobias, "may even turn out to be as exciting as the discovery of King Tut's tomb or the city of Troy."

And if the treasure is still beneath the island, Tobias predicts that it will be "something of incredible value; maybe hundreds of millions, maybe billions of dollars."

CHAPTER SEVENTEEN

Borehole 10-X

It BEGAN QUITE INNOCUOUSLY IN THE SUMMER OF 1970 AS just another water-flow test hole, and was designated on the grid map as Borehole 10-X by the Golder geophysicists working for Triton. But it would become the deepest, most controversial, and, for Dan Blankenship, most dangerous shaft ever sunk beneath Oak Island.

Borehole 10-X is 180 feet northeast of the Money Pit and the same distance away from the center of the Cave-in Pit. Oddly enough, it falls precisely on the line of the two drilled rocks found by Gilbert Hedden in 1937. This had nothing to do with deciding its location, though considering what was found in 10-X, there may well be a connection within the scheme of the original Oak Island project.

The hole was initially bored for Triton by the Bowmaster Drilling Company with a six-inch-diameter rotary drill. At 140 feet in the hard glacial till, the drill dropped into a five-foot cavity. A similar void was encountered 20 feet later. Bedrock was reached at 180 feet, and at 230 feet the drill hit another five-foot cavity.

The drill was pulled out, steel casing inserted, and high-pressure air was injected to blow up any loose material. From a depth of 165 feet, two handfuls of thin metal were blown to the surface. When it came up, the metal was soft and the color of lead. But within minutes it began oxidizing and became brittle, indicating that it had been starved for oxygen for a long period. Pieces of wire, chain, and angular sections of steel were also later blown out from approximately the same depth.

Samples were sent to be analyzed by the Steel Company of Canada. (Stelco). A. B. Dove, Stelco's senior development metallurgist, reported that it was a low-carbon type of steel (perhaps Swedish) that "in all probability was produced prior to 1750."

The discovery of the metal and cavities in a virgin area where no previous searchers had ever dug or drilled prompted Triton to ream the hole large enough to permit cameras and searchers to be lowered into it. Borehole 10-X thus became a full-fledged shaft, the deepest one ever put down on the island.

Statesman Mining Co. of Aspen, Colorado, had a piece of equipment that seemed perfect for the job. It was a cross between a hydraulic clamshell digger and a drill capable of scooping out a twenty-five-inch-diameter hole. Blankenship and Tobias flew out to California to meet with representatives of the company, and a contract was signed. (One of the owners of Statesman was film actor John Wayne. There was some talk at the time of getting him to do a documentary on Oak Island, but nothing came of it.)

The machine arrived in October 1970 and began reboring 10-X. At a depth of forty-five feet it brought up more of the metal that had been found earlier. But the drillers soon ran into difficulties getting through boulders, and by the end of the year they were only eighty-five feet down. So the machine was pulled off the job.

That winter Blankenship called up Parker Kennedy, a professional well driller from Halifax. Kennedy, whom Dan describes as "the best damn driller I've ever had on the island," agreed to come out that spring to finish the hole with a large Bucyrus-Erie churn drill. The shaft was eventually completed, rebored to twenty-seven inches in diameter. A quarter-inch-thick steel casing was put down to bedrock at 180 feet, with the rest of the hole left uncased to 235 feet.

While it was being drilled, a large quantity of spruce was brought up from 167 feet. The wood, to everyone's bewilderment, was carbon-dated to the future date of A.D. 3005. It was later found that this impossible reading was due to the wood having at one time been coated with pitchblende, which centuries ago was often used as a preserving agent on ships' hulls and mine-shaft supports. (Pitchblende is a uranium ore and would render the dating process meaningless by affecting the radioactive carbon-14 content of the wood.) Some wood and metal came up from about 140 feet, and pieces of wire and broken chain were also brought up from between 155 and 165 feet. The chain was analyzed by Stelco and found to be hand-forged prior to 1750.

The drill also extracted chunks of cement from the 165-foot level. It was later analyzed by W. S. Weaver, manager of research and quality control for Canada Cement Lafarge Ltd. In his report Weaver stated, "It is likely that these materials reflect human activity involving crude lime. . . . Furthermore, the presence of rust [on some of the samples] indicates contact with a man-made iron object."

In addition, bits of seashells, glass, and bird bones—apparently from the beach area—were often churned up by Kennedy's drill. This debris and the fact that seawater filled the shaft to forty-four feet from its top (which is sea level on that part of the island) convinced Blankenship that the cavities in Borehole 10-X were connected to one or more flood tunnels. Several pumping holes were sunk around the shaft in an attempt to drain it, but the water, entering at a rate of about 500 gallons per minute, could only be lowered to about the 100 foot level.

Triton now had more than enough evidence to proceed with the next stage of exploring this promising hole. The first visual investigation of 10-X was made in August 1971 when an underwater television camera was lowered into its depths. No one was quite prepared for the pictures it would send back.

Blankenship was sitting in a nearby shed watching the

closed-circuit monitor as the camera reached the chamber at 230 feet. One of the first things he saw was what appeared to be a half-clenched hand still covered in flesh and severed (probably by the drill) at the wrist. Dan, disbelieving his eyes, called Parker Kennedy, Dan Henskee, and another worker in one at a time and asked them what they saw. Each stated it was a human hand. It hung suspended in the water and remained in range of the camera lens for several minutes before the camera accidentally touched it and knocked it out of sight.

Recalling the incident many years later, Kennedy told me: "I was outside and Dan called me in. He said, 'My God, Parker, there's a hand down there; I want you to see it.' Of course, he was excited, but I wasn't; I never did get that excited about the island. But nevertheless, I seen the hand, like it was just hanging there and waving. And we all had the same impression; it was a hand when we seen it." Kennedy, who'd always been skeptical about the Oak Island treasure hunt, also acknowledged that, as a professional driller, he was impressed by the earlier findings. "When I brought up those pieces of metal and chain, I knew there was something down there that shouldn't have been. It was down there all right. How it got there, I don't know; but it sure as hell was down there."

A later probe with the camera picked up what seemed to be three chests (one with a clearly visible handle) and several large wooden logs or beams on the bottom toward one end of the cavity. A pickax and several planks with spikes or dowels protruding from them also came on the screen. And then suddenly the camera focused on what appeared to be a human body, complete with flesh and hair, slumped against a wall of the chamber.

Photographs were taken of all these findings. But most of them lack clarity and are inconclusive. The video camera's recording system was inoperative, and the photos were shot with a flash camera directly off the monitor screen, lending them a quality not unlike trash-tabloid pictures of UFOs.

The photo of the apparent corpse was later studied by a Montreal physiologist who reported: "This is the outline of a body. Jaw and mouth very realistic; perhaps too much so. No teeth in evidence. Suggests body in a sitting position origi-nally, then toppled over." And a leading Halifax pathologist agreed that it would be possible for human flesh to be pre-served "over a long period of time" if it were buried in a saline and airless environment under the island; in effect, pickled in brine.

The next step was to physically explore Borehole 10-X. Triton's pump was capable of handling 450 gallons per min-ute, enough to temporarily lower the water level, but only to 100 feet. So Atlantic Divers Ltd. of Brooklyn, Nova Scotia, was hired to send professional divers into the bottom of the pit.

The first dive was made by Phil Irwin. Wearing a wet suit and a helmet through which he received air from a surface compressor, he was lowered by cable into 10-X. At 170 feet Irwin radioed up that the water was starting to get murky. As he passed 180 feet (where the steel casing ended) he reported a current of water so strong that it was twisting the helmet on his head. He went lower, but the visibility was now so bad that he couldn't see his hand in front of his face.

He was hauled out and a check was made of Smith's Cove. In one section the water had been muddied up. "We had been doing that with our pumping," said Blankenship. "There's no question that we had stumbled on one of the flood tunnels." He theorized that the tunnel passed by 10-X above bedrock and that the drilling had rerouted the flow to down below the casing.

A bulldozer was used to pile tons of clay on the suspected tunnel entrance, and a week later Irwin and other divers made separate descents into 10-X. This time there was no rush of water below 180 feet. At the bottom of the hole, the divers were suspended in a large cavern which they said was about seven feet high. But even with strong underwater lights its lateral extent couldn't be seen through the murky water. Be-cause of the shaft's confined space, the divers' shoulders were rubbing against the soluble anhydrite rock walls, and this im-mediately clouded the water, turning it a milky color. They groped around the bottom but found nothing other than loose stone.

Later that year and again in 1972, Blankenship himself made several dives to the bottom. But he too encountered impossible visibility and found nothing worth bringing to the surface. "The chamber is really big," says Blankenship. "You go down into it, and you're just hanging from a cable like a pendulum in this big void. But the things I'd like to get at are too far away; it's too dangerous to move away from the shaft opening."

He discovered in subsequent dives that the pumping had caused considerable erosion, and the original cavity had become a large bottle-shaped cavern about fifteen feet high. Also, the bottom was filled with additional rubble that hadn't been there before, indicating that the chamber was gradually caving in. So further diving was ruled out as too risky.

The inconclusive results of the underwater photography and diving led to a minor schism in the Triton camp. Because of its dramatic appeal, that particular phase of the operation elicited sensationalistic media publicity. While Blankenship and a few others maintained at the time that the TV pictures of the hand and other items were what they appeared to be, some within Triton weren't so sure. Tobias, for one, has always downplayed the pictures. "I never put much stock in them," he told me. "For one thing, we had no idea of the scale" of the objects. "They could have been anything." (His skepticism eventually rubbed off on Blankenship, who, in a 1986 letter to Triton shareholders, said, "Your eyes can play tricks on you underwater, so we now minimize the importance of those photos. The same can be said of the results of our underwater diving.")

Still, there was no disputing the tangible evidence drilled up from 10-X, and Triton wanted to find out where the wood and metal was coming from and how it got there. It was about this time that Bill Parkin, a designer of weapons systems for the Pentagon, joined Triton. He was interested in the scientific possibilities posed by the search, and he began designing and adapting electronic equipment to be used on Oak Island. Among the gadgets he has made are one for measuring the speed and direction of flow of underground water, a conductivity meter to measure the salinity, and a hydrophone unit to record and measure underwater sound and thereby determine the nature of the ground between the hydrophone and the source of the sound.

But it was Parkin's sonar equipment that particularly interested Blankenship. Encased in a four-foot tube, it could detect the presence of cavities outside of steel-encased holes. It was used extensively in 10-X and located many possible voids above bedrock, the largest ones appearing to be east of the shaft and ending several feet away from the casing.

Triton decided to explore those areas to determine whether the cavities were natural or man-made. But first a pump had to be found that, working in tandem with the existing one, could get the water level down to 180 feet. A pump with a capacity of over 1,000 gallons per minute was eventually purchased in 1975, and the exploration of 10-X resumed the following summer.

In the meantime, Blankenship had returned to his drilling program on other parts of the island. On the basis of drilled rocks and other surface markers, Dan put down a series of small boreholes several hundred feet north of the Money Pit in 1973. Core samples from a few of the holes yielded wood from almost 100 feet down. At one spot, 660 feet north-north-east of the Money Pit, a two-inch piece of wire came up from 110 feet underground. The drill also bit into what Dan was sure was a solid metal plate slightly lower down. The wire, similar to the pieces that had been retrieved from 10-X, was analyzed by Stelco as "a corroded low-carbon material which has been drawn by cold workings, probably in the 1500s to 1800s."

Triton decided to put a cribbed 12-by-6½-foot pit (known as the Triton shaft) down in that spot. It was started in October 1973 and finished the following spring, all of it excavated by hand. Digging through the firm clay was difficult, and large boulders had to be drilled and blasted apart. At about 100 feet, the amount of fresh groundwater seeping from above became unmanageable and the project was abandoned. The source of the wire and the metal plate was never found.

In the summer of 1976, Blankenship did some more drilling in the Money Pit area, again getting samples of wood from between 160 and 190 feet. In August he was preparing to examine the ground behind the casing of Borehole 10-X above bedrock. Two pumps capable of drawing up to two million gallons a day were hooked to the bottom of nearby pumping holes. They ran continuously for almost a week trying to get the water below 180 feet in 10-X. Bill Parkin was up from Boston running various tests in the hole. One interesting discovery was that the water being pumped out had a low salinity count, indicating that the water flowing into the area beneath 10-X was more fresh than salt. A check of the water levels in other open drill holes and the Triton shaft showed that the pumping of 10-X was apparently lowering the island's entire water table. Yet after several days, as the water level fell the salinity count increased, until it was almost the same as the surrounding bay.

Just about the time the Triton workers succeeded in holding the water to below 160 feet, the drive shaft on the large pump snapped. Within two days the level was again near the surface of the pit, and the descent into 10-X was put off for a month while the pump was repaired.

In late September the first of many eight-inch-diameter observation holes was cut through the casing with an acetylene torch. Only shallow natural voids were found, and these were probably caused by the initial drilling. During the next two months Blankenship and his twenty-seven-year-old son David made several more excursions into the shaft looking for evidence of artificial workings behind the casing.

Then one day in mid-November Borehole 10-X ceased to exist.

Blankenship was 145 feet down in 10-X, while at the surface David operated the winch for the cable from which his father was suspended. A headset telephone kept them in constant touch with each other, and (as was done on all their dangerous descents) a tape recorder kept track of everything that occurred. The following incident was recorded on that tape:

Blankenship had just started scooping clay out of the hole he'd cut with his torch. Suddenly there was a deep rumbling in the background, like something heavy thumping against a metal drum. Blankenship felt small pieces of debris falling on his head and shoulders. He realized what was happening, and shouted into the headset: "Bring me up; bring me up! Out, out, out, out!"

David ran the winch at full speed. But the sound of rock against metal got ominously louder, and Dan knew the noise was still well above him. His yelling became more frantic: "Keep bringing me out. Don't stop! Bring me up! It's still over my head. Over my head! Bring me up! Bring me up!"

Blankenship passed the ninety-foot mark and looked down. The casing, designed to withstand thousands of pounds of pressure, was being crushed like an eggshell, and thick wet mud was spewing in from outside. As he continued his ascent, the thumping and crashing increased in volume. But he was now safely above the chaos. And, like a child who'd ventured into an area where he'd been told not to play, he radioed his son, "For God's sake, don't tell your mother, David."

Thirty-five seconds had elapsed between the first warning at 145 feet and the time Blankenship passed the 95-foot level, where the casing gave way. Had it taken five seconds longer he would have been entombed deep in the interior of Oak Island.

The next day Blankenship descended the shaft and found himself standing on firm ground at seventy-three feet. He later drilled through it to ninety-five feet, where the bit met twisted steel, the former casing of 10-X. "There was tremendous pressure down there," he says, "and the break [at ninety-five feet] forced debris upward for twenty-two feet." Blankenship surmised that the collapse was indirectly caused by a man-made flood tunnel that he was sure passed near 10-X at about ninety feet. The continuous pumping of the shaft may have created an artificial fault that finally collapsed downward and into the side of the casing.

Following that incident, 10-X was temporarily abandoned and Blankenship went back to drilling. In 1977 he carried out a hit-and-miss drill program around 10-X and the Money Pit, looking for traces of the flood tunnels and any other under-

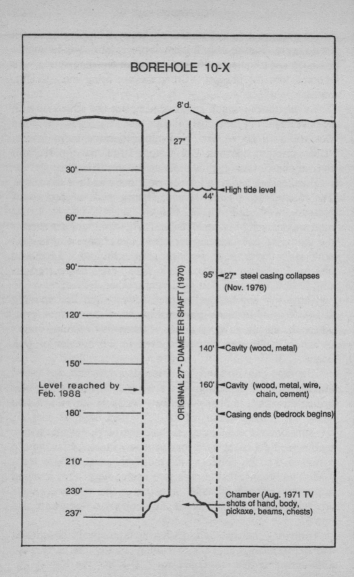

BOREHOLE 10-X

8' d.

27"

30'

High tide level

44'

60'

90'

95' — 27" steel casing collapses (Nov. 1976)

ORIGINAL 27"- DIAMETER SHAFT (1970)

120'

140' — Cavity (wood, metal)

150'

Level reached by Feb. 1988

160' — Cavity (wood, metal, wire, chain, cement)

— Casing ends (bedrock begins)

180'

210'

230'

Chamber (Aug. 1971 TV shots of hand, body, pickaxe, beams, chests)

237'

ground work, but he found nothing of significance. He was determined, however, to find his way back into the bowels of Borehole 10-X.

The next summer Blankenship came up with a novel and relatively inexpensive method to re-excavate 10-X. Four railroad tank cars, each thirty-four feet long and almost eight feet in diameter, were purchased and trucked out to the island. With their ends cut off, these were used as the new casing for Borehole 10-X, providing a lot more digging and exploratory room than the original manhole-sized casing. Moreoever, their half-inch steel shells were twice the thickness of the former casing, and interior cross-bracing was added for additional lateral strength.

Re-digging the hole, however, was slow and tedious work. Essentially, it involved standing the upended tank car over the center of 10-X and then excavating the interior by jackhammer, pick, and shovel, hoisting the fill to the top and dumping it some distance away. As the earth around the circumference of the casing was undermined, the weight of the five-ton tank car would drive it further into the ground. Once the first car was driven down its length, a crane was used to hoist a second one on top of it, the two were welded together, and the scooping process was repeated.

For two summers Blankenship and Henskee, occasionally assisted by hired local labor, continued this backbreaking toil. The project was often interrupted by flooding problems and equipment breakdowns. By August 1980, when they'd reached only 126 feet at a cost of $35,000, Borehole 10-X was again put on hold—this time for almost six years.

This was a severe personal setback for Blankenship. He, more than anyone else, believed that Borehole 10-X could provide the quickest and cheapest route to Oak Island's treasure. But some of the Triton partners, particularly Mel Chappell, felt that the syndicate should be concentrating its time and finances on the Money Pit rather than 10-X.

Chappell had sold his Oak Island property to David Tobias in 1977 for $125,000. However, he remained a Triton director and its third-largest shareholder, with an 18 percent interest (versus 31 percent held by the Tobias family and 19 percent by

Blankenship). Chappell's obsession with the search dated back to 1897, when, as a boy of ten, he had seen his father and Fred Blair drill up the piece of parchment and other evidence from the Money Pit. Ever since then, he believed that a thorough excavation of the Money Pit was the only way the treasure would be recovered.

During the 1970s the gaunt six-foot-three Chappell, whose youthful vigor belied his age, occasionally visited the site from his home in Sydney, Nova Scotia. With amazing clarity and accuracy he would recall specific search attempts made many decades before. He'd then point with his cane to a nondescript piece of ground, noting the exact location of a long-forgotten filled-in shaft or the route of a tunnel dug by some searcher at the turn of the century.

I last met Chappell in August 1978 to interview him for a television documentary on the island. We were standing beside the Money Pit, and he told me that while he had unquestioning respect for Blankenship's dedication to the search, 10-X was "not where we should be digging." He then rapped his cane on the ground and said, "*This* is where father brought up the wood and parchment, and *this* is where the treasure is." As it happened, that was his last visit to the island. On December 21, 1980, at the age of ninety-three, Melbourne Russell Chappell died without finding the treasure he'd spent most of his life pursuing.

Blankenship and Tobias earnestly wanted to solve the mystery before Chappell (or "M.R." as they and his other close friends knew him) passed away. And a major open-pit excavation of the Money Pit area was indeed contemplated in the late 1970s. However, the estimated cost of the project was $2 million, far more than the Triton members were willing to put up. A public share offering in the U.S. was considered, but the enormous underwriting costs and the red tape required to clear such a prospectus through the Securities and Exchange Commission eventually left that plan in limbo.

Moreover, Tobias was then heavily involved with expanding and diversifying his Montreal firm, Jonergin Inc., thus cutting into the time and money he could spend on Oak Island. So in the early 1980s Blankenship had to content himself with a scaled-down operation on a severely limited budget with antiquated and unreliable equipment. Still, it was costing Triton about $30,000 a year ($12,000 of which was Blankenship's subsistence salary) just to maintain its presence on Oak Island. And almost all of it was being financed by Tobias.

One curious discovery during that period occurred in February 1980. It was a particularly cold winter, and the sheltered waters off the island's south side had frozen over. One day Blankenship noticed four large holes that had mysteriously appeared about 700 feet off the South Shore Cove. The holes, spaced approximately 150 feet apart, had apparently been formed by warmer underground water percolating through the ice in those spots. Coincidentally, Blankenship had been pumping shafts the previous few days, thus circulating the water beneath the Money Pit area. Triton later consulted with geologists who concluded there was a link between the Money Pit and the strange ice holes, and they doubted that it was a natural connection.

The holes, which appeared again in the winter of 1987, greatly impressed Tobias. "I never really believed in the existence of a [south shore] flood tunnel until I saw those holes," he said. Several summers ago Tobias went diving in that area, where the water is fourteen to twenty-two feet deep. But he saw only rock and silt on the seabed floor. If there are flood tunnel inlets there, they presumably would be concealed beneath centuries of natural erosion.

In 1985 Tobias sold Jonergin, thus giving him the freedom to manage his family investments and pursue his two favorite hobbies, scuba diving and flying his Beechcraft Bonanza. More importantly, he was now in a position to fully concentrate on seeing the Oak Island treasure hunt to its conclusion.

However, a 1986 feasibility study (which itself cost about $15,000 to prepare) indicated that it could cost up to $8 million to seal off the water and thoroughly explore the Money Pit below bedrock. This was four times the estimate of ten years earlier (though for a much bigger hole), and the Triton partners (of which there were now forty-nine) had already poured $1,250,000 into the aptly named Money Pit. The project, they decided, would have to be financed from outside through either a private placement or public offering of shares.

That decision prompted Blankenship to make a renewed appeal to the Triton syndicate to allow him to return to his pet project—Borehole 10-X. His urgency to finish the hole was predicated on two things: his conviction that a major find awaited him in 10-X, and the fact that the injection of outside capital would water down his and everyone else's share of the treasure. In a March 1986 letter to Triton shareholders, Blankenship said he wanted to make "one final effort" to complete 10-X under the present Triton setup. To go to the market for $8 million, he noted, would mean "all of our shares will be greatly diluted proportionally."

In his letter Blankenship explained that "there are two main depths [in 10-X] that we are interested in. The one at 140 to 145 feet, and the one from 150 to 165 feet." He added that the bottom void at 235 feet had now been "discounted by the use of sonar profiling which indicates a large cavity there, but without an access tunnel leading into it, which leads us to assume it must be natural."

Blankenship's lobbying paid off. He was given the go-ahead and a $70,000 budget (half of it from Tobias) to continue the hole that he'd left at 126 feet six years earlier. But again the work was backbreaking and the initial results discouraging.

For the next eighteen months Blankenship and Henskee, sometimes aided by hourly-paid laborers, drove the tank cars deeper, eventually replacing them with a ten-inch-thick casing of reinforced concrete. The job was tedious and at times dangerous. Several times Blankenship nearly suffocated at the bottom of the shaft when the surface compressor supplying fresh air cut out.

I was on the island in June 1987 when the hole was at 150 feet. From the surface platform it was like looking down a rust-streaked fifteen-story elevator shaft. The roar of the air compressor, electrical generator, drum-winch hoist, and turbine pump that spewed 600 gallons of water per minute from an adjacent pumping shaft created an ear-splitting din that made conversation impossible. But that was nothing compared to the racket at the bottom, where Henskee was using a pneumatic hammer to break up a stubborn boulder inside the eight-foot cylinder.

Riding inside the excavation bucket, Blankenship was winched to the top of the pit. A grin broke across his mud-caked face. "We're getting close," he shouted to me, referring to the level at which he hoped to find a man-made chamber and maybe even a tunnel leading to the Money Pit. It was stated with his typical enthusiastic optimism. I noticed a nasty red welt across his upper chest and arm. When I asked him about it he shrugged and said that he'd accidentally burned himself with an arc-welding torch. That insouciant shrug was also typical of the man.

Later that evening, as we sipped pre-dinner martinis in a restaurant overlooking Chester harbor, Blankenship explained that Borehole 10-X could turn out to be an inexpensive back door to the treasure. "Who knows? We might get down there and find a tunnel, and it may be a shortcut to solving the mystery." Yet Blankenship is as much a pragmatist as he is an optimist. "We've made lots of trial-and-error mistakes, and we've struck out too many times on Oak Island," he acknowledged. "But often it was because we didn't have the money in place when and where we needed it. So if we're wrong about 10-X, then we'll get the money and go after [the treasure] through the Money Pit."

Outside, in the crimson hues of a midsummer sunset, a fleet of schooners and sloops bobbed silently on their harbor moorings. I asked Dan a question I'd posed several times during the seventeen years I had known him. What drives a man to dedicate his life in pursuit of a dream that has brought only misery and failure to all who preceded him?

Blankenship paused, then reached into his mind to paraphrase a quotation from the television evangelist and author Robert Schuller: "When faced with a mountain, I will not quit. I'll keep on striving until I climb over, tunnel underneath . . . or simply stay and turn the mountain into a gold mine." The Oak Island veteran smiled self-consciously at the aptness of the metaphor.

As we toasted Dan's mountain, it struck me that a genuine treasure hunter was more than just a man committed to a quest; he was a man manacled to an obsession.

Borehole 10-X, however, was one mountain that was reluctant to give up its gold. Two months later, after reaching 167 feet, the hole was again abandoned while Blankenship puzzled over why he hadn't yet found anything conclusive. The anticipated man-made cavities at 140 and 160 feet were apparently only pockets of loose sand blown away by the original churn drilling, and the still-unexplained metal and wood may have been washed elsewhere by years of pumping.

As far as Tobias was concerned, that was the end of 10-X. The project had consumed almost $300,000 by fits and starts over seventeen years, and he was prepared to write it off and concentrate on the 1988 Big Dig. In November 1987, as we sat in the Triton corporate offices in Montreal's fashionable Westmount Square, Tobias vigorously rapped the ashes from his pipe into a large ceramic ashtray. "We've been frigging around with 10-X, Smith's Cove, this hole and that hole far too long," he said. "We need to approach this thing as a whole, and that's exactly what we'll be doing as soon as we put the financing together." On the floor beside his desk and in the outer office were stacks of documents, photographs, drawings, and engineering plans. Tobias waved his hand toward the piles. "In there is everything and more that any prospective underwriter or investor would want to know about Oak Island and our proposal. After we get these packages out and get the money in place, we start the project."

Included in the package was something entitled "Engineering and Operational Plans Including Cost Estimates" for the proposed dig. The document, the size of a city telephone directory, was the result of three months' work by Cox Underground Research, an Ottawa-based consulting engineering firm that had put together various scenarios on how to explore physically the interior of Oak Island. The study, which Tobias said "cost us about $60,000 to prepare," recommended digging an eighty-foot-diameter shaft down through bedrock in the Money pit area. And the estimated cost of the project, including site preparation and auxiliary work, was in the order of $10 million.

While Tobias was preparing for the Big Dig, Blankenship, like a dog worrying over a gopher hole, was still intent on getting back into Borehole 10-X. Triton's consulting engineers and drillers told them that the metal and wood that had come out of the hole at the apparent depths of 140 and 160 feet probably were blown up from a deeper level when they'd used compressed air to clean out the hole. On that possibility Blankenship convinced Tobias to let him drive the shaft deeper. By January 1988 he was again in 10-X, ready to take it all the way down to 235 feet if necessary. Blankenship was still convinced that Borehole 10-X might provide a back door into the Money Pit, and he hoped to make an important discovery before a refinanced Triton (with diluted equity) was created.

Tobias, who tends to get a distracted look on his face when the subject of 10-X comes up, told me, "Dan's got a thing about that hole. And maybe he's right; I don't know." But immediately he added something he has expressed many times before: "Dan and I might not always agree, but there's no one else I'd trust as much on that island."

If Blankenship was wrong, Borehole 10-X would become just another of some thirty-one failed shafts relegated to the junk heap of Oak Island's history. But it would soon be followed, according to Triton's plans, by the widest and deepest shaft ever sunk on Oak Island.

The long-discussed frontal assault on the Money Pit hadn't been delayed only by Tobias's business commitments or by Blankenship's concentration on 10-X. In the previous five years Tobias had spent as much money on lawyers' fees and Blankenship as much time on legal research as they had on their quest for treasure. And all of it was directed against one man—Fred Nolan, Oak Island's other treasure hunter.

CHAPTER EIGHTEEN

The Lawyers Hit Pay Dirt

IF IT HASN'T YET MADE ANYONE ELSE RICH, OAK ISLAND HAS been a source of treasure for at least one particular group—the Nova Scotia legal fraternity. This is the result of five years of bitter litigation between David Tobias and Frederick G. Nolan, a sixty-year-old land surveyor from Bedford, Nova Scotia. Between them they have spent over $150,000 in legal fees to establish ownership of and access to Oak Island.

The origin of the dispute dates back to 1935, when Gilbert Hedden (through his New Jersey lawyer, George Grimm) purchased part of Oak Island from the heirs (three grown children and nine grandchildren) of Sophia Sellers. At the time, the Sellers family jointly owned Lots 5 and 9 through 20, or thirteen of the island's thirty-two four-acre lots. The deeds on file at the Registry Office in Chester state that Hedden purchased Lots 15 through 20, or the eastern end of the island where the Money Pit is located. No other lot numbers are mentioned. However, also on file is a survey plan dated September 9, 1935, described as "Selvin Sellers (who represented the heirs) to George W. Grimm—52 acres." By measurement this appears to take in Lots 5 and 9 through 20.

Nevertheless, when the property in question was sold by Hedden to John Whitney Lewis and then by Lewis to Mel

Chappell in 1950, again only the numbers 15 through 20 were recorded on the actual deeds. Chappell, who was under the impression he'd bought Lots 5 and 9 through 20 (as well as eight other lots unrelated to the dispute), later purchased the rest of the island from other landholders. By 1960 he was, or so he assumed, the sole owner of all of Oak Island's 128 acres.

Then along came Fred Nolan. He had first visited Oak Island as a tourist in 1957, and the treasure hunt sparked his interest. In the summer of 1960 he went to Chappell (who held the treasure trove license) and asked for permission to look for the treasure. Chappell, who already had a contract with Bob Restall and was seeking a well-financed group to eventually take over the search, turned him down. Yet Nolan was determined to have some role in the investigation, so he asked if he could do some surveying on the island. Chappell agreed, and Nolan spent the next two summers locating and plotting positions of shafts and various markers such as the stone triangle and the drilled rocks. But, as Chappell later discovered, that wasn't all he was plotting.

While he was on the island, Nolan surveyed the boundary lines that separated the various lots. Then, on a hunch, he visited the Registry Office in Chester and conducted a title search of the island. To his delighted amazement he stumbled across a glaring ambiguity. Lots 5 and 9 through 14, comprising almost a quarter of the island, appeared never to have been transferred from their original 1935 owners. Nolan promptly tracked down the remaining Sellers heirs (several elderly women living in Chester and Massachusetts) and paid them a total of $2,500 to sign quit claim deeds to whatever ownership interest they might have on Oak Island.

In April 1963, with the notarized deeds in hand, Nolan went to Chappell and offered to convey the lots to him in exchange for the right to take over the treasure hunt at the Money Pit. Chappell was horrified by this development. But as the lots in question were some distance from the Money Pit and because he believed Nolan's claim could eventually be overturned in court, he told Nolan to get lost.

Chappell had badly misjudged his adversary. Nolan was,

and still is, as dedicated to finding the treasure as Chappell, Tobias, or Blankenship. And, as those three were to find out, Nolan could put up a fight with the best of them.

Years of tit-for-tat skirmishes followed, with each side trying to wear the other down with harassment tactics. It began in the fall of 1965 when Bob Dunfield and Chappell built the causeway to the island. An armed guard was posted in the causeway to prevent Nolan from using it to get to his island property. Nolan retaliated in 1966 by paying $3,000 for a quarter-acre section of the mainland at Crandall's Point that abutted the causeway, and then barricading it. This created the ridiculous stalemate of both parties having to get to and from the island by boat.

The following year Tobias and Blankenship entered the picture. Since they were anxious to get their drilling equipment over to the island, they signed a six-month agreement with Nolan, paying him $1,000 to cross his property at Crandall's Point. The accord was later extended, with Tobias exchanging a few shares in his venture for right-of-way on Nolan's property and for some survey work in the drilling area. It was a brief compromise. By 1969, when Triton was formed, the agreement was terminated, with each side accusing the other of violating its conditions.

Nolan again chained off the causeway entrance on his mainland property, forcing Triton to reach it by an inconvenient bypass route. Reciprocally, Triton erected a gate at the causeway's island end (which was on Chappell's land) to prevent Nolan from getting to his own property, most of which lies in the central marshy portion of the island. (The causeway itself, because it crosses navigable waters, is on federal Crown property and was at that time considered a public access route.

In 1970 Nolan applied to the provincial government for a treasure trove license covering the disputed seven lots. Chappell tried to block the application by seeking a court order declaring that he was the owner of the entire island and that Nolan was trespassing. But the suit got nowhere, and Nolan got his license.

However, to conduct his parallel treasure hunt Nolan had to take a boat from the mainland to Joudrey's Cove, where his lots had water frontage on the island's north side. In revenge for not being able to cross Chappell's land, Nolan chained off the section of island road that ran through Lots 9 to 14. Now Triton was unable to drive from the island's west end to the Money Pit. Blankenship promptly cut the chain, claiming that the roadway was public access. Nolan then used a truck boom to block the road with huge boulders. A furious Blankenship threatened to bulldoze the obstruction away.

Matters heated to the point where, according to Nolan, "Blankenship comes down one day and he's got a rifle with him. So we said, this is ridiculous; we're not going to get our heads blown off. So we called in the Mounties. They came over, and Dan said he had the gun to protect his property. But they confiscated it from him."

Triton was eventually forced to spend $14,000 to build a road to the Money Pit that detoured around Nolan's lots. But each side continued to make life miserable for the other.

In November 1971, in an attempt to end the guerrilla warfare and get on with the search, Triton and Nolan again formulated an agreement allowing each other access across Crandall's Point, the causeway, and their respective Oak Island lots. The pact also stipulated that the parties would share information pertaining to their individual treasure hunts and that Triton was entitled to a 40 percent share of any treasure found on the disputed lots. In addition, each side was precluded from commencing any legal action over title to Lots 5 and 9 through 14 during the term of the agreement.

This uneasy truce lasted twelve years, though, as a Nova Scotia Supreme Court judge remarked in 1985, "The agreement was marked more by the breach than the observance, particularly by the defendant, Nolan."

Through the 1970s, while Blankenship was working in the Money Pit area and Borehole 10-X, Nolan conducted a detailed survey of his seven lots. He ran hundreds of transit lines between various surface rocks (some with ancient ring bolts imbedded in them) that he claims are monuments left behind by the original depositors. He has plotted all of his findings on detailed charts that he says indicate the locations of "a massive treasure" distributed in many separate caches around the island. He has yet to find any of this treasure, most of which he is sure lies under his property. He also dug a few shallow pits and drilled into the swamp, retrieving pieces of wood and metal.

Nolan exhibited these artifacts in a museum that he built on Crandall's Point. His museum competed with another one on the island, thus creating considerable confusion among tourists. The Oak Island museum and tours were originally operated by the province's Department of Tourism, which had to pay Nolan a percentage of the take in exchange for crossing Crandall's Point. In 1974, when the Department of Highways built a wider bypass road leading to the causeway, Nolan insisted it had been put through his property, and he immediately added an extension to his museum across the roadway. The feisty treasure hunter had now taken on both the Department of Highways and the Department of Tourism. In 1976 the tourism department threw up its hands in despair and turned the operation over to Triton. But it wasn't until much later that a court order finally forced Nolan to remove the part of the museum that obstructed the new roadway.

During the term of his agreement with Triton, Nolan, who claimed he was "conned into signing it" by unscrupulous lawyers, saw himself as the little guy fighting "the millionaire Tobias, and Triton with their influential friends in the [Nova Scotia] government." In 1975 Nolan described the conflict to me as "a chess game; one move then another move, that's the way it's been." It will end, he said, with "one of us, either Tobias or myself, winning this game. They've pulled every dirty trick in the book against me on this thing, and you don't forget that easily. The name of the game is you don't back down. Once you do, you show weakness. If I give in [on access through Crandall's Point] then they'll attack me on my position on the island and try to take my lots away. It's like the domino theory."

This period was marked by several direct confrontations between Blankenship and Nolan over the blocking of roads, trespassing, and over what Blankenship describes as "Fred's systematic removal and destruction of important markers and artifacts." On a couple of occasions the two got into nose-to-

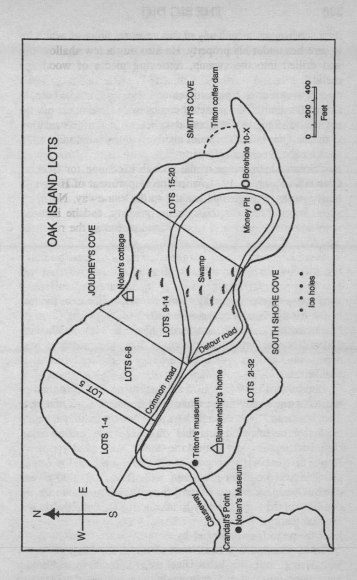

OAK ISLAND LOTS

Triton coffer dam

SMITH'S COVE

Borehole 10-X

Money Pit

LOTS 15-20

0   200   400
Feet

JOUDREY'S COVE

Nolan's cottage

Swamp

LOTS 9-14

Ice holes

SOUTH SHORE COVE

Detour road

LOTS 21-32

Common road

LOTS 6-8

LOT 5

LOTS 1-4

Triton's museum

Blankenship's home

Causeway

Crandall's Point

Nolan's Museum

N
W   E
S

nose shouting matches and came close to trading blows.

In January 1983 the "big guys" decided they'd taken all the sniper fire they could handle. Tobias, who'd acquired Chappell's Oak Island holdings in June 1977, launched a civil suit against Nolan over ownership of the seven island lots, access across Crandall's Point and the causeway, interference with tourism, and the removal and destruction of artifacts relating to the treasure hunt. The suit effectively terminated their 1971 "cooperation" agreement.

Tobias had two pressing reasons to bring the matter to court at this time. First, the ongoing dispute was making it that much harder to interest potential backers to join Triton's operation. Second, Nova Scotia's twenty-year statute of limitations to launch a civil action to recover land would run out in three months.

For the next two years Blankenship replaced treasure hunting with evidence hunting, spending almost all his time researching archival documents, interviewing people, conferring with lawyers, and generally trying to establish a case against Nolan for the discovery hearings before the Supreme Court of Nova Scotia. The case was finally heard in May 1985, with Triton's lawyers submitting some 1,100 documents in evidence, plus another five hundred pages of pre-trial and post-trial briefs.

December 17, 1985, was for Blankenship as dark a time as when he was nearly trapped inside of Borehole 10-X. On that date Supreme Court Judge A. M. MacIntosh upheld Nolan's claim to the disputed lots and dismissed the Tobias-Triton claim of trespass and damage to their Oak Island property. However, the court's sixty-six-page decision ordered Nolan to pay Triton $15,000 for interfering with Triton's $7,000-a-year tourism business and to remove his museum and any barrier that obstructed access to the causeway. It also upheld Triton's claim to exclusive use of the causeway under its twenty-year lease from the federal government.

Tobias decided to appeal the decision, despite being told by his lawyers that it would cost him about $20,000 in additional legal fees and that his chances of winning were "approximately one out of four." (Tobias's son, Norman, a Toronto lawyer, also advised his father not to pursue it.) The appeal was filed on May 6, 1986, citing errors of law and the inadmissability or acceptance of various documents pertaining to the original deeds covering the disputed seven lots.

Tobias, apparently, was also playing a game of bluff poker. The day after filing the appeal he made an offer (through his Nova Scotia lawyers) to purchase Nolan's seven lots for $125,000, which was the same price he'd paid Chappell nine years earlier for more than three-quarters of the island. Nolan (who in 1987 emphatically told me, "My lots aren't for sale to him at any price; not while I'm alive.") spurned the offer and challenged him to go ahead with his appeal. Nolan's lawyers also filed a cross-appeal on the ruling of damages and access to Crandall's Point and the causeway.

On the question of ownership, the appeal centered on the wording of the 1935 deed from the Sellers family to Hedden. The crucial paragraph of the deed referred to "all that certain tract or parcel of land being part of Oak Island near Western Shore, in the County of Lunenburg, *and comprising* [my emphasis] Lots 15, 16, 17, 18, 19, and 20."

Tobias's lawyers argued that the intent of the document was to transfer *all* of the Sellers family lots, and that the term "and comprising" was used in an expansive sense, citing those specific lot numbers as just one part of everything being sold. Nolan's lawyers, on the other hand, maintained that, as Justice MacIntosh interpreted it, the term had been used in a restrictive sense in that the Sellers family was transferring *only* those specifically numbered lots rather than their entire holdings. (Quite obviously the original deed had been sloppily worded. The legal culprit, as it turned out, was none other than R. V. Harris, who had acted on behalf of Hedden.)

If the day the Supreme Court ruling had been handed down was a black one for Tobias and Blankenship, April 15, 1987, was an even darker one. On that date the Nova Scotia Court of Appeals dismissed Tobias's ownership claim and accepted Nolan's cross-appeal to the extent of reducing damages for lost tourism revenue from the Supreme Court's assessment of $15,000 to a mere $500. However, Nolan didn't win the right to use the causeway and was again ordered to remove the part of his museum that blocked the access road. (In December 1987 he lopped thirty feet off the ninety-foot building.)

The conclusion to those years of litigation had been costly. ("My legal fees were about $75,000, and I'm still getting the bills," Nolan said in January 1988. Tobias estimates his own legal costs at $85,000.) But it had at long last resolved the ownership and access questions that had kept both sides at each other's throats for more than twenty years. Triton and Nolan were now free to concentrate on their respective quests for the Oak Island treasure.

Unfortunately, the messy legal maneuvers also created irreconcilable enemies out of two treasure hunters who at one time held each other in professional esteem. I can recall many separate conversations with Blankenship and Nolan during the 1970s and early 1980s in which each of them would rail on and on about what the other was doing to make treasure hunting and life itself more difficult than it should have been. Yet there was always a spark of expressed comradeship and begrudging admiration between them. They were, after all, two men sharing a common obsession. Today that spark is gone. Each borders on apoplectic rage when the other's name is even brought up.

"Sure, I'm very bitter about the outcome," Blankenship told me after the appeal, citing "the incompetence of the lawyers," from R. V. Harris on down. "But Fred [Nolan] has a lot to answer for, and someday he's going to have to. You wouldn't believe some of the things he did to win his case."

And from Nolan: "Dan did his best to destroy me in court. It was a dirty case. As far as I'm concerned, Dan and I may have been friends before, but not now; not ever again." Nolan said that, as they left the appeal hearing, "Tobias handed me one of those fat cigars he always smokes and congratulated me on winning" clear title to the disputed lots. "He's a businessman and accepted it. But with Blankenship it's a different thing. It's a cutthroat business, this treasure hunting, and Dan will do anything to try to stop me." (Nolan figures he's invested "about $250,000 so far, including time lost from my surveying business" in the Oak Island venture.)

From her home on Western Shore overlooking Oak Island,

Mildred Restall can only shake her head in wonder at the years of feuding and litigation. Still very bitter about the tragedy that took the life of her husband and son, she writes off Tobias, Blankenship, and Nolan as "a bunch of jackasses" with "nothing to show for all those wasted years." As she had told me before and again in July 1987, "Based on my experience living there, I don't believe there is any treasure on that damn island." She adds that the "whole fight over property is ridiculous, because they're fighting over nothing. Nothing at all."

Nevertheless, as Blankenship prepared for the 1988 autumn of the Big Dig in the Money Pit and Nolan got ready for yet another season of searching in the swamp, they were at least in agreement on one point: that the treasure they would find, no matter on whose property, would originate from the Spanish conquest of the New World.

CHAPTER NINETEEN

The Spanish Connection

OF ALL THE QUESTIONS THAT HAVE BEEN ASKED ABOUT OAK Island in these two centuries of fruitless digging, the predominant one is: Who buried the treasure?

The question, of course, accepts the conclusions presented earlier in this book: that the deep underground workings exist; that they were built to hide something of great value; and that there's a good chance the deposit is still down there. Since no one has ever come across a map or document that conclusively identifies Oak Island's creator, answering the question becomes a matter of deduction—weighing all the possibilities in the light of known facts, valid assumptions, probability, and logic.

In my eighteen-year association with this curious island—writing, making films, and lecturing on the subject—I have interviewed, corresponded with, or examined the records of every person who has ever taken part in the search. I have also been in contact with dozens of others who have studied the enigma from afar. In that time I have heard every conceivable guess as to the origin of the deposit, guesses that range from the plausible to the outright ridiculous. Each theory has been measured according to both what has been discovered on the island and documented historical facts. Against those two yardsticks, the majority of Oak Island theories (including the most prevalent ones—that it was built by individual free-lance pirates or by the early French or English colonizers) quickly fall apart.

There is only one general whodunit theory that corresponds with everything that has been found under the island and which fits within a plausible historical framework. And that is why I associate the project with the Spanish—specifically, during their conquest of the New World. But even here there are several variables: The deposit may have been made by the Spanish themselves, or by the people whose wealth they were plundering, or by others who relieved the Spanish of their ill-gotten loot. In my opinion, the first is the most likely possibility.

Some of those associated with the search also accept a relationship between Oak Island and Spain's conquest of the Americas during the sixteenth and seventeenth centuries. Dan Blankenship, who is generally reluctant to discuss what he expects to eventually find, concurs that the project was probably built "in the late 1500s or anytime in the 1600s." And he notes, "There was one great source of wealth during that period—the Spanish and the people they took it from."

For more than two hundred years after Columbus's first voyage, Spain was the envy of her European neighbors as she stuffed her coffers with the discovered riches of Mexico and Central and South America. In the early years of the conquest (till about 1550) the booty consisted mainly of gold and silver artifacts as well as pearls and emeralds taken from the Incas of Peru and the Maya and Aztecs of Mexico. The artifacts were usually melted down and returned to Spain in the form of bullion. Beginning in the latter half of the sixteenth century, the Spaniards went straight to the Indians' source—the rich gold and silver mines. They spent most of the next two centuries bleeding the mines (with enslaved Indian labor) of billions of dollars worth of valuable ore, all of it smelted on the spot into Spanish coins or ingots.

The cargoes were usually loaded on galleons at Caribbean ports in Colombia, Panama, or Mexico. From there the ships sailed to the Spanish stronghold of Havana, where they were assembled into convoys for the voyage back to Spain. This measure was taken primarily to protect the vessels from pirates and from English, French, and Dutch naval squadrons. Convoys were also a safeguard againsts possible embezzlement by a single ship's captain or crew.

Originally the route home was approximately due east across the Atlantic from Cuba to the Canary Islands. But after 1545 the accepted course was changed to the easier one following the Gulf Stream up the southeast coast of America and then turning east at about 38 degrees latitude on a heading for the Azores and Spain. On this route (which tracked the Gulf Stream as high as 40 degrees latitude) the fleets commonly passed within three hundred to four hundred miles of Nova Scotia.

These treasure expeditions were normally private ventures, often underwritten by the merchants and explorers of Seville. Provisions, munitions, and settlers were transported to the New World, as were tons of mercury, used for extracting silver from its ore. The same ships would return laden with gold and silver, tobacco, indigo, and other goods from the colonies. The Spanish Crown was entitled to one-fifth of all the treasure brought back, though in the early years of exploration the Crown's share was sometimes as much as half.

The Spanish fleets were often scattered apart during bad weather, and a single ship would sometimes straggle home days or weeks after the others. And if the ship and her crew were unlucky, they wouldn't get home at all. Records in the Archive of the Indies at Seville list hundreds of vessels that disappeared during storms on their way to or from the New World. In many cases the approximate location is known (from the accounts of other ships in the convoy), but in others it is simply stated as lost *"en el Golfo"* (in the deep part of the Atlantic).

Some of the vessels that sunk carried incredible wealth to the bottom. For example, the six-hundred-ton galleon *Atocha*, which was part of a twenty-eight-ship convoy, had approximately $400 million worth of gold and silver aboard when she went down in a hurricane off Florida's Marquesas Keys in 1622. (Treasure hunter Mel Fisher spent sixteen years looking for the wreck and finally found the motherlode in July 1985.)

Other such cargoes, some even more valuable, are recorded in the Seville archives as having been unaccountably lost on the voyage home, presumably plucked from the sea by either the elements or roving buccaneers. Is it possible that the treasure of one or more such ships may have found its way, either by accident or design, to a small uninhabited island in Mahone Bay?

Consider what is known about Oak Island:

The depth and magnitude of the subterranean workings suggest an operation undertaken by intelligent, ambitious, and coordinated people. Whatever it was they sought to hide was surely greater than a few chests of coins and trinkets; only an enormous treasure would be worth the work and masterful engineering that went into the project. The Spanish ships carried valuable cargoes; they were manned by disciplined crews (as many as two hundred sailors and soldiers on the larger galleons), and they sometimes ferried mining engineers and superintendents back to Spain.

The project, according to Triton's consistent carbon-dating results, was executed around 1575. The absolute margin of error is plus or minus eighty-five years, but a fifty-year leeway on either side is considered a reliable outside limit. Consequently, the Oak Island workings were almost certainly constructed between 1525 and 1625, at the height of the Spanish conquest, when homeward-bound galleons routinely sailed within a few hundred miles of Mahone Bay, at a time before the region was settled.

There are some who say the project couldn't date back to the 1500s because, they argue, the large oak tree found at the Money Pit in 1795 couldn't have lived that long. (The tree, with its cut-off limb, had apparently been used as a hoisting support to excavate the pit, and was therefore a mature tree when the pit was created.) But in fact, botanists at Harvard University's forestry division at Petersham, Massachusetts, have informed me that Nova Scotia red oaks commonly live for 300 years. And at an age of about 70 years such a tree would have an eighteen-inch-diameter trunk and branches stout enough to support hoisting equipment. If, for argument's sake, the tree in question was at or near the end of its life span in 1795 and had been employed at the age of 70, the project could date back to 1565. But that is not even the optimum case, since, according to the experts, it's quite possible for a red oak to live 350 years. So even a date as early as 1515 can't be ruled out.

Among the tangible clues that have been unearthed on Oak Island are the coconut fiber, the traces of mercury, the piece of parchment, and the wrought iron scissors. Coconut fiber was routinely used by the Spaniards as packing material in ships' holds. The Spaniards used mercury to separate pure silver from its ore. Their documents and charts were often written on sheepskin parchment. The scissors, according to the Smithsonian Institution, are Spanish-American, perhaps three hundred years old or older.

Granted, all of the foregoing is circumstantial evidence. But it nevertheless provides a strong case for a Spanish correlation to Oak Island.

One theory based on that connection was advanced in 1970 by Ross Wilhelm, a University of Michigan economics professor. He suggested that Oak Island was used by the Spanish Crown under Philip II (he reigned from 1556 to 1598) as a depot to repair ships damaged by North Atlantic storms on the way home. In order to allow the repaired galleon to continue its voyage unencumbered by cargo, the site was also used as a temporary repository for the gold and silver bullion, to be picked up later by another vessel or convoy. The island, in effect, was an unmanned safety deposit vault that may have been used many times over a long period.

According to Wilhelm's theory, the Spaniards designed a system whereby they could enter and reuse the vault under the Money Pit without springing the flood trap. The key, he says, lies in the inscribed rock found in the Money Pit in 1803. Wilhelm noticed that many of the symbols were similar to ones used by Giovanni Battista Porta, a sixteenth-century Italian cryptologist. Porta designed several cipher discs, consisting of a ring of symbols surrounded by an outer ring bearing the letters of the alphabet. By following a specified procedure, the inner ring is turned so many spaces until a particular symbol is aligned with a letter.

Using one of Porta's disks, Wilhelm translated the symbols into a Spanish plaintext message: *"A ochenta gui(a) mij(o) r(i)a sumideq(o). F."* The letters in parentheses were added by Wilhelm, who says they were probably left out of the original message for security reasons. Similarly, the last word is supposedly an intentional misspelling of *"sumidero."* Translated into English it reads: "At eighty (you) guide maize or millet (into the) estuary or drain. F."

Wilhelm says this means that the inscribed stone offered instructions on what to do before digging into the vault. That is, pour maize or millet into the drainage system at Smith's Cove to plug it up. The grain would swell and halt the flow of water. Then the wooden platform, or air lock, below the stone in the Money Pit could be removed, the shaft bailed out, and the vault entered. After the Money Pit was resealed, the grain would eventually rot and the trap would again be set.

Wilhelm adds that the reference to "eighty" indicates the level at which the stone was found (although almost all early accounts say it was discovered ninety feet down), and that the "F" stood for King Philip (Felipe in Spanish).

This curious hypothesis has a few bugs in it. First, it's unlikely those characters were the ones originally seen on the stone. In fact, Wilhelm arbitrarily changed a few of the recorded symbols in order to fit his interpretation from the disc. Also, if the Spanish government intended to have a temporary repository for disabled ships, why should they go to all the trouble of digging an underground bank? The area was uninhabited, and a small armed garrison could have been built far more easily to serve the same purpose.

The theory also runs into the same problem as do all others that seek to describe Oak Island as an "official" project planned and executed by a government and therefore known to many people. How could it have been kept such a total historical secret? Moreover, it implies that at least every captain of every Spanish vessel using that route would have had to be aware of the island and the purpose it served (as well as be provided with the appropriate cipher disc). If a ship ran into trouble, the captain would have to know where to go and what to do to hide his cargo. And then, of course, the entire crew of any vessel that had occasion to use (or to empty) the repository would subsequently know the secret as well. Yet no word of it seems to have ever leaked out. And the many historians who have pored through the official records and firsthand written accounts of Spain's New World activities have yet to find any mention of such a project.

In any case, Wilhelm is sure the vault has long been empty; that it was cleaned out one last time and the pit refilled in case of possible future use. This would obviously be true if it was used in the way he believes it was. The Spanish Crown would surely not have abandoned a treasure on Oak Island forever.

A more logical argument could be made for Oak Island's having been used as a repository by chance and not by design.

Consider the following scenario: Sometime around 1600 a convoy sails from Cuba on its way to Spain via the Gulf Stream route. Hundreds of miles south of Nova Scotia a severe storm is encountered, and a richly laden ship is separated from the rest of the fleet. The vessel is badly damaged, and the captain has no choice but to run before the storm. Two days later the winds subside. But the ship has lost most of her spars and is taking on water. A decision is made to find a sheltered area in which to make repairs, and Mahone Bay is selected. The bay is uncharted, and on the way in rocky shoals do more damage to the hull. But the ship is safely run aground off the east end of Oak Island. The passengers and crew, numbering more than a hundred, wade ashore, and a camp is established on the uninhabited island.

Over the next few days the damage is inspected and the Spaniards see that extensive repairs to the hull and rigging are needed to make the boat seaworthy. The ship's carpenters and riggers have all the tools they need, including a forge to shape iron fittings. But they estimate the repairs will take several months to complete, and that even then it will be a patch-up job. The ship's commander tells them to do the best they can, and then decides on a course of action. When the repairs are done, he'll try to sail to the nearest Spanish colony, Florida.

Or he may plan to rejoin the Gulf Stream and sail downwind to the Azores.

The ship's passengers include an auditor representing the Spanish Crown and agents of the Seville merchant who owns most of the cargo (their presence on board was common practice). Their particular concern is for the tons of gold and silver bullion and coins in the ship's hold. They and the commander agree that transporting such wealth on a damaged vessel unescorted through waters sailed by pirates and enemy corsairs would be foolhardy. It would be far safer to leave the treasure here and return for it later under the protection of a convoy. Moreover, the patched-up ship would be that much lighter and faster, improving its chances of reaching a Spanish port.

The island is ideally suited for their stay. It is tucked in behind the outer islands, so they can't be spotted by any enemy ship that might happen to cross the mouth of the bay. The island also has fresh water, game, hardwood for repairs and living quarters, and is a natural fortress against any Indians that may be in the area.

Perhaps also on board is a mining engineer, on his way home after supervising the opening of a new silver deposit in Bolivia. (Or substitute for him any intelligent officer or passenger with basic engineering knowledge.) The repository is designed to be completely tamper-proof should anyone stumble across it before the Spaniards can return. They have the manpower (besides the crew there may also have been black slaves aboard) to make it deep enough and large enough to contain a treasure that occupies most of the ship's hold. Digging tools are fashioned on the ship's forge from scraps of iron. The clay ground and anhydrite bedrock is water-free and fairly easy to excavate.

The Money Pit is dug first. Separate work crews tunnel out from it at various levels and directions, and large chambers are made at the end of each corridor some distance from the Money Pit. The treasure is placed in these vaults, sealed with puddled clay and a crude cement made from the island's limestone. At the same time at least two flood tunnels are dug, one toward Smith's Cove and the other to the South Shore Cove. Other crews have been constructing cofferdams at mean low tide in both these locations. The one at Smith's Cove also serves as the outer wall of a huge dry dock for the five-hundred-ton galleon that's being repaired on the slipway. The stone drains are built and covered over with the ship's coconut fiber dunnage, as well as eel grass, rocks, and sand.

Each vault has been carefully measured and mapped with respect to its position directly below the island's surface. The ship's commander has the valuable map, for it shows precisely where to dig through virgin soil to enter each watertight vault. The stone triangle and drilled rocks are set in place and are keyed to the captain's map.

Four months have elapsed. The entire crew has put in ten hours a day to repair the ship and build the repository. The galleon is riding at anchor now, and they are ready to leave. Every precaution is taken to destroy any evidence of their stay. Their living quarters are dismantled and burned. All garbage and other residue has been taken well offshore by the ship's longboats and dumped overboard. The cofferdams are dismantled and the flooding system becomes operational. The many tree stumps and disturbed earth in the Money Pit area provide the only clues that something happened here. But should any chance discoverer attempt to dig into the refilled shaft, he'd get no further than ninety feet before being flooded out.

The galleon sets sail and leaves Mahone Bay. The Seville agents are anxious to get to Spain and organize an expedition to return for the treasure. But they are satisfied with the project and know their fortune will still be there when they get back.

Three days out at sea. The weather has turned nasty, and the pumps are being manned around the clock. The makeshift clay-and-fiber caulking is not holding up as well as the carpenters had hoped. Worse still, there had been no time to properly season the new planking in the hull, and the wood is swelling and buckling in places. It's uncertain how long the patched-up hull will be able to withstand the pounding of the rough seas.

Suddenly a plank below the waterline springs loose. No amount of pumping can check the rush of water into the bilges. Soon the galleon is on her way to the bottom of the North Atlantic, and within an hour the last of the crew and passengers perish in the icy waters.

Included in the wreck some 2,500 fathoms down on the ocean floor is the commander's strongbox. Inside it is a carefully drawn map showing the location of Oak Island, what is buried on it, and how it can be retrieved.

Back in Seville the galleon and her cargo of bullion had already been written off several months earlier as having disappeared *"en el Golfo."*

This chain of events is imaginary. But who is to say it couldn't have happened? Spanish treasure ships *did* disappear without a trace, and something *was* buried on Oak Island. Could there have been a connection?

OTHER INVESTIGATORS WORKING WITHIN THE SAME TIME frame have suggested that it was not the Spanish who brought the treasure to Oak Island, but rather the Indians who were being systematically vanquished by those European conquistadors.

The earliest such theory (outlined in a previous chapter) was advanced in 1931, and attributed the project to the Incas of Tumbez, Peru.

In 1961, Eric Hamblin, an amateur historian and scuba diver from Chester, was part of a team of divers who searched the waters off Oak Island trying to locate a seabed entrance into the Money Pit. They found unnatural bow-shaped rock outcroppings off Smith's Cove and the South Shore Cove, which may have been the remains of ancient cofferdams, but little else of interest. Concurrently, Hamblin formulated a hypothesis to explain the origin of the mystery, one that would fit all the known facts about Oak Island. He concluded the project had been engineered in the sixteenth century by the Mayan or Aztec Indians of Mexico, either voluntarily (to hide their wealth and religious artifacts from the Spanish conquerors) or else under the direction of Spanish masters. In a thesis outlining his theory, Hamblin states in part:

The oak platforms [in the Money Pit] were set at a common distance of ten feet apart. Why ten feet? It is not a convenient height to climb in and out of or pass things up and down from. Nor was it, prior to the seventeenth century, a "normal" measure. Who might use ten feet as a standard measure? To date research has uncovered only one possible group. The Maya, praised above all things for the perfection of their systems of measurement, had a linear measurement similar to the royal cubit of ancient Egypt of 20.68 inches. In their system the next standard length was equivalent to six such cubits, or ten feet four inches, which, allowing for the thickness of the logs, could account for the spacing of the platforms with a precision and regularity not characteristic of Europeans of former days.

Oak Island in its southeastern end overlies a limestone deposit. The Maya and Aztecs both were well aware of limestone's capabilities, both as an ideal substance for tunneling operations and as a building material. Much evidence remains today of its use by those people in their native Mexico.

More important is the method used for more than 2,000 years by the Maya to manufacture lime from raw limestone. Briefly, a circular pile of logs was raised to a height of about four feet. On top of this were placed small pieces of limestone. Then the wood was lit through a hole in the center and allowed to burn through. The Maya have always believed that it was essential for a successful kiln to have absolutely no wind and a fire that burned evenly on all sides. To such people, needing to make a cement vault at the bottom of a pit, what would be more logical than to avoid all wind by placing it within the pit? Here may well lie the mystery of the layers of ash or charcoal [found in the Money Pit].

Hamblin concluded that "the complexity and permanence" of the workings are similar to the "strength, thoroughness, and details of construction" of the "drains and buildings uncovered [among Mayan and Aztec ruins] in Mexico."

A similar though more elaborate theory has more recently been advanced by some investigators in Phoenix, Arizona. This group, headed by Gary Clayton, a forty-two-year-old former Baptist minister, claims to have solved the Oak Island mystery through the use of ciphers, mathematics, and research.

According to their calculations, an intricate network of tunnels and chambers was built beneath the island by the Mayan or Aztec Indians sometime between 1480 and 1520. The purpose was to hide not just gold and silver but perhaps even Mayan codices relating to the history of the Maya culture prior to the start of the Spanish conquest under Hernán Cortés in 1519.

Such a discovery would certainly be astounding, as the few codices that exist today relate only to the Mayan calendar, astronomy, and religious divinations. Most of the Mayan hieroglyphic manuscripts, written on reams of bark coated with plaster, were destroyed in the sixteenth century by zealous Spanish priests who regarded the codices as pagan documents. Apart from these, many Mayan glyphs (primarily dealing with religion and astronomy) are found carved into rock in the Mayan pyramids and temples of Mexico's Yucatán Peninsula. Similar Mayan ruins have also been uncovered in Guatemala and Honduras.

The Maya were a sophisticated and highly intelligent people. By the tenth century they had developed a calendar more accurate than the Julian, and had precisely plotted the movements of the stars and planets. They were masters of mathematics, engineering, and architecture. They employed stone and mortar construction extensively, and constructed concrete tunnels, water drains, and bridges. Oddly enough, they never used the wheel, perhaps because they had no beasts of burden.

The Maya were also capable of extensive sea travel. On his second voyage to the Indies (1493–95) Columbus encountered Indians who said they were from the "land of the Maia" sailing large canoes off the south coast of Cuba. And Mayan glyphs have been discovered by archaeologists on cave walls on the Caribbean island of Bonaire, 1,400 miles southeast of the Yucatán.

The Phoenix group was formed in 1972 when Clayton read an article about Oak Island and began considering possible solutions to the riddle. With two partners, Lee Stahnke, a steelworker, and Arnold Gilson, an engineer, Clayton spent several years putting together the Aztec/Maya theory. They tried to get Triton and Nolan to allow them to dig on the island to prove their findings, but with no success. In 1976, Stahnke (financed by Clayton) visited the island for a few days—the only time any of them has ever set foot on the site. But according to Clayton, Stahnke (who has long since left the group) "just got boozed up every night and took a bunch of useless pictures [of the island]. It cost me $1,200 and got us nowhere."

Today, sixteen years after he started, Gary Clayton is still obsessed with his theory, defending its merits with the zeal of a preacher. "I've done 10,000 hours research on this, minimum, and I just *know* I'm right," he told me in January of 1988. "The individual who directed the [Oak Island] operation left clues and codes, and I've broken them all." Clayton says the current Phoenix group, informally known as the FHG (For His Glory) Corporation, includes "five or six very influential people who've confirmed and added to my knowledge" of the project.

Gilson, the other founding partner, is still with the group, though he tends to be more tempered than Clayton in his approach to the mystery. Still, he says, "When you see the evidence that we've come up with, it's very hard not to believe in it. Gary [Clayton] lives and breathes this thing; he's fine-tuned [the theory] to the point where it's impossible not to accept it."

The Phoenix team has drafted engineering blueprints of the interior of the island, showing the approximate locations of vaults, passageways, flood tunnels, and even underground living quarters used by the Indians who designed and built the project. Some of the drawings they've shown me incorporate data from the drilling and digging results of Triton Alliance and earlier searchers. But their "knowledge" of what's under Oak Island is in part based on false information. For example, one of their charts places the large cavern that is 230 feet down in Borehole 10-X a good distance away from the actual location. In their diagram it's in a position that was erroneously reported by a Halifax newspaper article in 1971 and then picked up (with the same error) by a later book on the subject.

However, most of their drawings involve subterranean workings at depths and locations on the island that haven't yet been explored. In that respect, the validity of their theory has still to be proven or disproven.

But where did all the information for these drawings originate? Clayton is not about to reveal the details, for he expects to eventually recover the treasure. He admits, however, that their solution incorporates the symbols on the inscribed rock found in the Money Pit in 1803 and those on the rock that Hedden found in 1936. Clayton says the symbols "must be used in conjunction with some very important factors, which I'm not at liberty to reveal, or else they are totally meaningless." He adds that the group has traced the characters to a "Mayan or Aztec source" (though they look nothing like Mexican Indian glyphs) and that by using these and other sources they have formulated "mathematical proof" of how the project was built. "We have cracked the code of measurement," says Clayton, "and it fits in with what is known" about Oak Island.

When I pointed out that it's pretty certain the inscription they're using was incorrectly copied from the 1803 original or is an outright fake, Clayton said this is ruled out by the fact that the group's measurements based on these symbols "work out to the inch" with what has already been found (by drilling) under the island. (But, as the errors on some of their charts show, this is not always the case.) Gilson, on the other hand, doesn't put as much credence in those particular symbols.

Clayton says he "can prove" that the Aztecs or Maya engineered the Oak Island project. As for how and why they came so far north, he claims to have "strong evidence" that the Indians were assisted by a group of Swedes who'd been shipwrecked off the Mexican coast in the late 1400s. These foreigners, recognizing the enormous achievements of the Aztec/Mayan people, organized an expedition to save some of their artifacts and historical records from the advancing Spanish conquistadors. The Swedes helped the Indians sail one-hundred foot ocean-going canoes from the Yucatán Peninsula, across the Gulf of Mexico, and up the eastern United States coast until they came to an area they were sure would be safe from the Spanish predators.

They dug beneath Oak Island and sealed their treasures and codices in waterproof vaults of cement. They later sailed home with a written account of what they had done and where they had done it. "It was to be left to a later generation to return for the treasure," says Clayton. He adds that a chart showing how to gain access to the vaults "was turned over to an Aztec or Mayan chieftain" but that "he was killed by Cortés before he could return." Clayton claims his group has, in effect, recreated that valuable chart. And they hope to use it someday to scoop the treasure out of the island.

THERE ARE SEVERAL OTHER OAK ISLAND THEORIES RELATED to the disappearance of Mayan or Inca treasures during the sixteenth century. For instance, the Inca king Atahualpa was taken prisoner by Pizarro in 1532 and, in order to secure his release, was told to have his subjects fill a seventeen-by-twenty-two-foot room once with gold and twice with silver artifacts as high as he could reach. Within eight months more than twenty-four tons of treasure (worth well over $100 million today) had been collected. Pizarro then expressed his gratitude by having Atahualpa garroted, and most of the ransom was melted down and sent back to Spain. But some of the legends insist that many of the artifacts intended for the ransom disappeared before they reached the Spaniards. One, supposedly, was a three-hundred-foot chain fashioned from ten tons of gold that had surrounded the square in the Inca capital of Cuzco.

Like Tumbez, a few other Inca cities were stripped of their wealth before the arrival of the conquistadors. One of these was Pachakamak, a few miles from modern Lima. However, its treasures are thought to be buried in the nearby valley of Lurin.

And in the early eighteenth century, a seven-foot solid gold statue known as the "Golden Virgin" disappeared from Panama just before it was to be shipped to Spain.

These and other "missing" Spanish-American treasures are sometimes rumored to be below Oak Island. But as with most other theories, it is all speculation.

FINALLY, THERE ARE THEORIES WHICH ACCEPT THAT OAK Island's treasure consists of New World plunder, but that it was put there by those who seized it from the conquistadors before they could get it home. As previously stated, sixteenth- and seventeenth-century European powers, England in particular, coveted Spain's lucrative monopoly over the Americas. And even when they weren't officially at war with Spain, these countries employed commissioned privateers to intercept home-bound galleons. Those ambushes usually took place on the high seas, as Spain controlled most of the ports and coastal waters of the Caribbean and Pacific seaboard.

Nevertheless, daring raids were occasionally made on Panama, Cartagena, Santo Domingo, and other Spanish New World ports. One such attack, by the British on Havana, forms the historical basis for Fred Nolan's theory about what he might find on Oak Island—or, more specifically, under his own lots.

In June 1762 a British naval force led by Admirals George Pocock and George Keppel, the Earl of Albemarle, attacked the Spanish stronghold of Havana and captured it after a ten-week siege. They occupied the city until July 1763, when it was returned to Spain in exchange for the Floridas. During their year of rule the British extracted millions of dollars worth of gold in ransoms from the Catholic Church and the Spanish nobility in the city. The records indicate that these prizes were shipped back to England.

But Nolan believes that some of those involved in the Havana expedition worked in conjunction with British military leaders in Halifax to sneak much of the loot up to Nova Scotia and bury it on Oak Island. The theory has two heavy strikes against it. It is almost two hundred years out of sync with Triton's carbon-dating results, and there is no known record or even rumor in British colonial history of the Havana gold being diverted on its way to England. Moreover, the Oak Island project could not have been undertaken in complete secrecy four years after Chester had been settled.

Oak Island's other landowner, David Tobias, also suspects a British-Spanish connection to the mystery. But he attributes the deposit to Francis Drake, the feisty red-bearded mariner who was the terror of sixteenth-century Spanish seafarers.

Although best known as the vice-admiral who humbled Philip II by defeating the awesome Spanish Armada in 1588, Drake was also very much a buccaneer. In the late 1560s and early 1570s he made several voyages from England to the Indies, where he raided and looted Spanish outposts on the Caribbean coast of Mexico and Central America. Some of these strikes, employing as many as six ships, were made in partnership with John Hawkins, another noted British sea wolf.

Drake's biggest haul was made in 1573, when he and the French privateer Guillaume Le Testu joined forces to ambush a mule train on its way across the neck of Panama. These caravans were used to transport bullion and other wealth from the Spanish Pacific coast fortress at Panama City across the isthmus to the Caribbean, where they were loaded on galleons for the trip back to Spain. The attack was a success (though Le Testu was captured and executed), and Drake returned to England a very rich man.

Drake then came up with a more ambitious plan. He'd seen that the bulk of Spain's booty originated from Peru and Bolivia on the west coast. And the Spaniards, who assumed they were safe from pirates in the Pacific, were delivering the gold and silver to Panama City on slow, unescorted galleons. So in 1577 Drake left England with a squadron of five ships and entered the Pacific under the tip of South America (via the passage that now bears his name). Two of the ships, damaged in the stormy voyage around Cape Horn, were scuttled. Soon after passing through the Magellan Strait (discovered in 1520 by the Portuguese navigator Ferdinand Magellan) another vessel sank and a fourth was forced to limp back to England. Drake was now left with only his flagship, the *Pelican*, which he then renamed the *Golden Hind*. Undaunted, he sailed northward up the coast of Chile, stopping briefly to raid the Spanish settlement of Valparaiso. Then, off the northwest coast of Ecuador, he intercepted a large galleon on its way to Panama. He captured it easily, relieving the Spaniards of some twenty-six tons of silver and gold plus chests of jewels and other valuables.

With the *Golden Hind* now crammed with plunder, the man the Spaniards called "El Draque" started for home. He sailed as far north as Oregon (perhaps even as high as Vancouver Island) in search of an eastward route into the Atlantic. Not finding it, he headed southwest, crossing the Pacific and Indian oceans and around Africa's Cape of Good Hope. He arrived in England in September 1580, almost three years after he'd left. He had become the first Englishman to circle the globe. And he had also soundly demonstrated the vulnerability of the Spanish Main.

Although he was knighted in 1581 for his circumnavigation, Drake's plundering exploits weren't publicly acknowledged by Queen Elizabeth, who was Philip II's sister-in-law. England and Spain were not then at war, so Drake was characterized by the British Crown as an independent maritime marauder. However, there is strong evidence that Elizabeth covertly encouraged and even helped finance his adventures. And she gladly accepted a major portion of his pirated loot.

Drake settled down for a few years in Plymouth, but longed to return to sea. In 1585, as the cold war with Spain heated up, Elizabeth openly backed Sir Francis's next foray into the Spanish Main. This time he led a fleet of twenty-nine ships and over 2,000 men to attack the Spanish bases at Santo Domingo in the West Indies, and Cartagena, Colombia. Although they routed the Spaniards, their take from those cities was relatively small. On his way home, however, Drake intercepted a large treasure galleon off the Azores. Its prize was more than enough to finance this latest expedition.

These brazen attacks helped goad Philip II into war with England, leading to the resounding defeat of his Armada. After that, Drake returned to Plymouth until 1595, when he set off with thirty ships for another voyage of plunder in the Caribbean. Less than a year later, on January 27, 1596, he was struck down by dysentery and buried at sea off Portobelo, Panama.

Tobias speculates that in the course of his expeditions Drake may have dispatched one or more of his vessels to set up a small secret colony on Oak Island as a place to temporarily store booty taken on the Spanish Main. The reason, Tobias suggests, could have been twofold: In the earlier voyages, from about 1567 to 1575, the raids would not have been sanctioned (at least not publicly) by the British Crown, which ostensibly was at peace with Spain. So the plunder may have been deposited in an isolated area of the New World until Elizabeth was politically in a position to have it brought home. A second purpose would be to provide a safe base on this side of the Atlantic where Drake's ships could be repaired and refurbished. (The British had no real foothold in the New World until the *Mayflower* landed at Plymouth, Massachusetts, in 1620. But as a result of John Cabot's voyages in the late 1490s, Drake and other British mariners were at least aware of the existence of the Nova Scotia coast.)

While Tobias's theory meets the requirements of proper time frame, motivation, and ability, it is, as he acknowledges, only hypothetically based. It is difficult to imagine that despite all of the historical research devoted to Drake and his adventures, not even a suggestion of such an enterprise has ever before surfaced. Granted, details of Drake's early voyages, including his circumnavigation on the *Golden Hind*, are rather sketchy, as his ship's logs were turned over to Elizabeth and have never been seen since. In any case, if the theory has any merit, it would have to be related to either Drake's early excursions or to his exploits from 1585 to 1587. The *Golden Hind* expedition definitely never ventured anywhere near the Acadian coast, and his final voyage in 1595 was too short-lived to have involved the creation of the Oak Island project.

Moreover, if the Drake hypothesis turns out to be correct, Tobias and his Triton partners should be prepared to find nothing of material value beneath the island. Queen Elizabeth, who reigned until her death in 1603, was hardly the sort of monarch who would leave a single ducat unclaimed in a New World piggy bank.

IF, AS I BELIEVE, THERE IS A SPANISH NEW WORLD ASSOCIA-tion with Oak Island's secret, the most plausible explanation is that the Spaniards engineered it themselves. But only time and further searching will establish the validity of this or any other theory.

Given the scope and engineering technology of Triton's Big Dig, the world may soon learn the identity of the genius behind the Oak Island enigma.

CHAPTER TWENTY

The Big Dig

"**T**HIS PROJECT, WHEN WE GET THROUGH WITH IT, MAY OR may not make us rich. But at least we will have solved one of the world's greatest mysteries." The speaker, David Tobias, was in a reflective mood as we sat in his Ilex Capital Corporation offices. Ilex, Tobias's family investment holding company, also doubles as office space for the Montreal headquarters of Triton Alliance Ltd. And the project he was discussing is the Big Dig—a $10-million hole in the ground that he sees as the final assault on Oak Island.

In late January 1988 Triton sent out its financing proposal to twenty-one Canadian and U.S. underwriters. The new capital, whether from a private placement or public stock offering, would still leave the current forty-nine Triton partners with 70 percent of the company's equity and, hence, a similar share in any treasure recovered. At that time Tobias had expected the money to roll in within a couple of months and the dig to be underway by early summer.

But now it was early July, with the funds still not in place and not a shovelful of earth yet scooped. "I've learned a lot about the world of financing in these past five months," says Tobias with a wry smile. "Black Monday (the stock market crash of October 19, 1987) has had a much bigger effect on

234

our financing plans than we thought it would. Underwriters and investors are being very conservative about new stock issues these days." Still, he adds, "We've had a lot of positive feedback," with investors "ready to put more than a million dollars on the table right now. But we're going to do this right, and we don't start until we've got the whole ten million dollars together."

Meanwhile, Blankenship (whom Tobias described as "getting kind of restless on the island") was preparing to deepen Borehole 10-X with a $100,000 budget from the Triton directors. "We'll definitely be doing preparatory work this summer" for the big dig, says Tobias, adding that "the shaft should be under way by autumn" and be completed within "four to six months."

Triton's president, a short and energetic man with curly gray hair and eyes that sparkle whenever he's discussing his favorite topic, Oak Island, has waited a long time for that conclusion. For more than twenty years he has financed and promoted the search from seven hundred miles away in Montreal. But for the dig, says Tobias, "I'll have a hands-on involvement; I'm going to move down there and see it through."

Tobias is ready to accept the possibility that the original depositor long ago retrieved the treasure. Nevertheless, as an armchair archaeologist and historian, he's excited by the prospect of soon knowing "who did it and why they did it, because that archaeological evidence is down there waiting for us to bring it up." He adds that "if we find nothing" at the bottom of the Money Pit, "it would mean that what I have seen or thought I saw with my own eyes doesn't exist. It would be like something out of *The Twilight Zone*, and I would have wasted all of these years." Tobias vigorously shakes his head. "That's just not possible. It's there, and we'll find it."

Tobias likes to point to the fact that "all of those drill holes we put down around the Money Pit [excluding Borehole 10-X] totaled only three square feet [on a horizontal plane] of actual exploration below the 170-foot level where we brought up most of our artifacts [wood, iron, brass, charcoal, cement, and china]." The proposed shaft, by comparison, will open up more than 250,000 cubic feet in the same depths and area.

The scale of Triton's Big Dig, North America's deepest and most expensive archaeological excavation, is indeed impressive. Bill Cox, a forty-eight-year-old underground engineer, is Triton's primary consultant on the job. He has calculated that since the discovery of the Money Pit in 1795 to the present, all the shafts, tunnels, and drilling by searchers have resulted in about 300,000 cubic feet of virgin material being excavated in almost two hundred years. This amounts to about 1,500 cubic feet a year, an accomplishment which, he notes, "could have been done by two men during their coffee breaks during the same period of time."

On the other hand, the Triton hole, 80 feet in diameter and at least 215 feet deep, encompasses most of the shafts ever dug around the Money Pit and will entail the removal of almost a million cubic feet of earth weighing about 50,000 tons —all in half a year's time. Significantly, says Cox, at least a quarter of this material is from unexplored ground beneath 170 feet. The perimeter of the shaft is being lined with steel plate and concrete, built in three-foot vertical sections, enabling the diggers to examine the walls of the hole as they go down. Any flood tunnels or water fissures are being plugged with cement grouting.

Electricity is being run out to the island's east end, four pumping stations will keep the water table down, and a $300,000 cofferdam is being built around Smith's Cove. (Plans for a similar dam around the South Shore Cove were dropped when it was estimated that it would cost about $700,000 to put it far enough out to contain the area where Triton had discovered underground water percolating through the winter ice.)

The entire project will eventually involve a crew of more than thirty men to sink the Money Pit caisson, plus another twenty or so employed in various support services such as site preparation, surveying, drilling, archaeology, and island security. It's an obvious boon to the Mahone Bay area economy, providing jobs and subcontracting. And in the long run the province anticipates an influx of tourism to the area, especially if a dramatic find is made on the island.

The scope of the excavation is far grander than anything

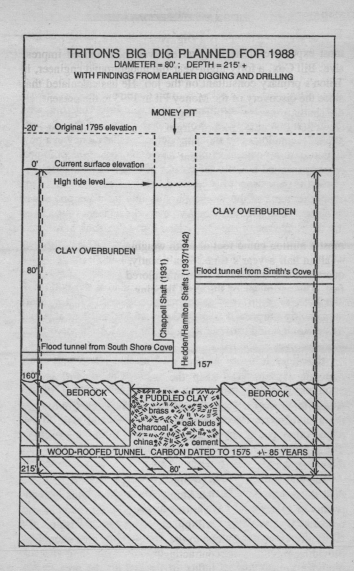

TRITON'S BIG DIG PLANNED FOR 1988
DIAMETER = 80' ; DEPTH = 215' +
WITH FINDINGS FROM EARLIER DIGGING AND DRILLING

MONEY PIT

-20' Original 1795 elevation

0' Current surface elevation

High tide level

CLAY OVERBURDEN

CLAY OVERBURDEN

80'

Chappell Shaft (1931)

Hedden/Hamilton Shafts (1937/1942)

Flood tunnel from Smith's Cove

Flood tunnel from South Shore Cove

157'

160'

BEDROCK

PUDDLED CLAY
brass
charcoal · oak buds
china · cement

BEDROCK

WOOD-ROOFED TUNNEL CARBON DATED TO 1575 +\- 85 YEARS

215'

← 80' →

237

ever undertaken on Oak Island (or, for that matter, almost anywhere else in the world). All of the wood-cribbed shafts dug by earlier searchers were confined to a relatively small area and were twisted out of plumb within their first fifty feet. Even Blankenship's work was often done on a shoestring budget with makeshift equipment that was held together with bailing wire and prayers. Now, armed with all of the state-of-the-art technology and modern equipment that money can buy, Triton is in a position to physically explore those depths previously reached by only the creator of Oak's Island's secret.

Bill Cox has spent his career digging holes all over Canada and other parts of the world, "but usually for water and sewer projects." The heavyset, bushy-bearded engineer is fascinated by the challenge of the Oak Island dig. "I've sunk harder and wetter shafts than this one, though maybe not as deep," he says. "But from what I've seen [while creating the engineering feasibility study] I know we can get down there."

As for what he personally expects to find at the bottom of the hole, Cox just shrugs. "I'm an engineer, not a treasure hunter. My purpose is to sink that shaft and not lose it. Once it's done, it could turn out to be the biggest joke or the biggest find that ever happened."

If it does turn out to be a $10 million joke, that would come as no surprise to several people who've been closely monitoring Triton's preparations for the final assault. One person with a direct vested interest in what the competition is up to is Fred Nolan. He has long believed that the Money Pit was constructed as a decoy to divert searchers from the real treasure locations; and most of those, he is sure, lie under his seven Oak Island lots, where he is continuing his personal search. (However, neither Nolan nor the few others who have offered that suggestion have been able to explain why such a deep and elaborate ruse would have been necessary.)

Nevertheless, Nolan is keeping a close eye on Triton's Big Dig. The reason is quite simple. The eastern boundary of his property is only 625 feet from the Money Pit. And he is enough of a pragmatist to accept the fact that the Money Pit, rather than being a decoy, is perhaps the "front door" to tunnels leading to treasure vaults some distance away.

That concept is shared by many others, including Bill Cox, who have applied engineering rationale to the original project. Whoever buried the treasure would have wanted to ensure two things: first, that nobody else could get to it before his return; and second, that when he did come back, he could reclaim it with minimum time and effort. With this in mind, the depositor would have dug the Money Pit, bobby-trapped it to the sea, then run tunnels from deep inside the Money Pit that sloped upward at a slight gradient to a point where they were above sea level, perhaps many hundreds of feet away. The treasure would then be stashed in vaults at the ends of these tunnels, with maps keyed to surface markers showing the depositor or his emissary exactly where to dig on the island to recover something that was no more than twenty or thirty feet underground.

Anyone who stumbled onto the secret would notice and be lured by only one thing—the Money Pit. But, exactly as the depositor designed it, no amount of digging would ever circumvent the flood traps. Elsewhere on the island, where neither the twig of a bush had been snapped nor a blade of grass flattened, lay a vast treasure that could be reclaimed with only a few hours of digging below totally virgin ground.

The distance of the cache (or caches) from the Money Pit is anybody's guess. Considering that the depositor was able to dig a 500-foot tunnel to Smith's Cove, there's no reason to assume he might not have run the treasure tunnels a much greater distance. It has even been speculated that a corridor could run to the mainland (600 feet off the island's west end) or even through bedrock under the sea (as do the coal mines of Cape Breton) to end up beneath Frog Island or Apple Island, a few hundred yards east of Oak Island. (Just to be on the safe side, Triton's treasure trove license extends 1,000 feet offshore and includes those two tiny islands.)

If a tunnel from the Money Pit leads to a vault somewhere beneath Nolan's twenty-eight acres, the Big Dig would indeed become an ironic cosmic joke. By virtue of common law and his treasure trove license, Nolan owns anything discovered on or beneath his property—no matter how or by whom. "Rest assured, we'll be monitoring what Triton is doing every step of the way," warns Nolan. "If they start tunneling toward my lots I'll hear about it pretty soon." Nolan, who some years ago built a modern waterside cottage on Joudrey's Cove, was intending to spend most of the summer and fall on the island.

In May 1988, Nolan approached me to see if I would act as an intermediary between him and Tobias to set up a possible accord between the two parties whereby Nolan could use the causeway and hook into Triton's electrical power in exchange for an agreement that any treasure discovered under Nolan's lots via a tunnel leading from the Money Pit would be split between him and Triton. It seemed a compromise that could benefit both parties; Nolan would be spared the trouble and expense of building a wharf at Joudrey's Cove and barging his equipment to the island, and Triton could ameliorate its worst-scenario fear of spending $10 million to uncover a treasure that was legally all Nolan's. Tobias was immediately receptive to such a discussion. But after several letters and phone calls between the two sides, it soon became apparent that neither could nor would trust the other. The negotiations broke down, and it would obviously be another season of competitive treasure hunters glowering at each other across their respective property lines.

While Nolan is keeping his eye on things from a few hundred feet away, another very interested observer is watching Triton's progress from a distance of 3,700 miles in Vancouver, British Columbia. Lavern Johnson, a seventy-four-year-old retired power engineer, has been on the trail of Oak Island's gold for almost thirty years. He is positive that he knows exactly where to dig, and that Triton is "wasting its time and money."

He first visited Oak Island in 1959 and was intrigued by the stone triangle and the two drilled rocks that Charles Roper had surveyed for Gilbert Hedden. Johnson is sure they were laid out as part of the original work, though he places no significance in the bearings and measurements that were on the Mar Del map.

Johnson doesn't claim to know who buried the treasure, but theorizes it was designed as a temporary repository by the crew of a storm-damaged Spanish or other European vessel sometime between 1650 and 1750. He also accepts that the Money Pit was the original entrance shaft, and that if the depositors had returned (he believes they never did) they'd have reclaimed their riches from a shallow vault some distance away from the Money Pit.

Johnson insists he has found the location of that vault, and that the answer lies in a "code" that he broke by studying the layout of the stone triangle and drilled rocks as they appear on the Roper survey. "The depositor," he explains, "set up the necessary code to lead him to the correct spot to dig if and when he could return for his deposit."

Johnson's first opportunity to test his interpretation of the code was in the summer of 1962, when he leased a small section of land north of the Money Pit from Mel Chappell. (Robert Restall was then working in the Money Pit and Smith's Cove.) Johnson dug a shaft about 240 feet north of the Money Pit, a spot selected on the basis of intersections of certain lines in his code as well as from a reading he got on a metal detector. He abandoned the shaft after reaching 30 feet and finding nothing of interest. A short tunnel driven from the 25-foot level also proved fruitless.

He returned three years later and bored about forty holes in the vicinity of his shaft. He used a pneumatic drill, forcing air into the ground in order to drive up the drilled material. In some of the holes between the Money Pit and his shaft the air traveled underground and was blown out many feet away through other drill holes and into the shaft itself. As the ground in that area is mostly solid clay, Johnson speculates that he may have intersected sections of the filled-in treasure tunnel. But he ran out of funds before being able to complete his search.

Today Johnson is still sure he was in the right vicinity and would like to test his theory further. He has tried many times over the years to have Triton enter into a limited agreement allowing him to dig for a short time on the island. With a Vancouver partner, Jack Lillico, he would fund the project and share the find with Triton. These overtures were being made in conference calls and letters to Tobias as late as January 1988.

Tobias, although impressed by Johnson's persistence, isn't about to give him the opportunity. "We, and Chappell before us, have been burned by people who come along with what they say is positive proof where the treasure is," says Tobias. "Then when nothing is found, they accuse us of not being in the right place or not going deep enough. That sort of thing can go on forever." He cites as one example his protracted dealings in the 1970s with the quixotic Johnny Goodman, who is referred to earlier in this book.

I met Johnson some years ago in Vancouver, and we've since corresponded and talked on the telephone many times. Unlike many others who claim to have "the answer" to Oak Island, Johnson appears to be a methodical and balanced individual. Still, I have no idea whether he's right or wrong. With good reason, he is not about to reveal how he came to his conclusions or where he thinks the treasure is buried. Therein lies his Catch-22 situation with Triton Alliance.

Johnson is certain of his findings, but he needs Triton's cooperation to test them. Triton would unhesitatingly cooperate if it knew what those findings were *and accepted* their validity. But who should trust whom? If Johnson gives Tobias all of his data up front, what's to stop Triton from using it to find the treasure on its own? And if Tobias signs an agreement that is predicated only on Johnson's personal conviction, Triton could waste time and effort (with potential legal problems) on yet just another misguided theory.

In an attempt to overcome that impasse, Johnson recently contacted Mendel Peterson, the former Smithsonian Institution curator who had authenticated some of Triton's finds. Johnson's idea was to have Peterson act as a nonpartisan middleman who would weigh the merits of his research and then advise Tobias whether or not it was worth following up. Peterson, after considering the legal implications, declined the role.

So as Triton spends $10 million on its current hole, Johnson sits at home in Vancouver waiting for the opportunity to find the treasure. "If I was given the chance," he told me in December 1987, "I could get the treasure out within a couple of months by digging a narrow trench no more than forty-three feet deep in a specific spot north of the Money Pit. The whole thing would cost $50,000, absolute maximum, and would prove my theory beyond a doubt."

Another would-be treasure hunter waiting in the wings boasts that he could locate the cache for half that cost and in a much shorter time. Gary Clayton of the previously mentioned Phoenix group says, "Give me $25,000 and I could uncover the real mystery of Oak Island within ten days, with nothing more than a laser transit and a pick and shovel."

Clayton scoffs at Triton's approach to the search. "The battle of Oak Island is going to be won in the mind, not by digging more useless holes. I've already won that battle, because I *know* what the treasure is, where it is, and how to get it out." He adds that Triton's Big Dig "is of no interest or threat to me; they're in the wrong place. Let them spend their millions."

Because some of the Phoenix group's charts indicate chambers dug by the Aztecs or Maya Indians in bedrock beneath the Money Pit, Clayton accepts that Triton's hole "may uncover some working areas, flood tunnels, and living quarters. But that's all they'll find. Any treasure will be well out of their reach" on another part of the island.

"By next August," Clayton told me in January 1988, "Triton will be discouraged enough to give up." And, he predicts, "I'll be right behind them. Within a year I expect to be on the island using my knowledge to solve the mystery."

Perhaps. Yet Tobias has file folders crammed with letters from people all over the world who are positive they have the answer and who are anxiously waiting for the opportunity to prove they are right. If Triton's current venture does fail, one can imagine a traffic jam on the causeway as searchers armed with secret documents, interpreted codes, genuine pirate maps, and treasure detectors scramble onto the island in search of glory and gold.

However, a more likely scenario is that Triton, when it completes its planned excavation of the Money Pit, will at the very least establish the source of all the unexplained clues that have teased searchers for almost two centuries. With luck, they may even find themselves following tunnels into vaults crammed with extraordinary monetary and archaeological wealth.

In any case, Tobias, Blankenship, and Nolan have already found an Oak Island treasure. As a result of a booming real estate market for waterfront property in Nova Scotia during the 1980s, the island is currently appraised at about $4 million. That's considerably more than any of them proportionally paid for their respective lots. (Nolan owns seven of the island's thirty-two lots. Of the remaining twenty-five, Blankenship owns and resides on Lot 23, which he purchased from Chappell in 1975. Tobias kept Lot 25 for his personal use and transferred half his interest in the rest of the island to Blankenship in December 1987. Under the 1988 financing plan, those twenty-three lots could be sold to the new Triton syndicate for $2 million.) Moreover, that value doesn't take into consideration the island's potential historical or archaeological significance. Given a major breakthrough in the treasure hunt, the island may soon be worth far more.

Even if the Big Dig proves inconclusive, that will not be the end of the treasure hunt. For there will always be someone who will be ready to match wits against the unknown genius who designed the Oak Island enigma.

That final chapter has yet to be written.

Bibliography

Baxter, James Phinney. *The Greatest of Literary Problems*. New York: Houghton Mifflin Company, 1915.

Bell, Winthrop Pickard. *The "Foreign Protestants" and the Settlement of Nova Scotia*. Toronto: University of Toronto Press, 1961.

Bird, Will R. *These Are the Maritimes*. Toronto: The Ryerson Press, 1959.

———. *This Is Nova Scotia*. Toronto: The Ryerson Press, 1950.

Bowen, Catherine Drinker. *Francis Bacon: The Temper of a Man*. Boston: Little, Brown and Company, 1963.

Brebner, John Bartlet. *The Neutral Yankees of Nova Scotia*. Toronto: McClelland and Stewart Limited, 1969.

Caso, Alfonso. *The Aztecs: People of the Sun*. Norman, Oklahoma: University of Oklahoma Press, 1958.

Clark, Andrew Hill. *Acadia: The Geography of Early Nova Scotia to 1760*. Madison, Wisconsin: The University of Wisconsin Press, 1968.

Clarke, George Frederick. *Expulsion of the Acadians*. Fredericton, New Brunswick: Brunswick Press, 1965.

Creighton, Helen. *Bluenose Ghosts*. Toronto: McGraw-Hill Ryerson Ltd., 1957.

————. *Bluenose Magic*. Toronto: The Ryerson Press, 1968.

————. *Folklore of Lunenburg County, Nova Scotia*. Ottawa: National Museum of Canada, 1950.

Crooker, William S. *The Oak Island Quest*. Windsor, Nova Scotia: Lancelot Press Limited, 1978.

Daley, Robert. *Treasure*. New York: Random House, Inc., 1977.

DesBrisay, Mather Byles. *History of the County of Lunenburg*. Bridgewater, Nova Scotia: The Bridgewater Bulletin Ltd., 1967.

Driscoll, Charles B. *Doubloons*. New York: Farrar & Rinehart Inc., 1930.

Evans, Millie; Mullen, Eric. *Oak Island*. Halifax, Nova Scotia: Four East Publications Ltd., 1984.

Fraser, Mary L. *Folklore of Nova Scotia*. Antigonish, Nova Scotia: Formac Ltd., 1928.

Freidel, Frank. *Franklin D. Roosevelt: The Apprenticeship*. Boston: Little, Brown and Company, 1952.

————. *Franklin D. Roosevelt: The Ordeal*. Boston: Little, Brown and Company, 1954.

Furneaux, Rupert. *The Money Pit Mystery*. New York: Dodd, Mead & Company, 1972.

Gage, Thomas. *A New Survey of the West Indies*. London: 1677.

Godwin, John. *This Baffling World*. New York: Hart Publishing Co., Inc., 1968.

Griffiths, Naomi. *The Acadians: Creation of a People*. Toronto: McGraw-Hill Ryerson Ltd., 1973.

Haring, Clarence Henry. *Trade and Navigation Between Spain and the Indies*. Boston: Harvard University Press, 1918.

Harris, R.V. *The Oak Island Mystery*. Toronto: McGraw-Hill Ryerson Ltd., 1958.

Helps, Arthur. *The Life of Pizarro*. London: Bell and Daldy, 1869.

Hoffman, Birney. *Brothers of Doom*. New York: G.P. Putnam's Sons, 1942.

Howard, Cecil. *Pizarro and the Conquest of Peru*. New York: American Heritage Publishing Co., 1968.

Kaulback, Ruth E. *Historic Saga of Leheve (La Have)*. Nova Scotia: Published by the author, 1970.

Kennedy, B.F. *Buried Treasure of Casco Bay*. New York: Vantage Press, Inc., 1963.

Leary, Thomas P. *The Oak Island Enigma*. Omaha, Nebraska: Published by the author, 1953.

MacMechan, Archibald. *Old Province Tales*. Toronto: McClelland & Stewart Ltd., 1924.

MacNutt, W.S. *The Atlantic Provinces*. Toronto: McClelland and Stewart Ltd., 1965.

McLennan, J.S. *Louisbourg from Its Foundation to Its Fall 1713–1758*. Sydney, Nova Scotia: Fortress Press, 1969.

Nesmith, Robert I. *Dig for Pirate Treasure*. New York: The Devin-Adair Company, 1958.

O'Connor, D'Arcy. *The Money Pit*. New York: Coward, McCann & Geoghegan, Inc., 1978.

Paine, Ralph D. *The Book of Buried Treasure*. London: William Heinemann, 1911.

Parkman, Francis. *A Half-Century of Conflict* (Vol. 2). Boston: Little, Brown and Company, 1892.

Quarrell, Charles. *Buried Treasure*. London: MacDonald & Evans Ltd., 1955.

Snow, Edward Rowe. *Mysteries and Adventures Along the Atlantic Coast*. New York: Dodd, Mead & Co., 1948.

Spedon, Andrew Learmont. *Rambles Among the Blue-Noses*. Montreal: John Lovell, 1863.

Thompson, John Eric S. *A Catalog of Maya Hieroglyphs*.

Norman, Oklahoma: University of Oklahoma Press, 1962.

————. *Maya Hieroglyphic Writing Introduction*. Washington, D.C.: Carnegie Institution of Washington, 1950.

————. *The Rise and Fall of Maya Civilization*. Norman, Oklahoma: University of Oklahoma Press, 1954.

Vaillant, George C. *Aztecs of Mexico*. New York: Doubleday, Doran & Company, Inc., 1941.

Van Doren, Charles. *Shakespeare: Reading and Talking*. Wayzata, Minnesota: Spring Hill Center, 1980.

Verrill, Alpheus Hyatt. *Lost Treasure: True Tales of Hidden Hoards*. New York: D. Appleton and Company, 1930.

————. *They Found Gold*. New York: G.P. Putnam's Sons, 1936.

Von Hagen, Victor Wolfgang. *The Ancient Sun Kingdoms of the Americas*. London: Thames & Hudson Ltd., 1962.

Wilkins, Harold T. *Captain Kidd and His Skeleton Island*. New York: Liveright Publishing Corp., 1937.

Wood, William. *Elizabethan Sea-Dogs*. Toronto: Glasgow, Brook & Co., 1918.

INDEX

About the Author

D'ARCY O'CONNOR is a Canadian free-lance journalist, author and screenwriter who has lived in Montreal, Argentina, Australia, New York, and Nova Scotia.

His fascination with Oak Island began in the summer of 1970 while he was a reporter for *The Wall Street Journal* and wrote a feature for that newspaper on the bizarre treasure hunt. He later wrote several follow-up articles on the subject for the *Journal* (the most recent in July 1987), and researched and coproduced several documentaries about Oak Island for U.S. and Canadian network television. He is also the author of a 1978 hardcover book, *The Money Pit*, on the Oak Island mystery.

When he's not writing, Mr. O'Connor pursues his other passion—sailing. In the early 1970s he spent three years circling the globe as a deckhand, navigator, and skipper aboard various sailing yachts of 30 to 72 feet in length, while contributing to *Yachting* magazine and other publications.

Today Mr. O'Connor divides his time between free-lance writing and teaching journalism at Montreal's Dawson College, and sailing his *Hobie Cat* with his family at their cottage on Lake Champlain in northern Vermont. He is currently working on a novel.

FACT
is stranger than
FICTION